MAPPING TAIWANESE CINEMA, 2008–20

MAPPING TAIWANESE CINEMA, 2008–20
Environments, Poetics, Practice

Christopher Brown

EDINBURGH
University Press

Edinburgh University Press is one of the leading university presses in the UK. We publish academic books and journals in our selected subject areas across the humanities and social sciences, combining cutting-edge scholarship with high editorial and production values to produce academic works of lasting importance. For more information visit our website: edinburghuniversitypress.com

© Christopher Brown, 2024, 2025

Grateful acknowledgement is made to the sources listed in the List of Illustrations for permission to reproduce material previously published elsewhere. Every effort has been made to trace the copyright holders, but if any have been inadvertently overlooked, the publisher will be pleased to make the necessary arrangements at the first opportunity.

Edinburgh University Press Ltd
13 Infirmary Street
Edinburgh, EH1 1LT

First published in hardback by Edinburgh University Press 2024

Typeset in 10/12.5 pt Sabon by
Cheshire Typesetting Ltd, Cuddington, Cheshire

A CIP record for this book is available from the British Library

ISBN 978 1 4744 7827 4 (hardback)
ISBN 978 1 4744 7828 1 (paperback)
ISBN 978 1 4744 7829 8 (webready PDF)
ISBN 978 1 4744 7830 4 (epub)

The right of Christopher Brown to be identified as the author of this work has been asserted in accordance with the Copyright, Designs and Patents Act 1988, and the Copyright and Related Rights Regulations 2003 (SI No. 2498).

CONTENTS

List of Illustrations	vi
Acknowledgements	viii
Note on Romanisation	x
1. Mapping Taiwanese Cinema	1
2. You Are Here	26
3. Back to the Woods	55
4. Indigenous Land and Sea	82
5. Love in a Designer City	110
6. House Style	139
7. Quiet Places	167
Conclusion	190
Bibliography	193
Filmography	204
Index	209

ILLUSTRATIONS

1.1	Antique map in *Amour-Legende* (Wu Mi-Sen, 2006)	2
1.2	Old map of the Republic of China in *Unwritten Rules* (Cheng Yu-Chieh, 2012)	8
1.3	Map on a school chalkboard in *I Didn't Dare to Tell You* (Mou Tun-Fei, 1969)	10
2.1	Wet map weighed down by a stone in *Island Etude* (Chen Hwai-En, 2007)	29
2.2	Hand-drawn map of a town in *My Missing Valentine* (Chen Yu-Hsun, 2020)	33
2.3	Affective cartography in *Somewhere I Have Never Travelled* (Fu Tien-Yu, 2009)	36
2.4	Rug with distorted map in *Somewhere I Have Never Travelled* (Fu Tien-Yu, 2009)	36
2.5	Globe at entrance to Rock Park in *Godspeed* (Chung Mong-Hong, 2016)	40
2.6	Coordinates for Ludao in *Aground* (Hsin Chien-Tsung, 2017)	46
2.7	Coordinates for Sendai in *Aground* (Hsin Chien-Tsung, 2017)	47
3.1	Globes in a jigsaw shop in *Starry Starry Night* (Lin Shu-Yu, 2011)	62
3.2	Chieh and the forest disintegrate in *Starry Starry Night* (Lin Shu-Yu, 2011)	66

3.3a–b	Production stills from *Forêt Debussy* (Kuo Cheng-Chui, 2016). Courtesy of Lu Yen-Chiu	76
4.1a–b	A view from the mountain cuts to a shot of the valley in *Lokah Laqi* (Laha Mebow, 2016)	90
4.2a–b	An aerial photo of the coastline cuts to a horizontal view in *Wawa No Cidal* (Cheng Yu-Chieh, Lekal Sumi 2015)	92
4.3	Panay's counter-map in *Wawa No Cidal* (Cheng Yu-Chieh, Lekal Sumi 2015)	94
5.1	Publicity photo for *Design 7 Love* (Chen Hung-I, 2014). Courtesy of Chen Hung-I	112
5.2	Multicoloured palette in *Design 7 Love* (Chen Hung-I, 2014)	115
5.3	Poster for *Design 7 Love* (Chen Hung-I, 2014). Courtesy of Chen Hung-I	121
5.4	Lecture map and annotations in *Love* (Niu Cheng-Tse, 2012)	126
5.5	An's rooftop terrace in *52Hz I Love You* (Wei Te-Sheng, 2017)	129
5.6	Hsiao-Kuan's rooftop terrace in *Love* (Niu Cheng-Tse, 2012)	130
5.7	TV installation in *The Mad King of Taipei* (Yeh Tien-Lun, 2017)	134
6.1	Breaking down the door in *Exit* (Chienn Hsiang, 2014)	148
6.2a–b	Art design previsualisations of the house interior in *More than Blue* (Lin Hsiao-Chien, 2018). Courtesy of Yao Kuo-Chen	151
6.3a–b	Household appliances and clutter outside Chieh's apartment end up on the theatrical stage in *Dear Ex* (Hsu Yu-Ting, Hsu Chih-Yen, 2018)	162
7.1	Pao looks out at the landscape in *A Time in Quchi* (Chang Tso-Chi, 2013)	169
7.2	The hotel and backdrop in *Secrets in the Hot Spring* (Lin Kuan-Hui, 2018)	177
7.3	Hsiao-Chin's ghost-map in *Secrets in the Hot Spring* (Lin Kuan-Hui, 2018)	180
7.4	Close-up of Pao-Te's ear as he listens in *Father to Son* (Hsiao Ya-Chuan, 2018)	186
7.5	Pao-Te listens, filmed from above, in *Father to Son* (Hsiao Ya-Chuan, 2018)	186

ACKNOWLEDGEMENTS

I'd like to thank Piotr Cieplak for his unwavering support throughout this project, and Yu-Lun Sung for reading drafts and assisting with interviews; over the past few years, conversations with both have been invaluable in helping me shape this book.

Scholars and friends have all helped make this book possible, whether through conversations about cinema and filmmaking, or through their support and encouragement. Thanks to Pam Hirsch, Chris O'Rourke, JC Cheung, Dušan Petković, Gregory Sporton, Steve Kennedy, Jonathan Wroot, Elena Papadaki, Tommy Tse, and Jin Zhi. I'm indebted to Andrew Knight-Hill, Jan Tovey, and Alex Lichtenfels, who helped refine my thoughts on film practice while sharing what was surely the most productive table in our open-plan office. Thanks to Yi Wang for giving me the opportunity to introduce and discuss Taiwanese cinema at Queer East film festival, and to Bi-Yu Chang for inviting me to give a talk at SOAS University of London, where I first presented some of the ideas that would form the basis of this book.

Thanks to the film directors who generously gave up their time to be interviewed: Laha Mebow, Cheng Yu-Chieh, Hsu Yu-Ting, Kuo Cheng-Chui, and Bon An. Thanks also to Lu Yen-Chiu and Wang Jen-You, whom I interviewed in relation to their work on *Forêt Debussy*. The production photos from that film, included in this book, are courtesy of Lu, for which I am very grateful. Many thanks also to Chen Hung-I for giving me permission to use the *Design 7 Love* poster and publicity photo, and to Yao Kuo-Cheng for

ACKNOWLEDGEMENTS

permission to include the *More than Blue* art design previsualisations. I'm grateful to everyone in the various filmmakers' production offices who helped facilitate interviews, especially to Vita Ho, who also helped organise the book's cover image from *Dear Ex*, taken by photographer Franco Wang and courtesy of Dear Studio Co. Ltd. Thanks to Janet Ku and Amber Weifen Wu for helping me source some archive film material.

I was granted research leave at the University of Sussex that enabled me to complete this project, while the University of Greenwich funded research and conference trips.

Thanks to Gillian Leslie, Sam Johnson and the editorial team at Edinburgh University Press, and also the proposal and manuscript reviewers.

Finally, thanks to all of my family for their love and support.

NOTE ON ROMANISATION

Wherever possible, I have Romanised Chinese names using the form in which they are most known in English, minimising inconsistency.

The names of people in Taiwan are generally Romanised using Wade-Giles, so when the preferred spelling of a Taiwanese person's name is unknown, I have used Wade-Giles.

Sometimes inconsistency is unavoidable, notably in the case of place names, which in Taiwan might be commonly Romanised using either Wide-Giles (Taichung, Kaohsiung) or Pinyin (Xinyi, Ximen).

For Romanisation not involving names, I have used Pinyin.

1. MAPPING TAIWANESE CINEMA

La Bomba del Corazón

A man wakes up in the desert. Sleeping on the sand dunes next to him is a woman. In this opening scene of *Amour-Legende* (Wu Mi-Sen, 2006), onscreen text informs us that the action is set 'somewhere in South America, 2006'. The viewer later discovers that the location is an island called La Bomba del Corazón, previously adorned with meadows, but which has undergone gradual desertification. The Japanese man is called Oshima (Yôsuke Kubozuka) and has amnesia, though he experiences sporadic flashbacks to his daily life as an executive in Taipei. The woman (Rachel Ngan) claims to be helping Oshima locate his Taiwanese mistress May, who has disappeared. Yet with Oshima unable to remember much about his past, he cannot be sure that she is telling the truth. The woman might herself be May, taking advantage of his amnesia to extricate herself from their difficult relationship. Or maybe he has dreamed up a fictitious backstory and May is a figment of his imagination. The stage is thus set for a surreal excursion around the island that stylistically, draws on traditions of South American magic realism and European art cinema. As the couple travel towards the elusive 'snow mountain', they repeatedly get lost; Oshima's desire for geographical orientation reflects his figurative inability to locate himself.

An enormous map of La Bomba del Corazón appears in one scene set in a hotel, hanging from a wall behind the protagonists as they sit eating (Figure 1.1). The shot in which it appears is an unbroken take of almost three

Figure 1.1 Antique map in *Amour-Legende* (Wu Mi-Sen, 2006).

minutes, which gradually tracks forwards so that the map encompasses the bulk of the frame. Drawn in an antique style and annotated in Spanish, it purports to date from 1739 and recalls maps of colonial conquest. It privileges fantasy; the waters surrounding the island are filled with drawings of galleons and sea monsters, evoking high adventure in the manner of the frontispiece map in Robert Louis Stevenson's *Treasure Island*.¹ Later, however, the road map consulted by the characters clearly represents Egypt, identifying places along the river Nile, with palm trees signifying the desert and evoking colonial fantasies of unmarked places. Oshima complains that the two maps do not match, that the shape of the island is different. The viewer, however, is less equivocal. These maps are patently artificial – utterly inconsistent, both spatially and temporally, with the environment portrayed onscreen. Trying to figure out what is going on, the exasperated Oshima speculates that they have been going in circles, that they never actually left Taiwan, that La Bomba del Corazón does not exist. Countering this, the woman responds with a question: 'Can you tell me if Taiwan really exists?'

It's a fair question, in the context of mapping. After all, the old Kuomintang (KMT) maps of the Republic of China, spanning the Chinese mainland and with Nanjing listed as the capital, were no less fictitious than the spurious pseudo-colonial renderings on display in *Amour-Legende*, which displaces anxieties about Taiwanese identity onto a mythical South American island. As both a filming location and a concept, La Bomba del Corazón *is* Taiwan – or rather a dreamed version of it, an imagined product of the protagonist's reverie. Oshima translates as 'big island', and the character's presence seems intended to reflect on the legacy of the Japanese colonists; his amnesia attests to the organised forgetting that characterises much postcolonial experience. Furthermore, Bomba del Corazón is not a place, but a song by Eddie Palmieri, which translates as 'the pump of the heart'. The film conceives itself as a map of the heart, *amour* meaning love, and *légende* having a dual meaning: the mythical, but also the key that facilitates map reading through symbols (*légende de carte*).[2] In his archaeology of the imaginary city of Victoria (a place that both is, and is not, Hong Kong), Dung Kai-Cheung ironically remarks that as legends on maps came to serve an instrumental purpose, they became 'uniform, compulsory supplements without any imaginative power to speak of', with arid maps reduced to games in the exercise of power.[3] 'It is only when individual ways of reading legends return', Dung continues, 'that we can again read legends as tales of marvels.'[4] *Amour-Legende* strives to do just this, returning the legendary to the legend, sketching out an affective cartography of an island that both is, and is not, Taiwan.

Point of Departure

This book investigates Taiwanese cinema of the period 2008–20 from the perspective of mapping. Drawing on cartographic approaches to film research, I analyse the appearance of onscreen maps, but more fundamentally, my intention is to argue for the diverse ways in which recent Taiwanese filmmaking can itself be understood as a form of mapping. A desire to refocus attention on the *making* of films explains my decision to approach the raw material of screen mapping – the environments that are filmed – from the critical standpoint of film poetics. As a mode of enquiry that probes the ways in which a film is shaped by a process of construction, the poetics tradition enables us to think about Taiwanese cinema differently. By scrutinising the period 2008–20 from the standpoint of how films are made, where they are made, and why they are made in a particular way, we can gain new insights, not only into the creative work itself, but also its relationship with culture more broadly. At heart, mapping and filmmaking are both practices, and in exploring the interplay between the two, this book seeks to account for the unique characteristics of post-2008 Taiwanese cinema.

This first chapter sketches out the critical, cultural, and methodological contexts that inform these arguments, offering an introductory overview that will be complemented by more detailed commentary and analysis in subsequent chapters. Here, I examine the significance of cartography to Taiwanese history and identity, summarising the typical ways in which onscreen maps were depicted, and often suppressed, in twentieth-century films made in Taiwan. Arguing that the early twenty-first century witnessed a surge of interest in mapping the island, my attention shifts to academic perspectives on film cartography, and how these might inform an appraisal of recent Taiwanese cinema. I will then discuss, in turn, the book's three main areas of focus – environments, poetics, and practice – explaining my understanding of these terms and the concepts, histories, and approaches they evoke. I will begin, however, by discussing the importance of the year 2008 to accounts of Taiwanese cinema, which prompts some reflections on the adequacy of existing critical frameworks and periodisation. *Amour-Legende*, discussed above, was one of several films that signalled the emergence of a new kind of Taiwanese cinema in the years around 2006–8. This was epitomised by the release of *Cape No. 7* (Wei Te-Sheng, 2008), Taiwan's highest-grossing domestic film ever, that undoubtedly marked a turning point in the island's cinema.[5] Song Hwee Lim argues that Wei's film helped the industry to recover from a slump, injected new confidence in its products, and paved the way for a more popular mode of filmmaking.[6]

Yet while there is consensus that Taiwanese cinema after 2008 was different from what preceded it, little scholarship has attempted to justify this in thematic or aesthetic terms. Partly, this results from the enduring critical tendency to focus on noted directors and arthouse *auteurs*, such as Hou Hsiao-Hsien, Tsai Ming-Liang, and Ang Lee, all of whom continued to produce work after 2008. Attempts to take stock of the Taiwanese film industry's recent output in broader terms have been few and far between. An edited collection by Yingjin Zhang and Paul G. Pickowicz, focusing solely on twenty-first century Taiwanese cinema is a notable exception.[7] Sheng-Mei Ma's cultural study of globalisation and trauma in Taiwan, which incorporates a discussion of film, is another, as is Ya-Feng Mon's study of production and consumption circuits from the perspective of sensory theory.[8] Another edited collection by Emilie Yueh-Yu Yeh, Darrell William Davis, and Wenchi Lin offers wide-ranging coverage of six decades of Taiwanese cinema, including films made in the twenty-first century.[9] However, these monographs and collections are rare in approaching contemporary Taiwanese cinema from a perspective that does not privilege the *auteur*.

Commercial developments have been another area of critical focus. Financially, Taiwanese cinema after 2008 was certainly more profitable than in the previous decade or so; the 1990s had witnessed a significant decline in the production and domestic consumption of local films.[10] By 2002, Taiwanese films accounted for just 6 per cent of all the films shown in local cinemas, while their revenue generated just 0.7 per cent of the total box office, although a contemporary study into concentration ratios tempers the narrative of decline somewhat.[11] But from this perspective, improvements after 2008 were relative, simply reinforcing how bleak the situation had become in the 1990s. James Udden offers a measured appraisal of what he termed a 'commercial mini-resurgence' after 2008, suggesting that 'despite recent improvements and a few exceptions here and there, the sense that Taiwanese films are not actually for Taiwan's market lingers to the present day'.[12] Since 2008, Taiwanese films have performed erratically at the local box office. In some years, none made it to the top thirty, whereas in other years, local films were more successful.[13]

A difficulty thus emerges as we attempt to define what, if anything, made post-2008 Taiwanese cinema different from what preceded it. The commercial case seems decidedly modest, while studies of authorship emphasise continuity rather than difference, the endurance of a tradition of transnational art cinema. A related issue is the intense critical focus on the films of Wei himself. His work has deservedly received attention, and *Cape No. 7* undoubtedly had an enormous impact.[14] Institutionally, the film's success resulted in the government playing a more active role in developing Taiwanese cinema. Initiatives included holding conferences to attract investment, changing subsidy policies, launching a series of nationwide film educational programmes, and passing new laws on the cultural and creative industries in 2010.[15] Yet the critical focus on Wei's films has tended to skew our understanding of broader developments. It is questionable how representative his work is of recent trends, given that he produces large-scale projects and operates with sizeable budgets and resources, unlike most Taiwanese filmmakers.

Some of the critical discourse surrounding *Cape No. 7* can also appear myopic; in all the scholarly discussion of this film, how often do critics mention that 2008 was also the year of the global financial crisis? Although it is not my focus here, the impact of the crisis on the Taiwanese film industry is understudied and should be an avenue for future research. The stratospheric success of *Cape No. 7* has also obscured the impact of other films released around the same time which, thematically and stylistically, helped lay the groundwork for the cinema of the subsequent decade. Some were commercially successful; *Island Etude* (Chen Hwai-En, 2006) was a low-budget film that broke records as the most screened domestic film until that point.[16] *Eternal Summer* (Leste Chen, 2006), *Exit No. 6* (Lin Yu-Hsien, 2006), *Da Yu: The Touch of Fate* (Pan Chih-Yen, 2006), *Do Over* (Cheng Yu-Chieh, 2006), *Silk* (Su Chao-Pin, 2006), *God Man Dog* (Chen Singing, 2007), *The Most Distant Course* (Lin Ching-Chieh, 2007), *Winds of September* (Tom Lin Shu-Yu, 2008), and *Orz Boyz* (Yang Ya-Che, 2008) all helped establish aesthetic trends that would later become commonplace. All except the last of these films appeared before the release of *Cape No. 7*; firm temporal delineations elide the study of change that was inevitably more incremental.

Ambiguities in periodisation result partly from ongoing confusion regarding what exactly constitutes 'post' Taiwan New Cinema. Lim notes that the standard scholarly consensus has Taiwan New Cinema ending in the late 1980s, with 1990s films referred to as 'post-New Cinema', or as a 'second wave' or 'generation' of the earlier movement. This is problematic, he suggests, given that many directors who came to prominence in the 1980s continued to produce work afterwards, while there was a great deal of continuity on the production side.[17] Davis similarly argues that although it is valid to discriminate between the New Cinema proper and its later directions as post-New Cinema, 'it is convenient to let the name cover a longer period until the mid-1990s, and indicate the movement's overall *auteurist* tendencies and stylistic character'.[18] Others suggest that post-New Cinema did not really take off until the twenty-first century. Ting-Ying Lin, for instance, argues that 'it is the year 2008 that is generally regarded as the key year of the rise of the post-New Cinema'.[19]

I would prefer that we drop the term 'post-New Cinema', and instead focus on historical trends, hence my decision to analyse 'post-2008' Taiwanese cinema. Without a doubt, designating 2008 as a watershed year again raises questions about the adequacy of periodisation more generally, given that, as noted above, antecedents to many of the trends discussed in this book are apparent from around 2006. Nonetheless, despite reservations, I think it remains useful to consider 2008 as a turning point: as a symbolic moment that encapsulated and affirmed the effects of industry changes that were already underway a couple of years before Wei's film was released.

Style, for example, is perhaps the area where post-2008 changes have been the most obvious, with Zhang arguing for a 'radically different aesthetic look' in Taiwanese films of the twenty-first century.[20] Generally, this entails a more comprehensive adoption of the forms associated with the classic Hollywood model, yet few critics have unpicked the detail or implications of this. Moreover existing scholarship has not analysed a sufficient range of case studies to persuasively account for the Taiwanese film industry's recent output. Taking an extensive survey of national production, this book seeks to embark upon this task. This is not to imply a search for a distinctively national style. Chris Berry and Mary Farquhar argue that national identity in the cinema is not a unified and coherent form, but constructed and contested in multiple ways.[21] Drawing on these ideas, Zhang conceives the national in cinema as discursive, fluctuating, and unfinished, observing that 'the boundaries of a cinema and a nation or state may not – and do not have to – fit perfectly'.[22] This is certainly true of Taiwan, which is not formally recognised as a nation by most of the world's countries, and is claimed as a province by China. I would suggest that mapping, as a practice in which geopolitical and representational boundaries might similarly fail to coalesce, offers a valuable means of approaching concepts of nation in cinema as necessarily propositional.

Maps of Taiwan

As instruments of power, maps have historically been associated with Western colonialism, while in the Taiwanese context they were used by the Japanese colonists and subsequently the KMT to exercise their authority. While maps are central to any construction of nationhood, they have nonetheless acquired a particularly vexed position in the Taiwanese imagination. For Denis Wood, mapping is fundamentally propositional, and mapmakers are 'extraordinarily selective creators of a world – not *the* world, but *a* world – whose features they bring into being'.[23] This was taken to an extreme by the Republic of China, which historically embodied the unusual paradox of being a state without territory; it laid claim to the Chinese mainland only through maps, without having any actual control there. Bi-Yu Chang has referred to this as a strategy of territoriality concerned less with the ontological existence of territory than an ideological struggle for the survival of Chinese *daotong*, the intangible traditions and cultures of Confucian orthodoxy that the People's Republic of China was alleged to have abandoned.[24]

Chang has examined how the KMT sought to naturalise its regime in postwar Taiwan by asserting strict control over cartography. Children were indoctrinated with maps in the iconic form of a begonia leaf, incorporating all of mainland China as well as Taiwan and other regions, with Nanjing listed as the capital city, reflecting an official position that was endlessly reiterated.[25] Review regulations were put in place to keep map production under close supervision. Few maps were published, and those that existed were of poor quality; outside of military settings, they were produced mainly by schoolteachers and used only in the classroom. The state deterred the public from reading, owning, and using maps, and as a result they were not generally used by the Taiwanese population.[26] Chang argues that the suppression of maps reflected the regime's hidden doubts about its own adequacy, its ability to achieve modernity as decisively as the earlier Japanese colonists.[27]

The unease surrounding maps was deep-rooted, however. Their role in the loss of territory under the Qing dynasty remained an anxious historical memory, especially in the context of the nationalist retreat to Taiwan.[28] China's defeat by the British in the first Opium War (1839–42), and the loss of territory in border disputes with the Russian empire and Korea, were all attributable to errors in surveying and mapping.[29] When seeking to justify the Taiwan expedition of 1874–5, Japanese diplomats deployed Western concepts of mapped territory and boundaries. They argued that the refusal of the Qing dynasty to accept responsibility for violence in Taiwan's indigenous territories rendered these regions 'unclaimed' and 'masterless', exemplifying what Robert Eskildsen terms recursive imperialism, whereby Japan selectively appropriated the ideas and practices of Western imperialism.[30] Taiwan, along with the Penghu Islands and the Liaodong Peninsula, was ceded to Japan in the Treaty of Shimonoseki following China's defeat in the first Sino-Japanese war (1894–5), and territorial encroachment continued into subsequent decades. These territorial losses were widely seen as humiliating. They bequeathed an emotive historical legacy and were central to later expressions of Chinese nationalism, including in films. In the pre-credits sequence of *Once Upon a Time in China* (Tsui Hark, 1991), Wong Fei-Hung (Jet Li) opens a hand fan inscribed with a map of China, accompanied by a list of 'unjust treaties' signed with other countries.

The legacy of this unease surrounding maps is aptly illustrated in Cheng Yu-Chieh's short film *Unwritten Rules* (2012). It is a comedy in which a group of filmmakers attempt to shoot a scene while avoiding the enormous national flag that is attached to the wall of their ill-chosen location. The flag cannot appear in their film for fear of making it unsellable in China, so the director orders his crew to remove it. But as the flag is torn away, he realises, to his horror, that something worse lies underneath: an old map of the Republic of China, incorporating the mainland (Figure 1.2). This is viewed by the young filmmakers with embarrassment, because it represented, of course, a geographical fiction. If earlier filmmakers faced actual censorship, then here Cheng suggests that contemporary filmmakers, with an eye on the Chinese market, engage in self-censorship. These are the unwritten rules of the film's title, and amidst the mockery lies a serious point; the question of how filmmakers should negotiate the industrial and geopolitical realities of the more commercial environment post-2008.

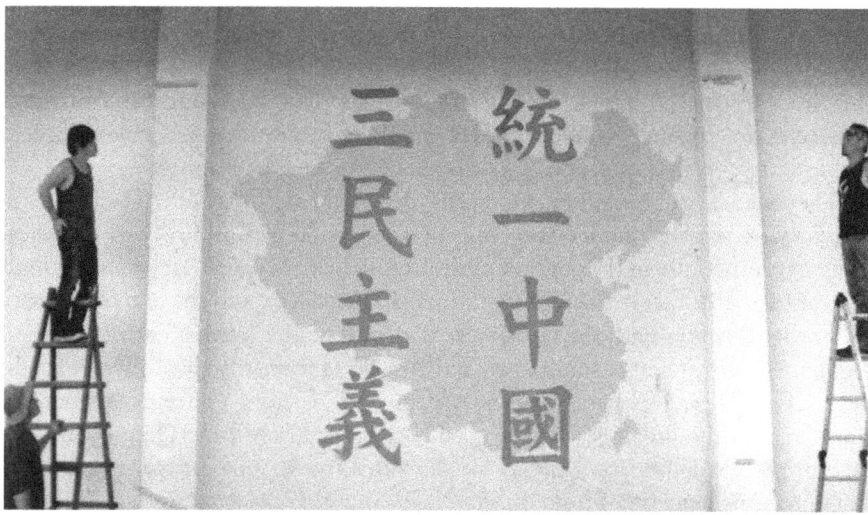

Figure 1.2 Old map of the Republic of China in *Unwritten Rules* (Cheng Yu-Chieh, 2012).

Intriguingly, maps feature onscreen in several noteworthy films released around the time that a new kind of filmmaking emerged in Taiwan, for example in *Da Yu: The Touch of Fate*, *The Most Distant Course*, and *Island Etude*. Some films, meanwhile, resulted in the offscreen production of maps. The success of *Cape No. 7* generated a tourist boom in Hengchun, located near Taiwan's southernmost tip, where the drama was shot; maps enabled tourists to visit the shooting locations and – as the advertising campaign put it – 'find the address of love'.[31] *Island Etude*, a travelogue film about a cyclist who journeys around the island's coastal circumference, popularised the *huandao* (around-the-island) trend that had been growing in popularity since the mid-1990s.[32] The film had a tie-in book which included detachable maps, along with suggested itineraries and restaurant recommendations.[33] This touristic interest in maps of Taiwan, in the early twenty-first century, strongly contrasts with what had previously been allowed and encouraged under the nationalist regime. Prior to the lifting of martial law in 1987, maps had been suppressed but in addition to this, the island of Taiwan tended to be de-privileged in nationalist discourse and imagery. As Chang's research demonstrates, the KMT education system, for instance, cultivated a national sense of place focused on mainland China, while neglecting Taiwan, thereby suppressing a local sense of place; this resulted, she argues, in children growing up with 'a distorted sense of place, a skewed worldview and an anchorless identity'.[34]

Cinema did not simply reflect these dynamics, but also helped shape them. The short 'national anthem films' that preceded film screenings from 1952 onwards featured a near-identical sequence of national iconography, including a map of the Republic of China incorporating the mainland; for a certain period, before the format diversified in the 1960s, audiences would have seen this map every time they went to the cinema.[35] It was reiterated as a form of banal nationalism, as was the case in classrooms, a process we see dramatised in the *taiyu* (Taiwanese-language) film *I Didn't Dare To Tell You* (Mou Tun-Fei, 1969). In the film, a teacher overseeing a geography lesson has chalked out a map of Greater China onto the blackboard, having copied it from a textbook. Her chalk rendering centres mainland China, and excises the lower half of Taiwan entirely, confirming the island's unimportance in the national imaginary (Figure 1.3). The protagonist Ta-Yuan (Yu Chien-Sheng) is asleep during the lesson and gets told off; more broadly, the depiction of his alienation in the context of authority resulted in the film being banned. Generally, when onscreen maps did appear in the nationalist era, their presence was carefully controlled in line with prevailing ideologies. Lin-Chin Tsai analyses the propaganda film *Beautiful Treasure Island* (Chen Wen-Chuan, 1952), which opens with a map of Taiwan, and uses animated road maps.[36] Lin argues that the audience is invited 'to participate in the process of settler colonial mapping', while the placing of Taiwan at the centre of the world map positions the KMT

9

Figure 1.3 Map on a school chalkboard in *I Didn't Dare to Tell You* (Mou Tun-Fei, 1969).

regime as the only legitimate embodiment of China.[37] Ideology notwithstanding, this does suggest that even in 1952, it was possible to prioritise island imagery over Greater China, even if this was not common practice.

There is evidence elsewhere of the suppression of maps in film. The *taiyu* adventure *Tarzan and the Treasure* (Liang Che-Fu, 1965) is a striking case in point. Tarzan (Kao Ming) must assist Tenn Siok-Hun (Liu Chin) in seeking to retrieve a hoard of treasure in Malaysia, with the aid of a map that reveals the location of the trove. Yet despite its centrality to the story, the audience never actually sees what is on the map. None of the characters consult it, nor do they comment on the directions, distances, or geography that it represents. Close-up footage of the map was probably censored or self-censored; perhaps the filmmakers were aware that audiences, unfamiliar with maps in their daily lives, may have had difficulty interpreting a cartographic rendering of a fictitious Malaysian jungle. For even at the height of martial law, non-propaganda maps do not appear to have been entirely forbidden. In *The Husband's Secret* (Lin Tuan-Chiu, 1960), a map is visible in the background of one shot, mounted on the wall of a police station. It serves no purpose in the narrative, seeming only to affirm that cartography is a form of knowledge permitted only to the authorities. Its position in the furthermost plane of the shot, out of focus, aptly encapsulates the place of cartography under the KMT regime – visible if you look for it, but definitely in the background.

Similarly, there was limited interest in exploring the island as a unique geographical environment. This began to change with the rise of the Taiwan New Cinema, yet maps appear infrequently in Taiwanese films prior to the twenty-first century. In one sense, this reflects changes in the national status of cartography. From the mid-1980s, tourism and democratisation led to more availability of maps, assisting national de-mythification; review regulations were formally abolished in 2004, after which the Ministry of the Interior discontinued maps that incorporated mainland China, and began to publish only maps of the Taiwan region instead.[38] It is striking that a new kind of filmmaking emerged in Taiwan at around the same moment that an outdated form of cartography disappeared; in the years around 2004–8. I would argue that these two things are linked, and that recent Taiwanese cinema can be seen to represent a new mapping impulse: a concerted effort to chart the island as a distinctive environment.

Cinematic Cartography

Like mapmakers, filmmakers creatively interact with the national, offering an historically situated interpretation of physical geography. An aerial map of an island may be etched in our minds as being Taiwan, but a map is not the same as a nation – which is not to say that for some filmmakers, this is not a useful fiction. The sheer volume of onscreen maps that appear in Taiwanese films from around 2008 is striking. Despite this, there has been no consistent attempt to consider recent Taiwanese cinema in these terms, despite the development of cartographic approaches to film studies following the publication of seminal works by Giuliana Bruno in 2002 and Tom Conley in 2007.[39] This feels like an omission, given the historical context described above and the heightened politicisation of Taiwanese maps given China's disputed territorial claim over the island.

Very few critics have studied the appearance of onscreen maps in Taiwanese cinema; a notable exception is Tsai, who in a recent article compares mapping in colonial (Japanese) and settler colonial (nationalist) propaganda films.[40] That said, Les Roberts refers to cinematic cartography as an assemblage of discourse clusters, rather than a clearly defined subject area.[41] Cartographic approaches to film studies do not necessarily have to entail the analysis of maps that appear onscreen, and indeed, what ultimately preoccupies me here is the ways in which cinema itself might be viewed as a form of mapping. This could involve a discussion of the historical and conceptual connections between filmmaking and cartography; the visualisation and sequencing of geography onscreen; films that foreground journeys and themes of travel; or the mapping of external environments in relation to internal emotional states. In this sense, I take up Teresa Castro's view that mapping can refer to 'a multitude of processes, from the cognitive operations implied in the structuring of spatial knowledge to the discursive implications of a particular visual regime'.[42] If film cartography is defined in these terms, then it is clear that processes associated with mapping have been far better served in studies of Taiwanese cinema, perhaps the best known example being Fredric Jameson's article on *Terrorizers* (Edward Yang, 1986), which has been criticised on a number of fronts.[43]

More recent examples include Ma's analysis of the national dreamscape in *Island Etude*, Jessie Liu Ssu-Fang's article on sound mapping in this film and *The Most Distant Course*, and Xiao Cai's discussion of the remapping of cities in Hou's films.[44] These discussions focus on case study films or individual directors, however; there has been no comprehensive attempt to approach Taiwanese cinema more generally from the perspective of film mapping. Focusing on the period 2008–20, this is what I propose to undertake in this book, carefully considering which critical methodologies are best suited to the task at different points. The first half of the book, for instance, will place heavier emphasis on the maps themselves, which, as Conley puts it, underline 'what a film is and what it does' while opening a rift or bringing into view 'a site where a critical and productively interpretive relation with the film can begin'.[45]

One challenge, in arguing for the relevance of these ideas in the Taiwanese context, is that cinematic cartography as an analytical approach has developed primarily in terms derived from Western traditions. Film scholars have productively challenged cartographers to rethink their discipline.[46] Yet their tendency to focus on European and American case studies ironically replicates the oversight of an earlier generation of cartographers. In a series of seminal chapters published in *The History of Cartography* in 1994, Cordell D. K. Yee argued against the critical appraisal of Chinese maps in relation to Western models emphasising scientific and mathematical measurability.[47] On the one hand, as J. B. Harley and others have argued, the claim to objectivity and abstraction obscured the hidden agendas of Western cartography and its legitimisation of colonial conquest.[48] However, Yee's articulation of the Chinese tradition of mapping – as accommodating subjectivity, relativism, and emotion – makes a case for its qualitative difference, and moreover anticipates some of the formulations around cinematic space and affect that would emerge a decade later in film studies.

The Chinese word for map, *ditu*, is comprised of *di* 地 (earth, ground, soil) and *tu* 圖, which can mean a map, but also a picture, drawing, diagram, or chart. This reflects how, in the Chinese historical tradition, maps and images were more closely intertwined than in the West, and until the late Qing period, were more clearly aligned with the arts. In particular, there was significant aesthetic overlap between maps and paintings.[49] Within this representational context, Yee argues, a good map 'did not necessarily tell how far it was from one point to another' – the ostensible purpose of a Western map – but might 'tell us about such things as power, duty, and emotion'.[50] We might trace a line from this understanding of mapmaking to later cinematic representations in Taiwanese cinema, in a manner that enables us to culturally situate concepts of affective mapping. For example, Huang Chun-Ming's 1974 documentary, *The Homecoming Pilgrimage of Dajia Mazu*, follows the crowds that accompany the statue of the sea goddess on an annual pilgrimage to Beigang. 'If these people did not have faith in Mazu', the narrator remarks, 'this 250 km journey would feel like nothing more than a long walk'. That it transcends this is down to the affective power bestowed on the journey by the participants. In visualising and sequencing – mapping – a route that is as much emotional as geographic, the documentary tells us a great deal about the endurance of religious faith in an ostensibly secular society.

Taiwanese cinema has been influenced by various traditions of mapping, which helped produce the geographic space that we now recognise as Taiwan. The island did not appear on Chinese maps until 1684, following its annexation by the Qing dynasty, while under Dutch rule, 'Taiwan' had referred to the settlement that is now Anping in Tainan.[51] The name gradually came to encompass more territory, but even by the early eighteenth century, Kangxi pictorial maps attest to a certain ambiguity concerning whether the name referred to a region or the whole island.[52] It was much later, in the latter half of the nineteenth century, that the Qing began to map and thereby assert definitive control over the whole island, which became a province named Taiwan in 1887. As Thongchai Winichakul argues in his classic study of the emergence of modern Thai nationhood, maps do not simply reflect the geography of a nation, they actively imagine, model, and create it.[53] Similarly, the mapping undertaken by Taiwanese filmmakers can be conceived as the modelling of possible, desired, or future geographies.

Environments

Any discussion of cinematic mapping requires consideration of the raw material being mapped: the environments depicted in the films. Filmmakers since 2008 have demonstrated considerable interest in charting Taiwan as a distinct geographical environment, and in portraying its varied regions, districts, and locales. While environmentalism, in the political and ethical sense of the term, is a central concern in several of the chapters, my discussion is not focused solely on the ways in which filmic representations of place dramatise ecological anxieties. Rather, I use the term 'environment' in its broadest sense, as an aggregate of surroundings and conditions, in order to capitalise on the scope of the terminology to assist analysis of a range of themes and case studies. So in the chapters that follow, an environment might refer to, for example, the whole of Taiwan, a general region (the east coast), a named region (Chiayi County), a named city (Taipei), a type of natural ecology (forests), or a type of domestic environment (apartments). The films mostly depict environments situated in Taiwan, but aside from that, I have not imposed limitations on their size or scope, nor restricted definitions to physical geography alone (cultural, sonic, gendered, and atmospheric understandings of environment are also discussed).

Post-2008 cinematic portrayals of the island's geography differed quantitatively and qualitatively from those of previous representations. Prior to the arrival of the Taiwan New Cinema in the 1980s, earlier generations of practitioners had not demonstrated much interest in depicting Taiwan's geography as unique; locations frequently appeared as stereotyped backdrops, or doubled for elsewhere (often mainland China, as was the case in many martial arts films and historical dramas). Until the 1980s, Dennis Lo summarises, rural location shooting in Taiwan had been used largely for aesthetic expedience or propagandistic purposes: 'the picturesque locales usually stand in for a Chinese imagined community, rather than uniquely local identities and histories based on Taiwanese lived experience.'[54] For instance, 'healthy realism' of the 1960s and 1970s sought to conjoin the techniques of Italian neorealism with narratives alleging the ways in which Taiwan's population thrived under KMT rule.[55] Yet although these films represented rural life in relation to nationalist ideologies, directors associated with healthy realism did use some impressive location shooting, while Guo-Juin Hong notes the meticulous quality of their interior sets.[56]

In this respect, it is worth considering the question of historical antecedents to the trends discussed in this book. Briefly addressing post-2008 developments, Hong cautions that in contemplating the possibility of a new kind of Taiwanese cinema, we resist the temptation to define newness in terms of a definitive break, 'lest the celebration of the new blocks the historical paths to an understanding, many understandings, of the present'.[57] In this book, I have tried to take one of these historical paths, making a case for the novelty of post-2008 cinema not by arguing for some kind of temporal rupture, but by historicising the analysis of contemporary case studies. While a detailed appraisal of twentieth-century Taiwanese cinema is outside the scope of this book, each chapter will nevertheless discuss how a range of different films made in the period 2008–20 engaged with the legacy of earlier work, modes, and filmmakers.

Antecedents to the trends considered in this book are perhaps most apparent in the Taiwan New Cinema and its 1990s iteration. Cai argues that *The Boys from Fengkuei* (Hou, 1983), for example, about a group of young men from Penghu who travel to Kaohsiung, is structured as 'an outsider's city map'.[58] The scene in *Rebels of the Neon God* (Tsai Ming-Liang, 1992), in which the protagonist's blood drips onto a page full of Taiwan maps in a textbook, has been interpreted as an AIDS metaphor, but would also seem to have implications for Tsai's views on nationhood.[59] Yet the context and creative rationale for these films was vastly different to those of post-2008 cinema, which impacted on the films' geographical spread and focus. The *auteurs* of the New Cinema filmed mainly in rural villages, contrasting the way of life with that of the cities. But they did not tend to set their films in rural areas on Taiwan's east coast, nor in its forested mountain regions, and rarely in the south. The focus of 1990s cinema, meanwhile, was overwhelmingly on urban life, with films predominantly shot in Taipei and Kaohsiung. By contrast, after a slump in film production in the 1990s, virtually every part of Taiwan has been repeatedly subject to filmed representation since 2008; the sheer volume of filmmakers seeking to represent the full range of Taiwan's environments was also notable.

This could be seen as an effect of changes that occurred during and after democratisation; the emergence of concepts, agendas, and policies that sought to connect Taiwanese identity to the island's geography. Of particular significance here is *bentuhua*, or indigenisation, a type of nationalism that champions the legitimacy of a distinct Taiwanese identity.[60] This has different facets and has taken various forms over the years. In the transition to democracy, *bentuhua* was particularly associated with the integration of Taiwan-born politicians such as Lee Teng-Hui into the ruling elite of the KMT. This anticipated a broader shift in the balance of power, from mainlanders to those born on the island. *Bentu* expanded culturally in the 1990s and was often understood as grassroots localism: as advocating the importance of putting down roots locally, and reducing the cultural gap between rural and urban communities.[61] Ideas such as these seem to inform *Cape No. 7*. Numerous critics have elaborated the ways in which Wei's film presents southern Taiwanese and *taike* identity as distinctive, with protagonist Ah-Chia (Van Fan) ultimately opting to put down roots in Hengchun, rather than returning to Taipei.[62] Berry argues that the narrative about the formation of the music band allegorises and affectively mobilises 'the formation of a new Taiwan structure of feeling centred on the south of the island'.[63] The importance of locality is acknowledged by the film's title, which references the postal address on a decades-old letter that Ah-Chia must deliver. A mystery of orientation drives the narrative, as Ah-Chia seeks to identify the intended recipient based on geographical information – Cape No. 7, Hengchun – that has lost meaning and precision through the passing of time.

The term *bentu* has been applied directly to cinematic developments. In 2012, Davis argued for the emergence of a 'bentu style', a more commercial mode of filmmaking that began as a reaction against the New Cinema, and sought to target local audiences rather than international festival juries.[64] In comparison to *xiangtu*, or nativism, which Davis argues was an animating principle of the Taiwan New Cinema, 'localism seems more of a sentiment than an aesthetic or ideology because of its emotional appeal (something bracketed, if not avoided, in New Cinema) and its straightforward politics of "Taiwan first"'.[65] Defining post-2008 cinema in terms of an impulse to the local is persuasive. The difficulty with this formulation, however, is that it relies on a shaky distinction between aesthetics and ideology on the one hand, and emotion and sentiment on the other. In any case, films of the subsequent decade would not bear out claims of straightforward politics, while aesthetics and affect often combine in complex and powerful ways. Moreover, films do far more than simply reflect the cultural contexts in which they are made. Like maps, they actively shape geography; they make space.

POETICS

The relationship between film environments and mapping is arguably well suited to analysis through the methods of film poetics, a term derived from the Greek word *poesis*, or active making, as used by Aristotle when discussing what we now recognise as drama and literature.[66] Film poetics was pioneered by David Bordwell, who suggests that the poetics of any medium studies 'the finished work as the result of a process of construction', a process that includes a craft component and the general principles of composition, as well as functions, effects, and uses.[67] He distinguishes between three modes: analytical, studying particular devices across a range of works or in a single work; theoretical, laying out conditions for a genre or class of work; and historical, understanding how artworks assume certain forms within or across periods.[68] The focus is on three objects of study: thematics, large-scale form, and stylistics.[69] This articulation of the tradition can been understood as historical poetics, while neoformalism, as developed by Kristin Thompson, can be considered a distinct though overlapping branch of film poetics.[70] Bordwell refers to poetics not as a theory but as 'a set of assumptions, a heuristic perspective, and a way of asking questions', elsewhere referring to it as 'an inductive, empirical discipline'.[71]

Recent adherents include Gary Bettinson, whose monograph on Wong Kar-Wai was intended as a corrective to the dominant critical tendency to interpret the director's films in line with theories derived from cultural studies. Summarising his misgivings, Bettinson expresses concern that many cultural theorists apply pre-existing theory to case studies, a top-down approach that tends to confirm the theory, obscuring, or even misrepresenting what the film might have to offer.[72] Inheriting Bordwell's scepticism of Grand Theory, he argues that a preoccupation with ascertaining meaning takes precedence over examining how a film is structured and made, one result being that 'culturalists often imply authorial intention, but problematically this intention is not always taken to be conscious on the part of the filmmaker'.[73] These arguments seem relevant in the context of Taiwanese cinema, which is routinely alleged by critics to represent, embody, or allegorise national identity, cross-strait relations, and the island's contested political status. The case has been made persuasively by some. But far more often, the existence of a political subtext is taken as given, rather than properly considered and evidenced.

The risk of theoretical generalisation is one reason I am also hesitant to conceive this project in terms of the Sinophone, the cultural studies paradigm first comprehensively outlined by Shu-Mei Shih in her seminal 2007 work, *Visuality and Identity*. In critiquing the concept of diaspora and identifying the site of the Sinophone as 'a network of places of cultural production outside China and on the margins of China and Chineseness', Shih is driven by an ambition to resist essentialism and imperialism, and to decouple notions of homeness and origin.[74] The Sinophone can certainly be conceived as a mapping exercise, which is also true of the critical controversies over the territories it is perceived to incorporate.[75] On the one hand, my work deals with films about Taiwan's indigenous tribes, who by Shih's own admission sit at least partially outside the remit of the Sinophone.[76] More generally, however, I share the concerns of critics such as Flair Donglai Shi, who cautions that proponents of the Sinophone, in seeking to challenge the hegemony of Western theories, risk replacing these with another ideologically reductionist paradigm.[77] The theoretical preoccupations of Sinophone studies potentially conflict with the inductive methods of film poetics.

A full consideration of these issues is evidently outside the scope of this book, although I would add that the two approaches are not intrinsically at odds; indeed the value of some recent work on the Sinophone has been to refocus attention on the acts and practices of cultural production, as was intended by Shih.[78] Ultimately, I probably have more sympathy for culturalist interpretations of cinema than others researching in the poetics tradition, and will often work from initial hypotheses rooted in cultural contexts. But hunches need testing against the evidence of the films themselves, and the methods of poetics are uniquely placed to facilitate this. One advantage of commencing the book with a consideration of onscreen maps, for instance, is that they are visualised and *there*. The presence of a map provides initial confirmation that the filmmakers are thinking about representations of space (and possibly national space, depending on what the map purports to depict). My intention is emphatically not to conceive of cinematic mapping as a theory, but instead to examine the ways in which, as a conceptual framework, it might be approached through the prism of historical poetics, through a focus on histories, thematics, stylistics, and large-scale form.

Of the latter, Bordwell argues that narrative is the most prominent research domain, but unlike in literary studies, film scholars lack 'a term for those transmedia architectonic principles that govern the shape and dynamics of an entire film'.[79] Mapping, insofar as it helps structure the shape and dynamics of a film's representation of space, arguably deserves consideration as a large-scale form of this type. Thinking about it in this way could be a means of connecting the conceptual rationale behind a film to its stylistic traits. Castro, for instance, describes mapping as a mode of thought relating to processes and formal strategies.[80] In this respect, it is worth noting the complex relationship between mapping and design. An onscreen map is a stylistic component of production design, yet the shared characteristics of the two disciplines are not merely stylistic. Conceived as a 'large-scale form', there is much conceptual, etymological, and practical overlap between mapping and designing. Fundamentally both activities involve intent, articulated through a plan or a scheme, which has implications for the spatial patterning of narrative.

The identification of patterns among a body of work, suggestive of underlying principles, is an object of study in film poetics.[81] In order to competently appraise these, I have viewed over 200 Taiwanese films produced in the twenty-first century – listed in the filmography – as well as numerous others from earlier periods. I have sought to explore the particulars of these films, in order to identify recurring norms, standardised practices, and formal and stylistic patterns. My aim in selecting case studies from this viewing has been to offer a sample that is broadly representative and gives an overview of some significant trends in recent Taiwanese cinema. This includes films of varied production types and budgets; popular genre entertainment and arthouse cinema; films aimed at different kinds of audiences, domestically, and abroad; examples of work by directors considered *auteurs* and those who are not.

Looking at a broad range of case studies redresses an imbalance in the scholarly output of film poetics; the tendency to focus on the work of single directors (Bordwell's study of Hong Kong popular cinema being a notable exception).[82] In this respect, a remark made by Yeh, offering an early formulation of film poetics in relation to the work of Hou, has stuck with me. What is significant, Yeh argues, 'is not identifying or capturing aspects of authorship, attributable to Hou, but instead showing how a corpus impinges on cinema as a narrative art'.[83] In effect, I have tried to scale up this approach, by analysing the films of a wide range of directors for their contribution to more general aesthetic trends. By doing this, one begins to see the reiterative effect of certain themes and forms being repeated over time, which can ballast more speculative arguments around nationhood and identity.

Practice

Film practice – the process of making a film – is an object of study in the poetics tradition, and in approaching post-2008 Taiwanese cinema in these terms, I will investigate the diverse ways in which screen environments are *made*. Discussing representations of place in films shot in mainland China and Taiwan, Lo disapproves of the critical tendency to interpret these depictions as 'semiotic signs that symptomize ideologies of nation building, globalization, or the cultural logics of modernity, postmodernity, and postcoloniality'.[84] Lo prefers to understand location shooting as 'place making', and advocates examining how narrative forms and stylistic motifs shape the viewer's experience of filmed locations by transforming them into places imbued with affective and symbolic meanings.[85] While the terms 'location' and 'site' are fairly neutral and will be used in this book to designate a given environment where filming occurs, 'place' is here understood as having affective value and as such something that is fundamentally made. This is where poetics, which Bordwell defines as a practice-based theory of art, overlaps with studies of production culture.[86]

This book is not intended as a comprehensive study of post-2008 production cultures, although I will draw on original interviews with several of the filmmakers whose work is discussed, as well as other interview material already in the public domain. A limitation is that most – though not all – of the interviews cited are with film directors and producers, rather than other crew members. It will become apparent, however, that my emphasis on recurring practices and representations calls into question some critical assumptions around film authorship. Nonetheless, to state that film directors sometimes engage with a shared set of preoccupations, and enact similar forms and styles, is not to deny the possibility of individual agency, innovation, and originality. Director Hou Chi-Jan puts it eloquently when he suggests that the emergence of a new kind of cinema was not solely down to a set of individuals, but marked 'the process of a particular time'.[87]

Mapping is a practice that involves a process of making, which opens up a range of questions and possibilities as I investigate its interplay with recent Taiwanese filmmaking. Examining the relationships between maps and narrative, Sébastien Caquard and D. R. Fraser Taylor observe that the first decade of the twenty-first century witnessed a post-representational shift in theories of cartography, with the production of maps conceived as a process of becoming.[88] Rob Kitchen, Justin Gleeson, and Martin Dodge argue that maps possess no ontological security; despite the semblance of being immutable and transferable across space and time, maps are always of the moment, are never fully formed, and 'unfold in context through a mix of creative, reflexive, playful, affective and habitual practices'.[89] With this in mind, it could be argued that the term 'remapping', frequently deployed by academics working in film and cultural studies, loses its value, in that it implies there was a stable map to begin with. These developments in cartographic theory can help inform a discussion of mapping as a film practice, noting that while a processual understanding of the map is a relatively recent development in the West, this is not necessarily the case in different traditions. Yee argues that traditional Chinese mapmaking, for instance, shared with painting an 'organismic and processual worldview' that differed from European traditions, in which space was defined as an abstract entity that was bounded and static, and therefore measurable.[90] While 'space' might be understood as a three-dimensional interval of distance between objects, this assumes stasis and fixity, and fails to acknowledge the ways in which space is always relational, undergoing continual construction, and is created through movement and transformation. Throughout this book, I assume a definition of cinematic space not as a thing in its own right, but as a continually evolving product of a creative process.

As an impulse that motivates cinematic depictions of environments, film mapping is a process of making and becoming: a practice of futurity. While in its most basic sense, film mapping is a metaphor – few Taiwanese filmmakers are likely to refer to their practice in these terms – I would contend that its principles help construct what we see onscreen. Mapping deserves consideration alongside narrative as a large-scale form that impacts upon practice at virtually at all stages of production. It might be, for example, conceptual (an outlook on the visual dramatisation of place), processual (the development of performances within a particular environment), or technical (the use of post-production software to construct a landscape). Filmmakers shape and craft their work actively and with idiosyncrasy, rather than passively reflecting cultural trends. Like mapmakers, they bring space into being.

Chapter Overview

This book examines what it means to map an environment in post-2008 Taiwanese cinema, with each chapter enabling critical scrutiny of significant developments in the post-2008 period. Chapter 2 argues that recent Taiwanese cinema can be understood in terms of a mapping impulse. I consider the breadth of screen artefacts that might be considered cartographic, whether defined conventionally (globes, wallcharts) or less so (cosmological diagrams, designs on interior furnishings), as well as elements imported from cartography, such as latitudinal and longitudinal coordinates. I begin by discussing films released in the years 2006–8, in which onscreen cartography recurs and is indicative of the filmmakers' broader interest in affectively and thematically mapping Taiwan. Turning to post-2008 developments, I analyse three case studies, *Somewhere I Have Never Travelled* (Fu Tien-Yu, 2009), *Godspeed* (Chung Mong-Hong, 2016), and *Aground* (Hsin Chien-Tsung, 2017). Contemplating questions around queer mapping and orientation, affective itineraries, cinematic salvage, and mapped representations of historical experience, I investigate how cinematic cartography is used to chart the island and its place in the world.

Chapter 3 examines the post-2008 reappearance of forests in films such as *Starry Starry Night* (Lin Shu-Yu, 2011), *Soul* (Chung Mong-Hong, 2013), *The Tag-Along* (Cheng Wei-Hao, 2015), and *Forêt Debussy* (Kuo Cheng-Chui, 2016). Forests have not featured significantly in Taiwanese cinema since the 1970s, so why did they return to cinematic prominence in the years after 2008? A discussion of the differing answers this question might provoke reveals tensions between the typical analytical frameworks of cultural studies and film poetics. We might account for this recent arboreal trend with reference to national identity, eco-cinematic agendas, developments in digital technology, the rise of genre cinema, and transnational business strategies. But fundamentally, these films can be understood as traumatic narratives in which the forest is mapped as something authentic that has paradoxically grown out of artifice. I nonetheless contemplate the possibility of this environment having an existence in and of itself, arguing for the capacity of the forest to impose its own aesthetic form on film practice.

Chapter 4 addresses questions of mapping in the fiction films that have emerged since 2008 about Taiwan's original inhabitants, the island's indigenous tribes. These include Laha Mebow's films *Finding Sayun* (2011) and *Lokah Laqi* (2016), *Wawa No Cidal* (Cheng Yu-Chieh and Lekal Sumi, 2015), *Pakeriran* (Lekal Sumi, 2017), and *Long Time No Sea* (Tsui Yung-Hui, 2018). Thematically, questions of land ownership and appropriation lie at the heart of these narratives, and I argue that visually, the trope of surveying – as a precursor to territorial acquisition – can be understood in relation to cartographic forms such as the aerial view. Thematically and formally, these films challenge abstract notions of space, for instance through onscreen depictions of counter-mapping, while at the level of practice, the use of non-professional actors requires us to consider the relationship between performance and environment. The chapter finally considers the significance of the sea to filmic depictions of indigenous experience, discussing how the waters around the island of Lanyu are depicted as productive of emotion.

Chapter 5 examines the relationship between mapping and design in post-2008 depictions of Taipei. *Design 7 Love* (Chen Hung-I, 2014) experiments self-reflexively with what it means to design, while other films including *Love* (Niu Cheng-Tse, 2012), *Zone Pro Site* (Chen Yu-Hsun, 2013), *The Mad King of Taipei* (Yeh Tien-Lun, 2017), *52Hz I Love You* (Wei Te-Sheng, 2017), and *The Story of the Stone* (Wu Hsing-Hsiang, 2018) may not feature design as a subject, but arguably share with Chen's film an impulse to construct Taipei as a designer city. This is undertaken by the creative decoration of the city's environments using multicoloured palettes, while the narrative recurrence of boutique stores points to dynamics of city-fashioning. More fundamentally, I argue that design is about the plotting of the future, with both narrative and design shown to be motivated by desire; in these films, love provokes the spatial and affective movement of ensemble casts along intersecting, mapped routes. In particular, Taipei's green and repurposed spaces, reimagined in line with a designer vision, set the characters on the path to conflict resolution.

Chapter 6 investigates the mapping of interior space in a range of recent films that have opted to situate significant portions of their dramas in relatively confined living quarters: flats, apartments, and houses. At stake in films such as *Exit* (Chienn Hsiang, 2014), *Black Sheep* (Bon An, 2016), *Sen Sen* (Bon An, 2018), *More than Blue* (Lin Hsiao-Chien, 2018) and *Dear Ex*

(Hsu Yu-Ting and Hsu Chih-Yen, 2018) are commonly accepted notions of what the domestic and the familial entail. Preoccupied with the home as an unhealthy, ailing space, these films arguably rework a Taiwanese tradition of recuperative family melodrama, with theatrical performance an important theme and mode. I examine tensions between the materiality of the home and psychological journeys, and discuss how the filmmakers construct domestic atmosphere and haptic portrayals of interior geography. Finally, I turn to cleaning, conceived as a movement of domestic material that facilitates narrative progress.

Chapter 7 examines how sound is used to dramatise the process of masculine change in 'quiet places' – the tranquil, sleepy settings common to otherwise diverse films including *A Time in Quchi* (Chang Tso-Chi, 2013), *The Great Buddha +* (Huang Hsin-Yao, 2017), and *Secrets in the Hot Spring* (Lin Kuan-Hui, 2018). From the characters' perspectives, these are backwaters in which they involuntarily languish, but while these films are ostensibly constructed in terms of urban centres versus rural peripheries, they are ultimately about character psychology; the filmmakers ask why it is that their male protagonists feel peripheral. I examine how the characters' affective journeys are articulated through soundtrack components including ambient sound, music, voiceover, and sound effects, looking at connections between depictions of environments and masculinity that is in the process of undergoing change. These films all require that the viewer must not merely hear, but must listen to, the soundtracks, and a final consideration of *Father to Son* (Hsiao Ya-Chuan, 2018) prompts an exploration of the connections between listening, mapping, and narrative patterning.

Some chapters look at each case study in turn, while others are structured thematically. Although I will offer detailed discussion of specific scenes and aspects of the filmmaking process, it is not my intention to provide comprehensive close analysis of entire films and their production. Certain areas are outside the scope of this book. First, I will analyse fiction films, rather than documentaries or television productions, although these will be mentioned for context. Second, while a diverse range of filmmakers will be discussed, I will not look in any depth at films made by Taiwan's most celebrated living directors Hou, Lee, and Tsai; they have received widespread critical coverage elsewhere, and this study is in part designed to counterbalance *auteur*-focused scholarship. Third, I will focus on depictions of contemporary Taiwan. This means I have had to exclude some significant cinematic trends, such as the rise of nostalgic time travel films including *Our Times* (Chen Yu-Shan, 2015) and *Take Me to The Moon* (Hsieh Chun-Yi, 2017). While filmic representations of time, history, and memory will be discussed in the context of the book's central theses, a detailed consideration of post-2008 films that primarily depict the past would require a separate study.

Notes

1. Stevenson, *Treasure Island*.
2. The French title under which the film was released internationally differs from the Chinese title, *The Suicidal Incident of the Squirrel*.
3. Dung, *Atlas*, 125.
4. Ibid., 125.
5. Lim, 'Taiwan New Cinema', 157.
6. Ibid., 157–8.
7. Pickowicz and Zhang, *Locating Taiwan Cinema*.
8. Ma, *The Last Isle*; Mon, *Film Production and Consumption*.
9. Yeh et al., *32 New Takes on Taiwan Cinema*.
10. For a summary of the reasons for this, see Yeh, 'Taiwan: popular cinema's disappearing act', 165.
11. Ibid., 159, and Weng et al., 'Concentration ratio', 122. Fewer local films were made and watched overall, but audiences focused on a smaller number of local successes.
12. Udden, 'Taiwanese comedies', 176.
13. Chinese Taipei Film Archive/Taiwan Film Institute/Taiwan Film and Audiovisual Institute, *Taiwan Cinema Yearbooks* (1991–2021).
14. See, for example, Chiu et al. (eds), *Taiwan Cinema*.
15. Wang, 'Memories of the future', 139.
16. Yang, 'Passionately documenting', 49.
17. Lim, 'Taiwan New Cinema', 158–9.
18. Davis, 'Second coming', 134.
19. Lin, 'Charting the transnational', 196.
20. Zhang, 'Taiwan film market', 29.
21. Berry and Farquhar, *China on Screen*, 9.
22. Zhang, *Cinema, Space, and Polylocality*, 21.
23. Wood, *Rethinking the Power of Maps*, 51.
24. Chang, *Place, Identity and National Imagination*, 44–5, 59–60.
25. Ibid., 155–206.
26. Ibid., 72, 89.
27. Ibid., 104–5.
28. Ibid., 104–5.
29. Yee, 'Traditional Chinese cartography', 194.
30. Eskildsen, *Transforming Empire in Japan*, 336–8. Also see 43–72 and 263–94.
31. Su, 'Multi-layered reconciliations', 104.
32. See Ma, *The Last Isle*, 27–9, 34–43. He suggests (43) that the *huandao* tour was previously associated with high school or college graduation trips, but had in recent decades become a more common endeavour. See also Liu, 'From visual fantasies to bodily trajectories', 199–213. She suggests (200) that the tour began to prevail as a personal travel itinerary and a publicly promoted agenda around a decade after the lifting of martial law in 1987.
33. Lo, *The Authorship of Place*, 175.
34. Chang, *Place, Identity and National Imagination*, 155–206 (quotation 198).
35. Misawa, 'The national anthem film'. The national anthem films began to disappear from the late 1980s, with Yilan County being the first to announce the discontinuation of screenings in 1988. Despite this theoretically breaching film laws, local governments failed to enforce compliance; these pre-feature cinema screenings seem largely to have ceased by the mid-1990s.
36. Tsai, 'Mapping Formosa', 306–9.

37. Ibid., 307.
38. Chang, *Place, Identity and National Imagination*, 77, 89–90.
39. Conley, *Cartographic Cinema*, and Bruno, *Atlas of Emotion*.
40. Tsai, 'Mapping Formosa', 295–319.
41. Roberts, 'Cinematic cartography', 69.
42. Castro, 'Cinema's mapping impulse', 14.
43. Jameson, 'Remapping Taipei'. For a critique of his arguments, see Yeh and Davis, *Taiwan Film Directors*, 127–31.
44. Cai, 'Borders and trajectories'; Ma, *The Last Isle*, 27–44; Liu, 'From visual fantasies to bodily trajectories'.
45. Conley, *Cartographic Cinema*, 2.
46. See Caquard and Taylor, 'What is cinematic cartography?', 5–8.
47. Yee, 'Reinterpreting traditional Chinese geographical maps', 35–70.
48. Harley, 'Maps, knowledge, power', 277–312.
49. Yee, 'Chinese cartography among the arts', 128–69.
50. Yee, 'Reinterpreting Traditional Chinese Geographical Maps', 67.
51. Teng, *Taiwan's Imagined Geography*, 44–5, 265.
52. Ibid., 141.
53. Thongchai, *Siam Mapped*, 130.
54. Lo, *The Authorship of Place*, 36, 102.
55. Wicks, *Transnational Representations*, 113.
56. Hong, *Taiwan Cinema*, 78.
57. Ibid., 189.
58. Cai, 'Borders and trajectories', 39–44.
59. Lim, *Celluloid Comrades*, 137–42.
60. Makeham and Hsiau, *Cultural, Ethnic, and Political Nationalism*, 1.
61. See Davis, 'Second coming', 144. Chang argues that the legacy of *bentu* can be seen in the establishment of the Ministry of Culture in 2012, although the term *nitu* (literally, earth or soil) was preferred to *bentu* or *xiangtu*. See Chang, *Place, Identity and National Imagination*, 210.
62. See, for example, Wang, 'Memories of the future', 145–7, and Berry, 'Cape No. 7'.
63. Berry, 'Cape No. 7', 317.
64. Davis, 'Second coming', 145.
65. Ibid., 145.
66. Bordwell, *Poetics of Cinema*, 12.
67. Ibid., 12.
68. Ibid., 12–13.
69. Ibid., 17.
70. Bettinson and Rushton, *What Is Film Theory?*, 132–3.
71. Bordwell, *Poetics of Cinema*, 20, and 'Transcultural spaces', 143.
72. Bettinson, *Sensuous Cinema*, 9–12.
73. Ibid., 9.
74. Shih, *Visuality and Identity*, 4, 189–90.
75. Numerous scholars have argued that the Sinophone fails to account for the diversity of cultural practice; as far as this applies to film, some propose to correct the geographical remit of the terminology (see Lu, 'Genealogies of four critical paradigms', 20–3), whereas others allege that the very premise is flawed (see Lim, 'The voice of the Sinophone', 72–4).
76. Shih, *Visuality and Identity*, 119.
77. Shi, 'Reconsidering Sinophone Studies', 333.
78. Shih, *Visuality and Identity*, 35.
79. Bordwell, *Poetics of Cinema*, 18.

80. Castro, 'Mapping the city', 154.
81. Bordwell, *Poetics of Cinema*, 24–5.
82. Bordwell, *Planet Hong Kong*.
83. Yeh, 'Poetics and politics', 175.
84. Lo, *The Authorship of Place*, 9.
85. Ibid., 19.
86. Bordwell, *Poetics of Cinema*, 22.
87. Hou in Q&A discussion. See Lin, 'New auteurs in Taiwan post-New Wave cinema'.
88. Caquard and Cartwright, 'Narrative cartography', 104–5.
89. Kitchen et al., 'Unfolding mapping practices', 481.
90. Yee, 'Chinese cartography among the arts', 144–5.

2. YOU ARE HERE

Introduction: Going Places

A woman consults a map of southern Taiwan at a roadside service station. An annotation in red indicates her current location, and the camera, moving diagonally up to the right, follows her gaze over the map in a point-of-view shot, anticipating where she wants to go: Taitung. The film is *My Little Honey Moon* (Cheng Yu-Chieh, 2012) and the protagonist's name is Chiung-E (Helen Thanh Dao), a Vietnamese immigrant who, following an arranged marriage, resides in the Hakka district of Meinong. At this point in the film – two-thirds of the way through – she has run away from her husband and is heading on a road trip with her daughter. Having barely travelled around the island at all, Chiung-E has decided to visit the friend who first taught her how to drive and now lives in Taitung. The roadside map gains affective resonance in this narrative context, with the point-of-view camera movement capturing how she mentally charts a course to her friend, embarking on a journey of empowerment. Assisted by this visualisation, 'You are here' morphs into 'You will be there', or more precisely, 'You want to be there'.

The scene underscores the importance of mapping to post-2008 Taiwanese cinema, an impulse also evident in films that do not feature onscreen cartography. In *Lokah Laqi* (Laha Mebow, 2016), shot in the indigenous Sqoyaw Village in Taiwan's central mountain regions, the character of Hu (Tsao Shih-Huei), returning to his hometown, takes his former teacher Lawa (Huang

Ching-I) on a scooter ride around the local area. They stop at a vantage point that offers a vista of the valley. Hu points to the village with his finger, indicating the location of his elementary school, and then his afterschool class. The entirety of the village landscape is spread out in front of them, enabling him to pick out geographical details. This is a cartographic image, and one with narrative purpose, signalling how both characters orient themselves in relation to their pasts, with an eye on the future. Places in which the pair previously shared experiences are now laid out spatially in front of them, at a moment when both characters are contemplating the future directions their lives might take.

In these examples, geographic imagery helps articulate and anticipate changes in characterisation; this is just one of the ways in which film mapping can be understood as a practice of futurity, a means of bringing narrative and affective space into being. The scene in *My Little Honeymoon* depicts an onscreen map, whereas the scene in *Lokah Laqi* does not, but both films arguably share an impulse *to map*, as a means of creatively approaching the relationship between environments, narrative, characters, and affect. In contemplating how these dynamics play out more broadly in post-2008 Taiwanese cinema, this chapter focuses on onscreen cartography, and what its appearance reveals about the principles, processes, and practices that shape filmmakers' construction of cinematic space. I will introduce the breadth of screen artefacts that might be considered cartographic, whether defined conventionally (globes, wallcharts) or less so (cosmological diagrams, geographical designs on interior furnishings), while also considering other elements imported from cartography, such as latitudinal and longitudinal coordinates.

Subsequent chapters will focus less on the maps themselves, and more on film mapping as a mode of poetics and practice; but as a starting point, it is useful to articulate the relationship between the two. This chapter will analyse the diverse ways in which a nation might be cinematically mapped, by focusing on films that directly depict national and regional cartography onscreen. On the one hand, these films seek to map Taiwan and its place in the world, yet they simultaneously embody what Tom Conley refers to as bilocation. This is where an onscreen map acts as a guarantee that the film unfolds in a particular location, but also signals prevarication, inserted to establish the fallacious authenticity of a place, and to invent new or other spaces.[1] The films considered in this chapter are all shot in Taiwan, but whether they can be said to *represent* Taiwan is another question – one that recurs in my discussion of the three principal case studies, all of which construct imagined and affective spaces. Before turning to these, I will first sketch out some context, examining the proliferation of screen cartography in Taiwanese films released around 2006–8, and the different uses to which onscreen maps have been put in the years since.

Onscreen Maps: From Island Circuits to Regional Itineraries

Amour-Legende (Wu Mi-Sen, 2006), discussed at the opening of this book, was among several Taiwanese films released in the years 2006–8 that signalled the arrival of a new kind of cinema, and also contained onscreen maps. These included the 'island-circuit' films such as *Island Etude* (Chen Hwai-En, 2007) and *The Most Distant Course* (Lin Ching-Chieh, 2007), which featured characters travelling around Taiwan, usually along its coastal circumference. These travelogue films consolidated a real-life trend for such trips, often undertaken by bike and replicated in YouTube videos, blogs, and exhibitions.[2] Using locations along the route as a prompt to discuss aspects of the island's history, the filmmakers contemplate various facets of contemporary Taiwanese identity. Karen Ya-Che Yang argues that the journey undertaken by Ming (Tung Ming-Hsiang) in *Island Etude* 'draws out a geographical Taiwanese nationalism shaped through topographical and cultural diversity'.[3] For Ssu-Fang Jessie Liu, the film's significance lies in its tactile depiction of geography and its embrace of Taiwan's multi-layered history, indicating an open and inclusive political sphere.[4]

A consideration of the maps that appear in *Island Etude* can enrich our perspective on these arguments. Near the end of the film, a map is shown chalked onto a blackboard in Ming's apartment in Kaohsiung. It is a rough aerial rendering of Taiwan that he has drawn himself. Only at this point is the viewer shown the whole of his mapped route and the entirety of Taiwan; we have hitherto seen close-up fragments of the maps that Ming consults while on the trip. This reflects how a sequence of discrete scenes, set in different locations along the route, come to cumulatively represent the wholeness that is Taiwan. Furthermore, the maps that Ming carries with him are presented in a recurring visual manner: they are opened out, placed on the ground, and weighed down with stones (Figure 2.1). The maps are repeatedly grounded, their aerial abstraction made to connect to the earth, at first sight implying a utopian view of cartography as proximate to the national geography it represents. This is a highly ocular depiction that runs counter to Liu's argument that the film emblematises an epistemological move from the visual to the sensorium.[5] Here, both work in combination to problematise mapping. Ming weighs down his maps with stones because he wants to avoid them being blown away by the wind – a preoccupation with tactility that is dramatised elsewhere, such as when a crab or beetle scuttles over one map, and when raindrops land on another. Open to the elements, these maps of Taiwan risk disappearance or disintegration, implying a more ambivalent view of national cartography under threat.

Sheng-Mei Ma examines how *Island Etude* embodies ambiguities and ironies, arguing that although it is a docudrama, the film has much in common

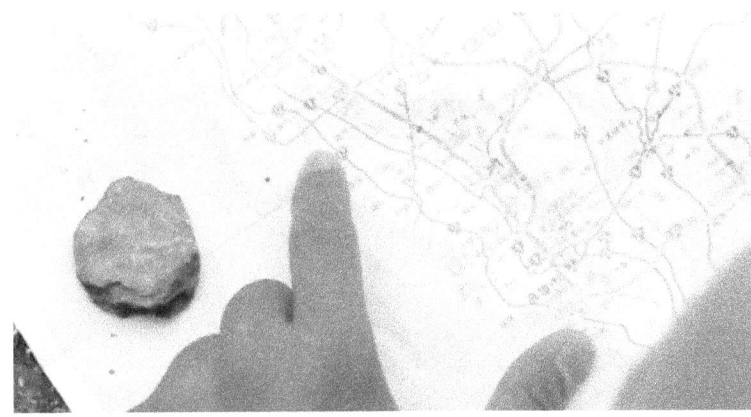

Figure 2.1 Wet map weighed down by a stone in *Island Etude* (Chen Hwai-En, 2007).

with the melodrama *Cape No. 7* (Wei Te-Sheng, 2008), in that both construct a 'romanticized dreamscape'.[6] This is emblematised, he suggests, by both films' sympathetic portrayal of the island's Japanese heritage, which Ma interprets as a reaction against the Chinese identity represented by mainland China and the former KMT regime.[7] Intriguingly, in this respect, one of the last films to adhere fully to the island-circuit format was a Japanese production, *Southern Wind* (Kôji Hagiuda, 2014), in which maps are ubiquitous.[8] Journalist Aiko (Mei Kurakawa) is sent to Taiwan to cover a cycling tour, and ends up travelling around the island with two locals, played by Chi Pei-Hui and Huang He. The maps they consult along the way help consolidate a strongly touristic aesthetic. The *Island Etude* format is reconfigured for a Japanese audience, as Aiko is taken on a guided tour of Taiwan, learning about its history and culture.

The island-wide travelogues were a relatively brief fad, and became less prominent in the years after 2008. *Anywhere Somewhere Nowhere* (Li Ting, 2014) was perhaps the last Taiwanese iteration, about a young film director who is scouting locations; onscreen titles indicate the names of the places he visits, and their distance in kilometres from his home. While the circumnavigation of the island occasionally surfaced as a secondary element in other narratives, more generally the legacy of the island-circuit trend was to facilitate depictions of regional life, a significant trope being characters who leave the cities and head out to the provinces. Ah-Chia (Van Fan) does this in *Cape No. 7*, travelling from Taipei to Hengshun, at the southernmost tip of the island. This new focus on the mapping of provincial regions contrasts with the bulk of 1990s cinema, which had been set mainly in cities. Taipei and Kaohsiung were widely visualised during this period, with urban experience a defining subject of works by *auteurs* such Edward Yang and Tsai Ming-Liang. There were isolated exceptions, such as *Tropical Fish* (Chen Yu-Hsun, 1995), which for James Udden represents a transitional moment in Taiwanese cinema formally and stylistically; yet his claim that it was 'a film of its particular time and place, but not thereafter', is more difficult to sustain thematically.[9] For the film deploys a trope that later became commonplace, the charting of itineraries from urban to rural environments, problematising notions of centre and periphery.

We see an early articulation of this in *Do Over* (2006), in which it often feels as if director Cheng Yu-Chieh is trying to offer a taxonomy of environments in northern Taiwan. This can be examined as a form of 'cartographic narration', which Giuliana Bruno argues collapses Michel De Certeau's distinction between the map and the tour – between seeing (the knowledge of an order of places) and going (spatialising actions).[10] One of the film's storylines, about Thai immigrant Ting-An (Huang Chien-Wei), commences on the periphery of Taipei. Ting-An drives along the motorway, passes a road toll booth, picks up his friend Kao (Kao Ying-Hsuan), and drives through a tunnel. Reaching a rural area, they leave their car and walk through a field, before finally reaching the seashore. There is a narrative purpose to this journey, to be sure; Ting-An has an ulterior motive in seeking to extract information from his friend. But these thirteen minutes of screen time simultaneously capture a spatial trajectory from the city to the coast, in which diverse environments appear sequentially.

Do Over offers an apt illustration of Conley's point that even films which do not feature onscreen maps bear an implicit relation to cartography.[11] This might be conceived in terms of an offscreen map, in which filmmakers plot the journey of their characters across geographical terrain, and make creative decisions about the sequencing of locations. Crucial here is what the historian of cartography J. B. Harley referred to as a 'mapping impulse', which he argues likely existed in human consciousness before maps appeared as physical artefacts.[12] For Teresa Castro, this 'is less about the presence of maps in a certain visual landscape and more about the processes that underlie the understanding of space'.[13] Filmic references to cardinal directions, for instance, usually imply mapping, even if cartography does not appear onscreen. A case in point is *Zone Pro Site* (Chen Yu-Hsun, 2013), in which master chef Hai (Yang Yo-Ning) arrives in a Tainan restaurant to show off his skills:

Hai:	'Northern Gourmet Doctor with 16 Knives' is my full nickname.
Ai Feng:	So you live in the north?
Hai:	Taoyuan.
Bystander:	Is Taoyuan considered the north?
Hai:	North of Taichung is considered north.
Bystander 2:	Welcome to the south!

The relative nature of orientation is here played for laughs; a particular place might be culturally designated with reference to points of the compass, but the accuracy of this designation is contingent upon where the subject is situated. In *Zone Pro Site*, this feeds into broader comic observations on regional identity.

In contemplating the appearance of maps in post-2008 Taiwanese cinema, it is worth distinguishing between screen cartography that is intended to be noticed by the viewer, and that which is not. The enormous map in *Amour-Legende* can hardly be missed, but others may go unnoticed by most viewers, if they appear briefly or in the background. In this respect, one can debate the degree to which, in certain contexts, maps have become decorative or generic. Cartography that appears in school classrooms, for instance, is routinely used to authenticate an educational setting. In the comedy *You Are the Apple of My Eye* (Giddens Ko Ching-Teng, 2011), several classroom scenes have as their backdrop a wallchart of a world map, pinned to a display board, with a globe placed on a nearby shelf. Yet even here, the cartography resonates narratively to some degree, its global breadth contrasting with the insularity of the protagonist's small-town existence: it is rare that a map is purely decorative. *Dear Ex* (Hsu Yu-Ting and Hsu Chih-Yen, 2018) similarly features cartography that is glimpsed in passing. A wallchart with a set of seven maps, depicting the world and its continents, is visible in the office where Liu San-Lien (Hsieh Ying-Hsuan) works. While this cartography signifies little as an element of production design, it helps affirm a contrast between the blandness of this globalised corporate space and the vibrant, localised authenticity of the film's main settings.

Many onscreen maps are designed to be noticed, however. Cartography appears three times in *Da Yu: The Touch of Fate* (Pan Chih-Yuan, 2006), first when the teenage runaway Da-Yu (Chang Yang-Yang) must decide whether to embark on a criminal lifestyle by pickpocketing for the first time. Waiting at a newly constructed bus stop, he stares at the route map while his older mentor cautions him: 'You've got to be sure. There's no turning back once you get on this path.' The onscreen cartography analogises a defining moment in Da-Yu's life. A map appears next in the estate agency where his mother works. She advertises new apartments to clients, using a map to indicate the proximity of real estate to future metro stations and planned commercial districts; by omission, the map confirms the effacing of the old neighbourhoods that the new residential complexes will replace. Finally, a police chief consults a map of Taipei while a cellular phone call is traced, setting in motion the climactic encounter between police and gangsters. The three maps assist plot and characterisation, while also evoking the ongoing redesign of the city around its new transport and technology networks.

Orientation is central to the surreal romance *One Day* (Hou Chi-Jan, 2010). A map appears in the opening scene, but it is the compass owned by protagonist Hsin-Ying (Hsieh Hsin-Ying) that holds the secret to her connection with Tsung (Chang Shu-Hao), whom she meets in a shared dream on a ferry in the Taiwan straits. She is dreaming in 2009; he is dreaming in 2010. But a whimsical love story that blossoms across time and space ultimately evolves into a tragedy. For in the dream, it is revealed that Tsung is wearing Hsin-Ying's compass around his neck, having acquired it after her death in an accident, which occurred prior to his dream in 2010. A wayfinding device becomes a plot device, and confirms the inexorability of fate. Invented in China, the compass is a navigational tool in and of itself, but its appearance in the context of cinematic mapping reflects how its history is closely intertwined with that of the map.

Scenes of map-reading, meanwhile, help us understand how a film might itself be considered to have a similar effect to a map, bearing in mind the affective qualities of movement described by Bruno:

> Like engaging with a map, experiencing film involves being passionately transported through a geography. One is carried away by this imaginary travel just as one is moved when one actually travels or moves (domestically) through architectural ensembles. Maps – like films and architecture – offer the emotion of motion.[14]

We see this at work in another film by Chen, *My Missing Valentine* (2020). It is a map that facilitates the transition from one protagonist to another midway through the film, and narratively helps the viewer to realise that Hsiao-Chi (Lee Pei-Yu) and Ah-Tai (Liu Kuan-Ting) are connected by a shared childhood history that Hsiao-Chi has forgotten. After travelling from Taipei to an unspecified town somewhere along the coastline of Yunlin and Chiayi counties, Hsiao-Chi finds a map in a post office locker. Hand-drawn by Ah-Tai when he was younger, it is a pictorial representation of the town and its landmarks, which are highlighted by bubbles containing drawings (Figure 2.2). This sketched rendering of local geography helps Hsiao-Chi reach a nearby beach that she has been searching for.

Were it to be consulted in reality, of course, this childlike map would barely be adequate to orient oneself within the town. As Sébastien Caquard observes, 'Unlike cartography, cinema can show maps that do not have to work. Cinemaps are author-orchestrated: they must only look like they work.'[15] In *My Missing Valentine*, the viewer is prepared to suspend disbelief, because literal wayfinding is less important than the interior, psychological travel that the map facilitates. For upon reaching the beach, Hsiao-Chi's memories flood back and she recalls her traumatic connection to Ah-Tai. She is taken onto a journey through time, back into her past, articulated here in a series of flashback scenes. A process of affective travel is dramatised onscreen, but also

Figure 2.2 Hand-drawn map of a town in *My Missing Valentine* (Chen Yu-Hsun, 2020).

occurs offscreen, on the part of the viewer: map-reading scenes offer a dual engagement with cartography and film, enabling affective moment.

Emotional mapping is central to the case studies discussed in this chapter, each of which is about travel: *Somewhere I Have Never Travelled* (Fu Tien-Yu, 2009), *Godspeed* (Chung Mong-Hong, 2016), and *Aground* (Hsin Chien-Tsung, 2017). In analysing these films, I have taken up Conley's view that screen cartography can make visible the history of the strategies informing what a film is projecting, and that quite often 'maps in films are archival diagrams that tell of the history and strategy of the surrounding film'.[16] The maps in *Somewhere I Have Never Travelled*, for example, assist the filmmaker in her strategy of presenting geography in relation to queer desire, an implied advocacy for the empowerment of minorities. The appearance of other cartographic elements within a film can also illuminate its formal construction and design. *Aground* is derived from a diagram, Hexagram 47, from the Chinese divination text *Yi Jing*, while its final sequence includes mapped coordinates superimposed onscreen.[17] In examining how the filmmaker connects the two, I will explore how onscreen maps have the capacity, as Conley argues, 'to make visible the history of the form producing the film, in other words, the archive held within and generating the tactics of the diagram'.[18]

The case studies reveal the heterogenous influences on recent Taiwanese screen mapping, and confirm Ting-Ying Lin's view that rigid dichotomies between the national and transnational do not exist in post-2008 Taiwanese cinema; rather 'transnational cultural flows have shaped, facilitated, and negotiated the development of Taiwan's national film industry and cinematic cultures'.[19] Despite variation in subject matter, genre, style, and intended audience, these films have one thing in common: they are set in Taiwan but situate their drama in relation to global geography, mapping the island and its place in the world.

Queer Journeys to a Tropical Island: *Somewhere I Have Never Travelled* (2009)

Somewhere I Have Never Travelled is a coming-of-age story about the close bond between Ah-Kuei (Li Yun-Yun as a child; Yu Hsin as a teenager) and her older cousin Ah-Hsien (Lin Po-Hung), who live on the outskirts of a southern port town in Taiwan. The film spans two timeframes. In the first third, Ah-Kuei is a child and Ah-Hsien is a teenager, while the remainder of the film takes place several years later, when she is fifteen and he is twenty. In exploring their transition into adulthood, the film draws a thematic parallel between Ah-Kuei's colour blindness and Ah-Hsien's homosexuality, aspects of their identity that leave them feeling alienated and lonely. Their experience of being different manifests itself as a shared, queer outlook on the world – which fuels their fantasies of travel and escape. A consideration of the film helps sketch out what a poetics of mapping might entail, with journeys thematically foregrounded; several onscreen maps are featured, while the film's title is inspired by the E. E. Cummings poem 'somewhere i have never travelled, gladly beyond', read by Ah-Hsien in a crucial scene.[20] Taking its cue from the poem, the film frames the experience of desire as the imagined traversing of space. Director Fu was mentored on the project by the film's producer Wu Nien-Jen, a key figure of the Taiwan New Cinema, for whom she had previously worked as an assistant.[21] She uses onscreen maps to prompt her characters' interior journeys, dramatising cartography as a site of tension between apparently objective form, and subjective possibility.

The most prominent map in the film is a Pacific-centric Mercator projection, purchased by Ah-Kuei and mounted on her bedroom wall. Ah-Kuei marks this up with a pen, tracing a route from Taiwan to Pingelap in Micronesia, an atoll with a land area of 1.8 square kilometres. It is Ah-Hsien who first makes her aware of this tiny island, which is notable for having a very high proportion of residents, around 10 per cent, who are colour blind, due to a recessive genetic disorder. Visiting a bemused travel agent, Ah-Kuei plots her escape. She discovers that the journey is complicated, entailing three flights – from Taiwan to Tokyo, then to Hawaii, then to the Marshall Islands – and finally a ferry to Pingelap. Ah-Kuei daydreams about her journey to this place that she has never visited. Her map offers an imaginative stimulus of the kind discussed by Bruno, who argues that cartography can substitute for travel.[22] Conventionally, a world map would be consulted vertically, from an aerial overview. But in one shot, Ah-Kuei leans in close, her face against the wall, as if trying to comprehend her route horizontally, as a path unfolding before her eyes (Figure 2.3). She envisions her itinerary not as a two-dimensional scribble, but as a situated exploration.

A climactic, dreamlike shot features two children running towards an idyllic tropical island, affirming that Ah-Kuei's view of Pingelap is hopelessly utopian; her whimsical dreams of escape ignore the costs and practicalities of relocation. The atoll is marked on her map by a childlike sketch, a mound of land rising as an oval from the sea, sprouting palm trees. This is the tropical paradise of fantasy, a treasure island. The markings on the map do not represent a journey from Taiwan to Micronesia that will actually be taken, but rather a desired affective route. In seeking to travel from an environment that marginalises people who are colour blind to an island where achromatopsia is normal, Ah-Kuei charts a course away from alienation. Ultimately, however, neither Ah-Kuei nor Ah-Hsien can leave their hometown; Fu conceives travel as an activity imagined from within confinement. As a child, Ah-Kuei rides a tricycle in Ah-Hsien's bedroom, proclaiming, 'I'm riding around the world!'. As a teenager, she treks around her own room wearing a rucksack.

Somewhere I Have Never Travelled also deploys onscreen maps to emblematise emotional conflict and confusion. When the viewer is first introduced to Ah-Hsien, two maps are visible in his bedroom. The first is a globe, a scale model of the Earth placed on a wooden chest, that is geographically accurate, if a little retro with its faded antique styling. On the floor, however, is something far more unusual. A circular rug depicts the Earth's continents, which remain roughly proportional in terms of land mass, but have been rearranged so that everything is squeezed within the circumference of a two-dimensional circle. The production design establishes a contrast. Within the same bedroom and the same cinematic frame, two maps of the world offer representations that are in conflict. The globe reflects a view of geography that is scientific and measurable, while the rug proposes an imagined geography in which space is creatively compressed and distorted. These discordant maps reflect how, in broader terms, Fu frames her protagonists' inner conflicts in terms of a struggle to reconcile material and emotional space. Ah-Kuei's yearning for Pingelap is a case in point, and the irony here is that the Mercator projection featured on her poster is itself a distortion of geographical reality. As Mark Monmonier explains, this type of projection is undertaken in line with conformality, whereby local angles are preserved on both globes and flat maps, resulting in massive distortions of scale towards the north and south poles.[23] Although interpreted by Ah-Kuei in a subjective manner, the map hardly offers an objective view of geography in the first place.

The map on the rug, however, is qualitatively different, a work of creative design that bears no resemblance to the surface area of the Earth, and becomes a site where Ah-Hsien's inner turmoil is dramatised. A hopeless romantic who fantasises about buying an apartment in New York and living there

Figure 2.3 Affective cartography in *Somewhere I Have Never Travelled* (Fu Tien-Yu, 2009).

Figure 2.4 Rug with distorted map in *Somewhere I Have Never Travelled* (Fu Tien-Yu, 2009).

in domestic bliss with his boyfriend, Ah-Hsien also dreams of travel. In an early scene, he explains to Ah-Kuei how people of different cultures greet one another. Standing on the rug, the pair light-heartedly mimic shaking hands, kissing, and embracing. But suddenly, Ah-Hsien's mood changes. Dejected, he holds Ah-Kuei tight; the physical contact has reminded him of his lonely desire for intimacy. The map on the rug is prominent at this moment. A close-up depicts the characters' feet, with Ah-Hsien standing next to Taiwan. Ah-Kuei's feet rise up on tiptoe from southeast Asia, emphasising the contrast with her cousin's height and maturity (Figure 2.4). She is still a child, whereas Ah-Hsien is coming of age, beginning to experience the alienation commonly faced by young people experiencing same-sex attraction. The map on the rug, with its skewed continents, becomes a site of emergent queer desire, capable of recasting conventional understandings of spatiality.

For just as the map on the rug pushes continents closer together, Ah-Hsien feels near to New York, referring to the city as if it were just within his reach. His affective remapping of space is inescapably intertwined with his sexuality. However the other, more conventional map in his bedroom – the globe with its rigid scale and insurmountable distances – challenges his reimagining of space, and over the course of the film, New York seems to retreat further away from Ah-Hsien. The price of rent in the city begins to dawn on him, and in a travel agency, the camera pointedly lingers on an old poster of the Manhattan skyline, dominated by the twin towers of the World Trade Center. The city that exists in Ah-Hsien's imagination is untouched by geopolitical realities, here emblematised by the architectural legacy of international terrorism.

That is not to say that Ah-Hsien has no sense of space. Indeed, changes in the production design of the character's bedroom across the film's two timeframes indicate the contrary. The younger boy's bedroom includes film posters and props that suggest the influence of Hollywood and European cinema in moulding his nascent longing for romantic escapism, reinforced by the presence of DVDs and books. But five years later, architectural models, designs, and plans are now scattered everywhere. As he has grown up, Ah-Hsien has cultivated a new interest in the design of built environments, implying that his view of space might have become more grounded and scientific. But in fact, the roots of his interest in architecture are romantic. At the end of the film's first section, he meets Mori (Chou Yung-Hsuan), a Japanese architecture student who is visiting Taiwan to take photographs of buildings. Ah-Hsien has an offscreen sexual encounter with Mori, who subsequently departs.

Tellingly, both Mori and the unnamed boyfriend who appears later are played by the same actor, suggesting that the object of Ah-Hsien's desire is less important than the experience of desire itself. 'I love you so much', he tells the boyfriend at one point, but the other guy evidently doesn't reciprocate these feelings, and cheats on him. Although the betrayal is cruel, Ah-Hsien overloads their relationship with significance, just as New York as an eventual destination seems ultimately less important than the yearning he experiences when fantasising about the city. Fu later permits a bleak joke at the character's expense when the boyfriend and his lover are overheard in a bookshop, mockingly remarking that nobody is likely to buy *The End of the Affair*, given that it has been accidentally placed in the travel section. Yet for Ah-Hsien, travel and emotion are more intuitively interconnected – as indeed they were for Graham Greene, the author of the classic novel, who was himself interested in the relationship between mapping and psychology.[24]

Ah-Kuei and Ah-Hsien share a desire to travel, and a conception of space that has been creatively remapped by their queer experience of difference. The film's Chinese title is phrased as a plea or request: *Take Me Somewhere Far Away*. It does not seem insignificant that in fantasising about escape, Ah-Kuei envisages another Pacific island as her destination. Her affinity with Austronesian culture might well tell its own story, and more broadly, *Somewhere I Have Never Travelled* anticipates a clear tendency in post-2008 Taiwanese cinema to refocus on the Pacific as both a location and a geographical idea. This has been interpreted as a gestural turn away from the Taiwan straits, associated with questions of Chinese identity, towards an embrace of global connectivity.[25] However, the degree to which this has occurred can be overstated and one could argue, bearing in mind Conley's notion of bilocation, that Fu's film is not really about the Pacific or Micronesia at all.[26] In dramatising Ah-Kuei's yearning for an island utopia, is Fu evoking the search for Taiwan itself? If utopia is defined as an unobtainable state, then given the island's contested status, the symbolism of a rearranged map is richly evocative. Yet at the narrative level, there is nothing much to suggest that the film is *about* Taiwan; issues of national identity are not directly addressed in the plot or dialogue.

However, bearing in mind the film's formal approach, which owes much to traditions of magic realism, it is the very absence of specificity that becomes significant. *One Hundred Years of Solitude* by Gabriel García Márquez is a point of reference, and mentioned in the film. Ah-Hsien has read the novel, and relates some of the plotlines to Ah-Kuei, which resonate thematically in their own lives.[27] Ah-Hsien tells his cousin about Macondo, the fictional town which recurs in Márquez's work, generally thought to be based on the author's childhood home, Aracataca, but intended to represent Columbian experience more generally. In shaping her young protagonists' unnamed hometown, Fu similarly reaches for a composite; the film is set in an unnamed harbour town in the south of Taiwan, an environment that comprises locations that span the entire island. The harbour settings are identifiable as Kaohsiung, and Ah-Hsien's home was filmed on a location in Zuoying, a district of the city. However, Gongliao, on the far edge of New Taipei City near Yilan, served as the location for Ah-Kuei's seafront house (one interviewer joked that Ah-Kuei's mother must be very robust to walk from Taipei to Kaohsiung every day to buy vegetables).[28] Other locations included the Yanshui Catholic church in Tainan, with its hybrid murals.

Like the map on Ah-Hsien's rug, the filmmakers squeeze disparate geographic locations close together, and within this new configuration, shape an imaginary filmic environment. This creative remapping occurs at the level of practice; that is, in the scouting and filming of locations, and in how footage of them is edited together. This came about for practical reasons. Fu's preferred location for Ah-Kuei's home, Hongmao port village in Kaohsiung, was demolished prior to the shoot; this led the crew to trek across Taiwan in search of an alternative.[29] But the geographical inconsistency was nonetheless in keeping with Fu's instincts; she questioned the need for realism as she felt that once a setting was identified, the audience would expect it to appear in a certain way.[30] Her approach seemed to have more in common with the magic realism of García Márquez, while there is a question mark over the degree to which Fu was even thinking about Taiwan, visually at least:

> The environment in the film was reconstructed by me. The characters speak Taiwanese and so the setting is clearly Taiwan, but I hope not to give clear geographical hints, and even to deliberately blur things. Later, I came to discover that what I wanted to create in the film was a scene of a fishing port in the Japanese countryside. This was different from many Taiwanese fishing ports. It was an atmosphere I assembled from the elements I wanted to see, my own impression; an environment that was created.[31]

Is there general experience to be evoked from this collage of disparate locales? Ah-Kuei's reverie takes her to an island utopia, a striving for civic perfection, which here seems to evoke Taiwan's failure to offer adequate support for minorities – facing discrimination and stasis, they are left to dream of other places. This is a theme that would be taken up frequently in the cinema of the next decade, with mapping offering empowering possibilities for minorities – both filmmakers and fictional characters – seeking agency over their environments.

Fu's film, however, concludes in a downbeat manner, with Ah-Hsien left in a coma following a suicide attempt. The distorted map on his rug returns to visibility in the poignant scene in which he resolves to kill himself. A slow track away from Ah-Hsien brings the rug into view, allowing the continents to unfold while, in a voiceover read tenderly in English, actor Lin recites the Cummings poem from which the film takes its title. Notwithstanding the importance of the Pacific in the film's imaginary, the approach here recalls the aesthetic conventions historically shared by Chinese art and cartography. Poems often inspired maps, and were frequently inscribed on them; they might be the same artefact, as was the case with painting, and were meant to offer poetic, subjective expression as well as geographic information.[32] In this scene in *Somewhere I Have Never Travelled*, the map and the poem are visual and aural components of the same filmic artefact that together affirm Ah-Hsien's commitment to emotional geography, rather than observable terrain and distances. While imagined itineraries may be liberating, equally they may be damaging to vulnerable characters such as Ah-Hsien. Some journeys, perhaps, should not be taken.

WETLAND ITINERARIES: SALVAGE, PLACE, AND PATTERNS IN *GODSPEED* (2016)

Travel is central to the black comedy *Godspeed*, the Chinese title of which, *Yilushunfeng*, is similarly an idiom that means to have a good and safe journey. While *Somewhere I Have Never Travelled* features several cartographic objects, *Godspeed* includes just one, an object that exists on location rather than a prop, and that appears roughly halfway through the film. A concrete globe welcomes visitors to the decrepit Rock Park in Taichung, on top of which presides a rather kitsch statue of a general, probably Chiang Kai-Shek, riding a horse (Figure 2.5). The Asian side of the globe faces frontally, offering the viewer a glimpse of the places featured or referred to in the story: Taiwan, Thailand, Hong Kong, and mainland China. The ironic presence of the statue, towering over the Earth's sphere, alludes to an earlier period in history when the KMT envisaged the Republic of China as encompassing much of the landmass that is faintly visible. The encroaching moss and rot, however, make a mockery of this discreetly abandoned territorial claim.

This disused amusement park, located in the Waipu district of Taichung, adopts a prominent position in the narrative. Criminal boss Ta-Pao (Dai Li-Jen) instructs petty thief Na-Tou (Lin Na-Tou) to transport a drugs package from Taipei to the park, which gangster Brother Tou (Tou Tsung-Hua) uses as his hideout. Na-Tou travels by taxi with the unsuspecting driver Old Hsu (Michael

Figure 2.5 Globe at entrance to Rock Park in *Godspeed* (Chung Mong-Hong, 2016).

Hui Koon-Man), but things spiral out of control when Ta-Pao suspects there is a traitor in their organisation. Though most of the action (everything after the first fifteen minutes) is set in Taiwan, the globe in the Rock Park reminds us of the global influences that have shaped the film's style. Hsu emigrated from Hong Kong, while Hui, the actor who plays him, is strongly associated with the territory's satirical comedy tradition, to which *Godspeed* pays homage. The prologue, meanwhile, features a brutal fight scene staged in a Thai cinema. The high-contrast red lighting and the presence of actor Vithaya Pansringarm intentionally recall *Only God Forgives* (Nicholas Winding Refn, 2013), and establishes the film's Buddhist themes and aesthetics. A consideration of how *Godspeed* represents ideas and forms derived from Buddhism is outside the scope of this book, but is discussed by Victor Fan in his analysis of the film.[33]

Transnational connections concern me here insofar as they help shed light on the film's mapping of Taiwanese environments. For despite Chung's ironic perspective, Taiwan is nonetheless conceived as a central node on the East Asian map, the single place that narratively connects the characters. Ta-Pao travels from Taiwan to Thailand and back; Hsu left Hong Kong twenty years ago; Tou takes an offscreen trip to Henan province in China. The flightpaths taken by the characters connect the island to overseas locations, like a series of invisible lines, and the film is similarly structured in relation to a network of itineraries within Taiwan, a series of road trips. One straightforward route taken by the characters follows a north–south axis from Taipei to Taichung, along the motorways and roads of the island's western corridor. Other routes entail far more circuitous journeys, as the characters must navigate the maze-like lanes of the wetlands located on the western seaboard.

Chung demonstrates an impulse to map that takes various forms. Shooting mainly in Yunlin and Chiayi counties, he takes the opportunity afforded by the road movie format to depict the vast stretches of wetlands, aquaculture pools, and levees that span much of this coastline; the infrastructure of industrial fisheries. The film was partly shot around Kouhu in Yunlin, a subsiding landscape that is below sea level. The overuse of groundwater in industry and agriculture, compounded by annual monsoons, typhoons, and climate change, has transformed the previously arable lands around Kouhu into wetlands.[34] The area was seriously flooded following Typhoon Morakot in 2009, captured in Huang Hsin-Yao's documentary short film *Nimbus* (2009). Huang worked as the making-of videographer on *Godspeed* and collaborated the following year with Chung on *The Great Buddha +*. The area is also highly polluted. Kouhu lies a few kilometres southwest of the petrochemical plants at Mailiao and Taixi. It was featured two years later in Shih Ho-Feng's documentary *The Scenery Through the Smog*, which explores how industrial pollution has been linked to high cancer rates in the area, as well as other health and social issues, including depopulation.

Ivy I-Chu Chang argues that the inchoate landscape imagery of Chung's earlier film, *The Fourth Portrait* (2010) offers 'clear proof that not only the city, but also the countryside as well, has been altered in a frantic effort to keep up with the pace of global capitalism'.[35] The environments in *Godspeed* have also been indelibly marked by human intervention, but the emphasis here is on the aftermath of intervention. The places we see are largely devoid of population, while the placement of ruined architecture amidst watery expanses lends it an almost arbitrary, contingent quality; many buildings are partially ruined and on the brink of being submerged. These places are now backwaters, forgotten by those in the cities they used to serve. A cameo by *Tropical Fish* director Chen Yu-Hsun, as a small-town vet, evokes that earlier cinematic excursion from Taipei to the island's less prosperous provinces.

A salvaging impulse is evident in the dramatisation of these decaying environments, and the approach here has something in common with that of Urbex photographers such as Huang Bo-Wen, who has documented abandoned industrial infrastructure across Taiwan.[36] In *Godspeed*, Chung seeks to document, on film, culturally important sites that may soon disappear (as a result of land subsidence, climate change, post-industrial decline, changing leisure habits, and depopulation). Crucial to the salvage aesthetic is the retrieval of what culture has judged no longer to have value, an allegiance to the visual preservation of forms that will, materially, probably be lost. Even when shooting in central Taipei, Chung has a predilection for older and traditional sites that incongruously endure amidst rapidly redeveloping environments. Na-Tou visits 'Pan's 60-year-old beef noodles stall' on Huayin Street, the kind of small family-run shop that has become increasingly rare in central Taipei, while a later scene occurs next to another historical survivor, an enormous tree with outstretched branches, located in Yizhu township, Chiayi County.[37] This impulse to salvage exists outside the narrative, but also helps contextualise it. Viewers unfamiliar with the Rock Park, for instance, are given enough information to understand its allegorical significance as a relic of the nationalist regime and its bygone leisure habits, its occupation by hoodlums decidedly ironic.

The film thus unfolds on two levels: as a comedic gangster thriller, and as an affective documentation of landscapes in decline, which affords a material basis for the characters' interior journeys. 'It's like a maze here', Hsu mutters as he and Na-Tou try to exit the wetlands, having escaped some gangsters. 'There's no street signs or anything. I keep getting lost, can't find the way.' The pair lack a map. Environmental and psychological navigation are aligned, as the network of levees morphs into an ethical maze. At a low ebb, Na-Tou produces a photograph of a man he claims is his father. Hsu responds by furiously berating his passenger for failing to confront life's hardships: 'Don't take some guy's fucking picture and say it's your dad!' Na-Tou starts to cry. As this cathartic moment plays out, it seems the pair might have managed to escape the wetlands; emotional progress is shown to match advancement through the landscape. So it is especially crushing when, at this bleakest moment, Na-Tou receives a phone call from Ta-Pao asking him to drive back and collect another package. 'Go back' is a spatial instruction to return to the wetlands, but also signals an affective movement backwards. Na-Tou is being asked to revisit the criminal lifestyle from which he is now desperate to flee.

If navigation is central to the characterisation in *Godspeed*, then the spatial orientation of the viewer is also a preoccupation. This is notable in the scenes set in the Rock Park. The film's opening conversation between Ta-Pao and Tou is initially shot using close-ups that reveal little of the environment. But gradually, the shots encompass more of the space, until after thirteen minutes, it becomes clear that the location is a bowling alley. The exterior of the building is then shown briefly as Ta-Pao suspiciously converses with Tou's associate Ah-Wen (Chen Yi-Wen). The opening of *Godspeed* thus permits the viewer to orient themselves within the bowling alley, and just outside it, but no broader geographical context is provided. However as the film progresses, Chung gradually situates the location. By the time Na-Tou delivers his package to Tou, forty-seven minutes into the film, the viewer has learned that the gangsters' hideout is located near Taichung. Its position is gradually mapped, first in relation to Taiwan as a whole, as Hsu and Na-Tou drive there from Taipei, and subsequently in terms of its placement within the amusement park. Na-Tou enters the front gate, passing the roundabout with the overgrown globe as its centrepiece. As he makes his way into the decrepit park, its layout, and the exact location of the bowling alley are unveiled. This visual sequencing requires the viewer to approach a known location from an unfamiliar spatial perspective.

Mapping could also be said to occur through the type of cinematography and its subject matter. Throughout the film, Chung includes several drone shots of cars moving through the landscape. These are mostly filmed from an oblique angle, one of two perspectives that dominated classical cartography historically (the other being the vertical aerial view). This was sometimes known as the *perspective militaire* and was based on the use of a grid to create the impression of perspective when drawing on a flat surface, something that filmmakers can achieve by raising the camera vertically and angling it downwards.[38] In *Godspeed*, the aerial footage of the road network evidences the imposition of human patterns on nature; indeed the oyster beds divided by levees even resemble a grid. This reflects more broadly the film's preoccupation with patterns: that which is ordered, arranged, and recurring. Patterning can be both visual and narrative, here intricately connected, given that Chung is both director and cinematographer.[39] There is, for instance, a recurrence of straight lines in the visuals, often accentuated by the aerial *perspective militaire*.

Shots of vehicles advancing along straight roads are plentiful; in one drone shot, we can observe that the road runs parallel to a railway, which is itself bordered by a line of small greenhouses. Straight lines are elsewhere prominent in the form of levees, the edges of salt and oyster pans, driftwood logs, telegraph wires, the lanes of the bowling alley, and marker sticks protruding from the water. A subtext here may be *feng shui*. Among traditional practitioners, straight lines were regarded as signs of malign influences, of a lack of *qi* – spatial energy – and historically Chinese painters and mapmakers held them in low esteem.[40] Here, the straight lines appear narratively in the context of malign activity: moral corruption, drug smuggling, and murder.

The film's interest in spatial patterning and design is articulated early on. In the film's opening scenes, Ta-Pao explains to Tou that he will again be using Na-Tou as his drugs courier, and we later learn that he first recruited him a year ago. The film then jumps back a year, relating how Na-Tou responded to a newspaper advertisement by calling a phone number. The five-minute sequence that follows sets Na-Tou on an urban tour of Taipei, organised for him by Ta-Pao, who is keen that the drugs handover should avoid detection. Na-Tou's itinerary demonstrates Ta-Pao's obsession with security and his fear of betrayal, lightly poking fun at the paranoia and arcane methods that permeate many gangster thrillers. Ta-Pao first instructs Na-Tou to go to 100 Huayin Street, and to take the stairs to the ninth floor. He is then to enter a hotel and to walk to room 906. Once in the hotel room, the phone rings, Na-Tou answers, and Ta-Pao instructs him to return downstairs, visit a noodle stand, and order pork noodles with pickles. The proprietor brings him a mobile phone, and the instructions continue. This time, Na-Tou is asked to visit a sauna in the East District at 4 am, order porridge in their café, and wait two hours before returning to his locker, where he can finally pick up the illicit parcel. The ludicrously elongated excursion is played for laughs, as the bewildered courier wanders around gormlessly, trips over the doorframe in the hotel room, and endures unwanted homoerotic attention in the sauna.

This sequence establishes mapping as a central preoccupation of the film, despite it not involving an onscreen map. Instead, the itinerary designed by Ta-Pao connects disparate Taipei locations as part of a grand scheme that is ultimately as misplaced as it is ridiculous. For Ta-Pao's paranoid, excessive mapping of Na-Tou's movements is not matched by due diligence elsewhere. He fails to prevent Tou's death at the hands of Ah-Wen, who is clearly unreliable but has unfettered access to the inner circle, and fails to spot other dangers that are signposted early, such as the visual impairment of his henchman Wu (Wu Chung-Tien), which ultimately causes a fatal car crash. Nonetheless, this urban tour establishes Ta-Pao's paranoia, his tendency to see patterns where there is only randomness, and his resolution to deploy a counter-pattern: a mapped itinerary.

An intriguing editing choice reveals that the drugs drop-off may also follow a temporal, as well as a spatial, pattern. At the end of the sequence, Na-Tou waits for a taxi and is eventually picked up by Hsu. However, a temporal jump has occurred somewhere here, as previously the viewer has been under the impression that this was a flashback. Na-Tou was first recruited a year ago (depicted at the beginning of the sequence), but his meeting with Hsu (depicted at the end of the sequence) takes place two weeks after the events of the film's opening scene. With hindsight, the editing hints that Na-Tou's movements around Taipei represent a composite experience of multiple trips; in the opening scenes, Ta-Pao explains that he has previously used the courier a few times. So this arcane mapped route around the city has acquired the force of habit – has become a pattern. Like the tyre tracks that can later be seen overlain in the dirt roads of the wetlands, the footage of Na-Tou's trips around Taipei acquires the characteristics of a palimpsest. If there is a starting point to Na-Tou's journey, it is ambiguous. Fan goes further, arguing that *Godspeed* is best viewed as a temporal helix with neither a beginning nor an end, noting the film's reference to the Buddhist concept of *saṃsāra*, a cycle of becoming driven by ignorance; an inability to recognise that one is trapped in a cycle of suffering.[41]

Again, our understanding of the film's themes is enriched when we consider the significance of its real-life locations. A final example is fitting in this respect. Number 100 Huayin Street in Taipei, where Na-Tou is first sent by Ta-Pao, exists in real life. But the address is not a stairwell leading to a hotel; it is in fact the Puji Temple, a location that provides extra-filmic confirmation of the film's Buddhist themes and subtext, dangling clues and inviting critical speculation. Possibly significant here is the Buddhist monk Puji who self-immolated in the year 581, and whose story resonates with the journeys we see onscreen.[42] In an amusing flashback near the end of the film, an outraged Tou recalls how he received an erroneous calendar update on his phone, mistakenly stating that he was 1,400 years old. The scene is poignant, given that Tou has sacrificed his life by this point in the story. Turning the clock back 1,400 years, of course, takes us back to the lifetime of the monk Puji, who also sacrificed himself, and spatially, back to where the film started – 100 Huayin Street.

Confined Mapping: Practical Cosmology in *Aground* (2017)

Aground is an experimental drama that takes inspiration from the ancient Chinese divination classic *Yi Jing*. It seeks to dramatise one of the text's sixty-four hexagrams, which in this context is a set of six stacked horizontal lines comprising two trigrams, symbols of Taoist cosmology representing principles of reality.[43] Each hexagram is accompanied by a descriptive statement of six lines, akin to a parable. The film's Chinese title refers to Hexagram 47, *kun* 困,

which evokes confinement, oppression, and exhaustion. Its six accompanying lines appear on intertitles placed throughout the film, which thematically resonate with the drama. The composition of each hexagram from two trigrams finds a contemporary parallel in the mapped coordinates that appear in the final scenes of *Aground*, as onscreen text accompanying footage of locations previously unseen in the film: '22.6 degrees North, 122.5 degrees East, Green Island Prison (for political prisoners)' and '38.2 degrees North, 140.98 degrees East, Sendai, Miyagi, Japan (tsunami-stricken area)' (Figures 2.6 and 2.7).

In order to appreciate the significance of these mapped coordinates, it is first worth considering the film's central concept of doubling, which provides a rationale for how space is constructed. Two characters in the film have a doppelgänger, though in one case, this is not immediately apparent. Farmer Old Chi (Ban Tie-Hsiang) needs to make a trip, and leaves his rural home in the care of backpacker Chin, a dual role played by Chung Yao and Mariko Okubo. Shortly after Chi leaves, Teng (Hsu Kai-Hsin), a travelling puppeteer, arrives at the farm and asks Chin if he can stay there for a few days. Meanwhile Chi has travelled to a hospital where he cares for a disabled young man (Kuo Yi-Dai), whom we assume to be his child or grandchild. But when Chi takes him on an excursion to the west coast, it is revealed that the youngster is, in fact, the teenage Chi himself. The doubles of Chin and Chi are avatars of a single person's different characteristics. Teng's puppetry performances confirm Sun Wukong, the Monkey King from *Journey to the West*, as a source of inspiration, while Hsin also cites *Persona* (Ingmar Bergman, 1966) as an influence.[44]

Figure 2.6 Coordinates for Ludao in *Aground* (Hsin Chien-Tsung, 2017).

YOU ARE HERE

Figure 2.7 Coordinates for Sendai in *Aground* (Hsin Chien-Tsung, 2017).

The use of doubles in *Aground* facilitates its affective mapping, the implications of which cannot be fully grasped until the film has been watched in its entirety. Upon first viewing, Hsin seems unconcerned with adhering to the rules of conventional storytelling. But with hindsight, the characters' emotional trajectories are more readily identifiable; they must resolve inner conflicts that were brought about by their experience of traumatic incidents in the past. Most of the film takes place in just two environments; Chi's rural home in Taiwan's hilly inlands, and the sandbar at Waisanding, located in the waters off Chiayi and Yunlin counties (close to where *Godspeed* was filmed). However it is the locations that appear at the very end of the film, accompanied by mapped coordinates, that provide a spatial reference for Chi and Chin's trauma. The scene shot in Ludao (Green Island, located in the Pacific off Taitung) comprises drone footage of the former political prison located there, while the scene shot in Sendai shows Chin exploring an area devastated by the 2011 earthquake and tsunami. These locations are the sites where the characters' traumatic experiences took place – resulting in their internal conflict, embodied dramatically by the doubling. The viewer ultimately learns that the young Chi was a political prisoner on Ludao, and feels responsible for his mother's death following social ostracism, while Chin lived with her family in Sendai, where their home was destroyed by the tsunami.

Coordinates on a map, comprised of reference points on two axes (one latitudinal/horizontal, the other longitudinal/vertical) find a parallel in the structure of the *Yi Jing* hexagrams.[45] Each hexagram is similarly defined in relation to two references – an upper and lower trigram – which can be

47

consulted along vertical and horizontal axes in the King Wen Sequence, a tabular ordering of the diagrams. Diagrammatic and pictorial forms such as these can be conceived in terms of mapping if we accept that a map does not have to directly represent the surface of the Earth, but can depict other relations of space. In Chinese cosmology, each trigram in the *Yi Jing* corresponds to natural elements, as explained in the *Xici zhuan*, a third-century commentary: 'Looking upward, we use it to comprehend the signs in the heavens; looking down, we use it to examine the patterns of the earth.'[46] As Cordell D. K. Yee argues, even by this point in time, conventions might already have been established of 'interpreting abstract designs with no resemblance to the empirically observed objects as referring to reality'.[47] More broadly, this reflects how the two tendencies of Chinese aesthetic discourse, formal resemblance as a means of representing empirical reality, and that which sought to go beyond physical appearance, were not seen as opposed (as in many Western discourses around symbolism and realism), but as complementary.[48] Traditional mapping operated in this representational context.

Aground attempts a cinematic articulation of this aesthetic discourse by using natural elements and landscapes that are rooted in physical reality, while simultaneously transcending it. The film's titular hexagram *kun* is comprised of the trigrams *ze* (lake or marsh) and *shui* (water); the film's Chinese title 澤水困 comprises the characters for these. Although no direct translation is possible, the English title *Aground* captures a similar meaning, though it refers more to a process whereby something that should be waterborne runs aground, becoming stuck in sand or mud owing to the absence of sufficient water. Visually, the film takes its cue from the earthiness of marshy soil and mud. The footage is shot and colour-graded in a manner that accentuates brown and sandy hues. The vegetation surrounding Ji's farm, for instance, should be a vivid green colour, but instead the subdued, soil-coloured tones match the colour palette of the Waisanding sandbar. Water and marshy ground, interpreted here as land subjected to inundation (paddy fields, sandbars, the land flooded by the tsunami), feature heavily in the film.

Yet for all the rich interpretive possibilities offered by the film's allusions to the *Yi Jing*, we should not overlook the role played by practice in shaping its aesthetics. For it was not the case that Hsin developed his film in line with the concept of *kun* – that the theory preceded the practice. In fact, it was the other way around. The project initially bore the title *Dark Moon* (from the song sung in the film), which centres on the theme of self-hatred.[49] Hsin came to feel this was insufficient to represent the film, so began to search for a better title, consulting the Chinese classics:

> I started from the *Book of Songs* and the *Classic of Mountains and Seas*, then I stopped once I saw this oracle in the *Yi Jing*. It felt just right. It has

water, oppression. This prompted me to read into those meanings of this Hexagram, and I was surprised that these lines coincided with my film so well.⁵⁰

The references to the *Yi Jing* informed the film's editing, reflecting more broadly how the project was allowed to evolve over time, in line with Hsin's unusual production methods. He conceived the low-budget film as a collaborative venture; initially there was no script and barely even a concept. The story was developed in conjunction with the actors, in a deliberate rejection of conventional workflows whereby a filmmaker starts with a complete script, then proceeds to seek funding, and so on; the director cites the Dogme 95 manifesto as an influence.⁵¹

Remarkably, the film was shot in just nine days, two of which involved trips to Sendai and Ludao, meaning that the bulk of the film was shot in one week – impressive given the eighty-two-minute running time.⁵² Initially it was water, rather than the hexagram, that was conceived as the starting point for the development of the project:

> When I first had a discussion with the actors, the idea of *kun* hadn't yet been solidly contrived, only 'water', as well as environments with water. Mariko mentioned the earthquake, then I thought of a corporate video I had shot on Ludao, so everything linked together.⁵³

The film's traumatic locations, Sendai and Ludao, have Pacific water in common; and on set, the sense of confinement later expressed by *kun* initially entailed the construction of a *mise en scène* in which the characters are entrapped by water. Water is present visually or aurally in most scenes, while the characters are repeatedly made to undertake activities such as washing food, showering, taking a boat, boiling a kettle, and sheltering from rain. Water is omnipresent, meaning that the characters are unable to escape the traumatic associations of Sendai and Ludao.

When Chi visits his mother's grave, located in the wetlands near Chiayi, he finds it partially submerged by water, the result of rising sea levels. Here most overtly, but throughout the film, water signals the return of the repressed, aligning *Aground* with traditions of Sinophone eco-cinema, and more specifically recalling the films of Tsai Ming-Liang. The ubiquity of water – often displaced, flooding, or leaking – in Tsai's films has been variously interpreted as creating an *unheimlich* space that signifies ecological malaise; as representing urban antipathy and the collapse of family structures; and as an allegory for cross-strait relations.⁵⁴ Several of these themes are evoked in *Aground*; moreover, the displacement of water depicted in this graveyard scene has negative connotations from the perspective of *feng shui*, which is concerned with the siting of graves in auspicious locations so as to benefit the living and pacify the dead.[55] For those who believe in the cosmology underlying *feng shui*, the grave does not merely symbolise Chi's guilt and the figurative discontent of the dead, but retrospectively offers a material, environmental explanation for it: the events of the film occurred *because* a grave was inauspiciously sited.

In the markedly surreal scenes set on the Waisanding sandbar, water is similarly used to evoke the return of the repressed. It is left ambiguous whether Chi's excursion there exists entirely, or just partly, in his imagination. Visually, the environment is bleak and empty, comprised only of sea and sand, occasionally interrupted by deposits of driftwood. This recalls the displacement aesthetics of *Amour-Legende*, with its theme of desertification, and is suggestive of allegory. The nocturnal scenes set on the raised wooden shelter, designed as a refuge from rising tides, suggest a need for reconciliation with the historical crimes committed on the island.[56] The younger Chi suddenly becomes able-bodied and sings the national anthem, provoking a violent dispute with his older counterpart. The effects of propaganda are dramatised and the former nationalist regime is directly implicated as bearing responsibility for Chi's trauma. It does not seem accidental that these revelations emerge *in* the Taiwan straits, challenging the conception of clear boundary lines that distinguish one unit of sovereign space from another, which Thongchai argues is an important precondition for imagining nationhood.[57] *Aground* uses the sandbar to situate national experience spatially closer to China – albeit by a few kilometres – reminding us that Chiang Kai-Shek's regime, which was established following the nationalists' flight from the mainland, was an extra-territorial import.

The raised shelter on the sandbar comes to resemble a theatre; the beams of the structure create wooden rectangles enclosing the inky darkness of the night, recalling stage flats. Moreover, the action in the shelter is intercut with a scene depicting Teng's puppetry performance in Chi's home, drawing conceptual parallels between the two locations. As Teng releases the puppets from the confines of their portable stage and moves them around the room, it becomes clear that this home, too, was always a theatrical space. For although the house is visually less abstract than the sandbar, it is not significantly more realistic. Where, after all, is it? No precise location for the dwelling is given, and its trappings of actuality are curiously incongruous, such as the mobile phone that Chin uses while operating an antique sewing machine with a foot pedal. Hsin has spoken of Teng as being a Prince Charming who rides a bicycle instead of a white horse, and the environment certainly has a fairy tale quality to it.[58] Characters enter and exit the story via lush, overgrown lanes, lending the action a timeless, otherworldly quality.

Aground features a set of spatially discrete, enclosed environments, in line with the film's concept of *kun*. While these environments overlap psychologically and conceptually, we are given no indication as to how they might be connected geographically. This contrasts with *Godspeed*, which visualises a credible itinerary from one place to another, and *Somewhere I Have Never Travelled*, which compresses different locales into fictitious proximity. *Aground* does not reveal where Chi's home is located, or what route he takes to get the hospital or to the coast, or what city the hospital is in, and so on. *Aground* is structured as a map comprised of unconnected nodes. The degree to which authorial intention accounts for this impression of otherworldly confinement is debatable, which is no criticism. The production circumstances dictated that only a limited number of locations could be filmed, and many scenes were shot in a single take, for reasons of economy.[59] There would not have been the budget or the time to shoot scenes that visualised the characters travelling between the different locations; nor, aesthetically, would this necessarily have been desirable.

In this sense, absent coordinates are equally as important to the film's mapping as those provided in the final scenes, which inscribe longitudinal and latitudinal reference points for Sendai and Ludao. However, this final section is aesthetically very different to the material that precedes it. Notably, the locations are shot using a drone, a technique not employed elsewhere in the film. In Ludao, the drone flies inland from the ocean, towards the prison, through the entrance of the complex, then finally along the corridors and past the prison cells.[60] In Sendai, the drone rises vertically as Chin explores the ruins of the town in which she used to live. Both scenes visualise what the characters have repressed, and in contrast to the rest of the film, the perspective here gives the impression of objectivity. The onscreen text with the coordinates provides clinical precision, where previously there has been ambiguous reverie. Hsin explains why he chose to use this kind of shot:

> An aerial shot is like an omniscient perspective; recognizing our geographical location from the perspective of the sky also expresses the cruelty of history. Through the cold data of latitude and longitude, the cruelty is made more intense.[61]

In depicting locations associated with traumatic events, the apparently objective perspective of the aerial shot contrasts with the more subjective approach used elsewhere in the film. As in *Godspeed*, the drone shots in *Aground* bear a close resemblance to the visual forms of classical cartography, and the Sendai footage strongly resembles an actual map. As the drone rises from the ground, more of the ruined wall foundations come gradually into shot, until we are given an aerial overview of the town's former layout; a map of a place that no longer exists.

Epilogue: Land That Moves

Several of the environments discussed in this chapter pose a challenge to conventional notions of mapping, in that they undermine a view of geography as static. Many islands in Micronesia, including the Pingelap Atoll that Ah-Kuei dreams about in *Somewhere I Have Never Travelled*, are under threat from rising sea levels, as are the areas on Taiwan's western seaboard featured in *Godspeed* and *Aground*. The sandbar at Waisanding, meanwhile, is not static but has drifted several kilometres south over the past century, initially parallel to Yunlin County but now lying off the shores of Chiayi County. This resulted in a minor territorial dispute in 2006, when Chiayi requested the transfer of jurisdiction from Yunlin, which was rejected.[62] But more significantly, the sandbar raises questions regarding what we consider worthy of being mapped. The sandbar does not appear on some maps, including Google Maps, for instance, where at the time of writing, searching for it will identify a location in the ocean. Yet as *Aground* confirms, land certainly exists there.

As a geological formation, the Waisanding sandbar is not unique in moving – rather, the dilemma it poses for cartographers is that it moves quickly, within the span of human experience. In Japan, the 2011 Tōhoku earthquake and tsunami, responsible for Chin's traumatic experience in *Aground*, tragically reshaped Honshu's east coastline, while the ensuing Fukushima disaster revitalised the anti-nuclear campaign in Taiwan; protests in 2014 led to construction being stopped on the island's fourth nuclear plant.[63] Natural disasters are prevalent in Taiwan, and are referenced in a diverse range of films.[64] Yet they are rarely discussed in scholarship about the island's cinema, even though these events can challenge, or at the very least nuance, our neat periodisation of cinematic trends. The year 2008 is symbolically important in the history of Taiwanese cinema, yet for many local audiences, 2009 might well have been more significant, witnessing Typhoon Morakot, the deadliest storm to impact Taiwan in recorded history. Its effects are directly depicted in *Starry Starry Night* (Tom Lin Shu-Yu, 2011) to be explored in the following chapter, which turns to forest environments.

Notes

1. Conley, *Cartographic Cinema*, 3–4.
2. Ma, *The Last Isle*, 27, 29.
3. Yang, 'Passionately documenting', 48.
4. Liu, 'From visual fantasies to bodily trajectories', 208.
5. Ibid., 206.
6. Ma, *The Last Isle*, 37.
7. Ibid., 37–8.
8. Also known as *Riding the Breeze*.
9. Udden, 'Taiwanese comedies', 176–7.

10. Bruno, *Atlas of Emotion*, 245.
11. Conley, *Cartographic Cinema*, 1.
12. Harley, 'The map and the development of the history of cartography', 1.
13. Castro, 'Cinema's mapping impulse', 11.
14. Bruno, *Atlas of Emotion*, 185.
15. Caquard, 'Foreshadowing contemporary digital cartography', 54.
16. Conley, *Cartographic Cinema*, 14.
17. *I Ching, or Book of Changes (Yi Jing)*.
18. Conley, *Cartographic Cinema*, 15.
19. Lin, 'Charting the transnational', 198.
20. Cummings, 'somewhere i have never travelled'.
21. Huang, 'Interview with Fu Tien-Yu'.
22. Bruno, *Atlas of Emotion*, 185.
23. Monmonier, *How to Lie with Maps*, 14–15.
24. See Airey, 'Graham Greene's *Journey Without Maps*', and Greene, *The End of the Affair*.
25. See, for example, Liu, 'From visual fantasies to bodily trajectories', 209–10.
26. Conley, *Cartographic Cinema*, 3–4.
27. For example, the storyline involving Remedios.
28. Huang, 'Interview with Fu Tien-yu'.
29. Ibid.
30. Mao, 'The meaning of travel'.
31. Ibid.
32. Yee, 'Chinese cartography among the arts', 158–63.
33. Fan, '*Godspeed*', 395.
34. Chang, 'Documenting life', 239.
35. Chang, *Taiwan Cinema, Memory, and Modernity*, 211.
36. See Chen, 'Taiwan, abandoned'.
37. In identifying some of these locations, I am indebted to Yang Ta-Ching. See Yang, 'Log into the film to go travelling'.
38. Caquard, 'Foreshadowing contemporary digital cartography', 49.
39. Nagao Nakashima, the Director of Photography, is a pseudonym.
40. Yee, 'Chinese cartography among the arts', 154.
41. Fan, '*Godspeed*', 388, 394–5.
42. See Benn, *Burning for the Buddha*, 80–1.
43. Each of the lines is either broken (*yin*) or unbroken (*yang*).
44. Hsieh, 'Wading into the deep water'.
45. A third axis that can be used is elevation.
46. Yee, 'Chinese cartography among the arts', 131.
47. Ibid., 131.
48. Ibid., 131.
49. Hsieh, 'Wading into the deep water'.
50. Ibid.
51. Ibid.
52. Ibid.
53. Ibid.
54. Mi, 'Framing ambient *Unheimlich*', 22–4; Wu, 'Postsadness Taiwan new cinema', 82–4; Marchetti, 'On Tsai Mingliang's *The River*', 118–20.
55. Henderson, 'Chinese cosmographical thought', 216.
56. This recalls what Wafa Ghermani observes as the difference between visible geography and the protagonist's 'own cartography of memory' in *Super Citizen Ko* (Wan Jen, 1994). Ghermani, '*Super Citizen Ko* (1994)', 226.

57. Thongchai, *Siam Mapped*, 56.
58. Hsieh, 'Wading into the deep water'.
59. Ibid.
60. High winds meant that two shots had to be combined using CGI. See Hsieh, 'Wading into the deep water'.
61. Ibid.
62. Cottenie, 'A geographical oddity in Chiayi', 13.
63. Chang, 'Indigenous attitudes toward nuclear waste', 193.
64. For example, the 921 earthquake of 1999 provides the traumatic backstory for *Mad King of Taipei* (Yeh Tien-Lun, 2016) and was directly depicted in *Turn Around* (Chen Ta-Pu, 2017), while earthquakes appear in *20:30:40* (Sylvia Chang, 2004) and *You Are the Apple of My Eye* (Giddens Ko Ching-Teng, 2011).

3. BACK TO THE WOODS

Introduction: The Return of the Forest

Maps appear prominently in *The Tag-Along 2* (Cheng Wei-Hao, 2017), when Li Shu-Fen (Yang Cheng-Lin) sets in motion the search for her daughter, who is missing in mountain forests. In the rescue headquarters, the team leader explains the search strategy with reference to a range of cartography and CCTV. Shortly afterwards follows a scene that opens with a moving drone shot of the mountain forests, which tilts vertically downward to reveal – a drone, flying through the sky. The rescue team are shown commencing their search using walkie-talkies, the drone operator among them. This dramatises what can be inferred from the films discussed in the previous chapter, that the aerial visuality of drone technology operates in the same representational system as cartography, while technologies such as CCTV and walkie-talkies assist the mapping of space. Shu-Fen's daughter is sought using the tools of science and rationality, with their claim to objective accuracy. Unfortunately, none of this does much good. The girl is not found, while the discovery of a different woman confirms that malign demons, whom we later learn are able to reshape space for their own ends, have the upper hand in this environment. Maps and their enabling technologies are of limited use in this supernatural forest.

The reappearance of forests is a defining feature of post-2008 Taiwanese cinema. Several filmmakers have turned their attention to the tree-lined regions of the island's central and eastern mountainsides, using these environments as settings for their fictional narratives. Forests have not featured significantly in Taiwanese cinema since the 1970s, when they often appeared in *wuxia* films, notably in some classic works directed by King Hu. They appeared infrequently in representations of contemporary living, aside from brief interludes in romantic melodramas. Forests were (along with beaches) a go-to environment when lovers in Qiong Yao films needed to escape society and find momentary respite in nature, as Brian Hu has elaborated.[1] But after the mid-1970s, the woods were relegated to the margins of Taiwanese cinema. The New Cinema of the 1980s dramatised rural living but dealt largely with village life and farming, predominantly in lowland or coastal regions, while the focus of 1990s cinema was on urban environments.

In English, 'forests' are distinguished from 'woods' by their greater size and density, and culturally have connotations of being dark, inaccessible, and dangerous. There is, however, a degree of terminological slippage, especially in relation to fairy tales and horror; we might say that Little Red Riding Hood goes for walk in the woods, but this is portrayed using the tropes of a forest. The terms are used interchangeably here, but in the Taiwanese context, the environment under discussion is less ambiguously *senlin*, which translates as forest, rather than woods or *shulin*. It is also important to note that Taiwan's forests are located predominantly in mountainous regions, so there is an automatic association between the two; several films explore the thematic and aesthetic connections between forest vegetation and altitude.

After three decades of absence, forests are back. This is where two children escape the city to hide in *Starry Starry Night* (Tom Lin Shu-Yu, 2011); where a man possessed by a demon convalesces with his father in *Soul* (Chung Mong-Hong, 2013); where spirits torment visiting urbanites in *The Tag-Along* (Cheng Wei-Hao, 2015); and where a woman lives in seclusion with her mother in *Forêt Debussy* (Kuo Cheng-Chui, 2016). Aside from these four case studies, forests have appeared in a range of other films, achieving a new prominence regardless of genre, box office success, the scale or type of production, or the intended audience. *The Tag-Along*, for instance, was a massive commercial hit, making thirty million NTD on its opening weekend and ultimately becoming the most profitable domestic horror movie in a decade. *Forêt Debussy*, on the other hand, was aimed squarely at European arthouse audiences and its modest release was focused around international festivals. Before exploring the aesthetic implications of this return to the woods, I will first sketch out some possible reasons for it.

A Way through the Woods: Critical Orientation

Why were Taiwan's forests more cinematically prominent in the years after 2008, compared with previously? A discussion of this question, and the differing answers it might hypothetically provoke, reveals broader tensions between analytical approaches that are theory-driven and those that are practice-oriented, perhaps best embodied by the typical frameworks of cultural studies and film poetics. Questions of nationhood are emblematic of this tension. If a film location recurs in a set of films, as is the case here, then we have a pattern – an object of study in film poetics. If that pattern can be identified across films that are produced in a particular nation – and this provenance is a common factor – then to what degree can the pattern credibly be said to represent the national? Here, the cultural context appears compelling. The legacy of increased tourism and the wider availability of maps from the mid-1980s, coupled with the popularisation of concepts such as *bentu* in the 1990s, meant that people were encouraged to value the island's landscapes. Previously there had been an emphasis on the relative importance of 'Greater China', and indeed when Taiwanese forests did appear in *wuxia* films, they often stood in for China.

In this respect, it seems significant that the films under consideration all depict the forest as a place where one returns home: literally, figuratively, or both. There are, of course, longstanding associations between concepts of home and nation, not to mention metaphorical precedents in Sinophone culture involving trees. The Chinese commitment to the native land and ancestral home has been described as *luoye gui gen* – literally translated as 'the falling leaves return to the roots', and student textbooks in 1970s Taiwan used a tree and roots to construct a national myth of the ethnic origins shared by Chinese people worldwide.[2] The recent reappearance of cinematic forests could be seen to rework these arboreal tropes, resituating home on the island of Taiwan, rather than in mainland China. When summarising the possibilities of Sinophone studies in her book *Visuality and Identity*, Shu-Mei Shih uses the metaphor of tree roots, stating that her proposed mode of study 'allows us to rethink the relationship between roots and routes by questioning the conception of roots as ancestral rather than place-based', thereby decoupling notions of home and origin.[3]

A case might be made for the films' construction of a unique Taiwanese identity through the prism of environmental politics, the rise of which offers a credible explanation for the post-2008 emergence of films set in Taiwan's apparently pristine woodlands, warning against degradation and signalling the need to preserve the island's ecology. One environmental performance index compiled in 2018 ranks Taiwan at 23 and China at 120.[4] In this context, it might be tempting to view these films as an effort to distinguish Taiwan, its forests undeveloped and pristine, from China, overdeveloped and polluted. Tempting – yet these arguments would probably be greeted with scepticism by scholars who favour a bottom-up approach to case study analysis. Critiquing culturalist approaches to Hong Kong cinema, Gary Bettinson argues, for instance, that concepts of identity are often so vaguely defined as to be applicable to all case studies, and that assertions regarding the films' reflection of collective sensibilities rely on hermeneutic categories imposed by the critic.[5]

When watching the forest films, hard evidence for the above interpretations is distinctly lacking. None of the films considered here make any connection between Taiwan's forests and China, nor have filmmakers referenced this issue in interviews. Yet for some critics, this kind of silence may well be the point. Discussing the films of Wei Te-Sheng, Chris Berry draws on terminology first coined by Richard Dyer, arguing that 'the absence of any reference to China stretches the realist conventions that otherwise shape Wei's films, suggesting that it is more than chance. Perhaps we can consider it as a structuring absence.'[6] He views this as a space of erasure, a topic that is avoided and as such explains the prominence of Japan in Wei's films, which 'functions as a displacement, substituting a comforting image for the anxiety-producing image of China'.[7] Intriguingly, three of the case studies considered here evoke not China, but the legacy of Japanese colonialism, at significant narrative moments, suggesting that Berry's arguments have broader applicability – although the Japanese connection is not necessarily represented as benign.

The filmmakers certainly draw on the island's unique history and culture, including its postcolonial experience, in their depiction of the mountain forests. Cheng openly acknowledges that when making *The Tag-Along*, his intention was to make local Taiwanese myths accessible to an international audience. The relevance of this to questions of nation branding or soft power is more speculative, however, given that any comparison to other nations usually occurs by implication, and is not necessarily intended by the filmmaker. It also goes without saying that assertions of national uniqueness may be inaccurate, with formulations around environmentalism, for instance, becoming complicated once we consider the subtleties masked by generalised indices. If we were to argue that the portrayals of Taiwan's forests are intended to suggest a contrast with China, then this is a problematic formulation, given that reforestation has been steadily increasing in China since the early 1960s.[8]

That said, the notion of a structuring absence undoubtedly poses a challenge to film poetics, an approach that appeals to empirical evidence and examines the material components of the constructive process – neither of which, by definition, will reveal much about something that isn't there. Yet whether or not we choose to make the critical leap, it is worth considering Bettinson's advice that before proceeding to read a film for allegory, 'the viewer must first master the film as a film, that is, grapple and come to terms with the film's often complex surface level'; in moving directly to the secondary level of analysis, he argues, we risk losing sight of a film's surfaces, its appeal to emotions, and its sheer mastery of craft.[9] A consideration of craft is essential in this context. The increasing cheapness and portability of digital technology, especially in the decade after 2008, enabled filmmakers to shoot in Taiwan's often remote, inaccessible wooded regions; locations that are not easily, or in some cases at all, accessible by road. Digital technology made filming there far easier, and logistically more viable. It would have been extremely difficult, perhaps even impossible, to shoot certain scenes in *Forêt Debussy* using analogue camera technology. None of this had anything to do with cross-strait relations, green politics, or post-colonialism.

There is also a broader question of whether the themes and aesthetics common to these case studies are shared by films made outside Taiwan. Writing about forests in Southeast Asian cinema, Graiwoot Chulphongsathorn concludes with a question:

> Can we adopt the cinematic forest as a mode of mapping and imagining a new regional cinema beyond Southeast Asia? In films about forests, though they come from different parts of the world, these works share aesthetic parallels and thematic similarities that can link them together.[10]

The Taiwanese films considered here certainly engage with themes and forms artistically associated with forests internationally. The case studies cited by Chulphongsathorn are works of art cinema, but we might investigate whether the forest operates as 'a mode of mapping' in popular entertainment as well. From the perspective of market considerations in Taiwan, it is likely that once a few films appeared featuring forests, a trend took off. Audiences were simply interested in seeing something different, and the industry responded. This recent trend of films set in forests could be understood with reference to work on genre cycles.[11] I would not suggest that we refer to a forest genre, but it may be useful to speak of location cycles – moments in time when filmmakers and audiences are drawn to certain types of cinematic environment. Taiwanese horror proliferated following the success of *The Tag-Along*, and it would be useful to examine the role played by forest locations in helping establish this new cycle.

Poetics involves identifying the recurrence of narrative patterns, in order to draw out general characteristics from the particular. On the one hand, these films deploy universal storytelling forms. As John Yorke remarks in his book on scriptwriting, *Into the Woods*, 'in stories throughout the ages there is one motif that continually recurs – the journey into the woods to find the life-giving secret within'.[12] When examining how this motif is articulated in recent Taiwanese cinema, it becomes clear that in all of these films, the characters' return to the woods allows filmmakers to dramatise the experience of trauma; specifically, the reliving of feelings or memories associated with death. Yi-Chun (Hsu Wei-Ning) feels guilt for having had an abortion in *The Tag-Along*; Chuan (Chang Hsiao-Chuan) recalls the euthanasia of his mother in *Soul*; Mei (Xu Jiao) faces up to her grandfather's passing in *Starry Starry*

Night; the woman (Gwei Lun-Mei) in *Forêt Debussy* blames herself for the murder of her family. There is a sense that truth lies in the woods – that returning there yields knowledge and emotional growth, the prospect of coming to terms with repressed and painful events. By analysing how these narrative patterns are aesthetically expressed, we can then assess the evidence for allegorical possibilities. The traumatic narratives might evoke environmental degradation (*The Tag-Along*), the impact on rural communities of natural disasters (*Starry Starry Night*), or past cinema itself (*Soul*).

A notable effect of this, in all the films, is an acknowledgement that the forest environment is far from pristine. Though the filmmakers vary in the degree to which they find the fantasy of unspoilt woodland alluring, they each deploy a range of aesthetic strategies that ultimately deconstruct it. They sometimes do this by adopting the forms of eco-cinema, which I broadly understand as the filmic dramatisation of the interconnected human and non-human relationships that exist within, and between, environments. Chris Tong has argued that eco-cinema does not seek to reaffirm the binarism of urban versus natural, but is instead the cinematic representation of an eco-scape that seeks to problematise the easy categorisation of the objects it views.[13] In this sense, the construction of cinematic forests requires the filmmakers to consider what they understand by the urban. All the protagonists are city-dwellers, and it is urban life that shoulders the blame for their malaise. Thus in certain respects, these films subscribe to the critique of urban modernity associated with the New Cinema of the 1980s, albeit in a manner that is formally and thematically different. In contrast to the safe artifice of urban life, which protects but stifles the characters, the forest is portrayed as a realm of dangerous authenticity.

The filmmakers also challenge notions of pristine nature by dramatising its inevitable mediation. The characters are not blank slates, but arrive in the forest with emotional baggage, preconceptions, tastes, and habits. The films thus question how the forest might be experienced as authentic, in a manner like that elaborated by Wu Ming-Yi in his novel *The Man with the Compound Eyes*, also a traumatic narrative:

> Nobody has ever seen the forest he now beholds. It's like a forest in a novel that has grown into a real wood. This is not to say that the forest is not immense, peaceful, dark and deep. It is indeed immense, peaceful, dark and deep, just a bit unreal.[14]

This perspective on the forest, as something real or authentic that has paradoxically grown out of artifice, is shared by the films considered in this chapter, in which the *seeing* of the forest becomes a source of creative tension and formal experimentation. This is a matter of self-reflexive concern for some filmmakers. The forests around Alishan in Chiayi County, where *Starry Starry Night* and parts of *Forêt Debussy* were filmed, are remote but hardly untouched by human intervention; they are a tourist attraction. When making a film, at least, there is no such thing as a pristine forest.

Or is there? The notion of an eco-scape has limitations, as it requires that interrelations between the urban and the natural must form part of a film's subject matter; must be an object of study. The filmmakers considered here certainly emphasise the porous, mutually generative qualities of the natural–urban binary.[15] Yet in the case of forests, there is something eco-cinematic that cannot be entirely captured by this notion of interrelationships. Bettinson argues that in film poetics, we should master the film as a film.[16] In doing so, should we not also strive to critically accommodate the place as a place – to at least consider the possibility of a forest's existence in and of itself? The human geographer Yi-Fu Tuan argues eloquently that forests are experienced by humans in specific spatial terms, while the anthropologist Eduardo Kohn asserts that a forest has its own qualities and forms.[17] Practice in *Forêt Debussy* will be examined with reference to their ideas.

Forêt Debussy reminds us of perhaps the oldest storytelling motif in existence – getting lost in the woods. Mapping is a crucial consideration in these films insofar as the characters must situate themselves in an environment noted for being difficult to navigate. Forests tend to lack obvious landmarks, rendering many cartographic symbols redundant, while paths can become easily overgrown, altering marked routes. The boundary lines found on maps may appear entirely arbitrary in forests, something that has proven confusing to colonialists or to people otherwise not familiar with, or indigenous to, a particular environment.[18] In contemporary Taiwan, county boundaries that fall in the woods frequently exist only in maps, and are unmarked at ground level. And all this, before we must contend with mountain spirits leading us astray, an unwanted navigational intervention endured by the heroine of *The Tag-Along*. Questions of orientation are central to these films, in which all the characters become literally or figuratively lost, and usually both. How this is depicted aesthetically will be the focus of this chapter.

A Dissected Map: *Starry Starry Night* (2011)

Starry Starry Night is a coming-of-age drama, director Lin's adaptation of a graphic novel by Jimmy Liao.[19] It explores the friendship that develops between Mei and her new classmate Chieh (Lin Hui-Min), two thirteen-year-olds who live in Taipei. When Mei's beloved grandfather dies and her parents (Liu Jou-Ying and Yu Cheng-Ching) announce their intention to get divorced, she resolves to run away. Taking Chieh with her, Mei travels to her grandfather's home, an isolated cabin in the mountain forests – filmed in Alishan, Chiayi County – where she spent happier childhood days.

The film adopts the jigsaw puzzle as its central metaphor. In one scene, Mei and Chieh visit a jigsaw shop, seeking to purchase a single piece that is missing from her puzzle of Vincent van Gogh's oil painting *The Starry Night* (1889). Several globes are scattered around the shop, and feature prominently in the background of all the shots in this scene (Figure 3.1). Elaborating the connection, Chieh explains that the first jigsaw was created by an English cartographer in 1760, who placed a map onto a wooden board and cut around the borders of different towns. The cartographer asked his children to put the map back together, Chieh continues, so that when they had done so, 'they knew where they lived, where home is'. Jigsaws, as remediated maps, are one of Lin's original contributions to Liao's story, and did not feature in the original graphic novel. Chieh's explanation refers to the British cartographer John Spilsbury, who is credited with creating and popularising what were then called 'dissected maps', designed to assist the teaching of geography. The film takes some liberties with the truth in order to connect jigsaws more explicitly to the domestic; Spilsbury's work likely dissected nations and regions, rather than towns. But *Starry Starry Night* deploys the jigsaw more specifically to interrogate notions of home, and does so in the context of a character making the journey from city to forest.

Mei ostensibly wants to visit her grandfather's cabin in order to show Chieh the stars in the night sky, which cannot be seen in Taipei due to light pollution. But what subsequently unfolds is a rite-of-passage; on the cusp of puberty, the girl is pushed into womanhood by her experiences in the forest. This is the stuff of fairy tales, and the clothes Mei wears during the excursion (bright red shorts and a red rucksack, a striped red jumper) recall the imagery of *Little Red Riding Hood*, with its subtext of feminine sexuality and awakening. The pair's journey through the woods deploys similarly mythic tropes. There is

Figure 3.1 Globes in a jigsaw shop in *Starry Starry Night* (Lin Shu-Yu, 2011).

the winding forest path, in which the children are dwarfed by towering trees. There is the fork in the path, where the wrong direction is chosen. Finally, the heroes get lost in the woods, and tellingly, it is the marks of industrial modernity – train tracks – that help them get their bearings.

Mei's journey into the forest reflects how, more broadly, the film identifies travel as a prerequisite of personal growth. The budding artist Chieh is far more worldly than Mei, already drawing sketches of nude figures, which leads him into trouble at school. His growth into maturity has been accelerated by his family circumstances. He and his mother are victims of abuse by his father, and in order to escape the man's reach, they have lived an itinerant lifestyle, moving around Taiwan. Mei's mother, meanwhile, is an art dealer specialising in European impressionism, who as a student, studied in Paris. She aches to return and is dissatisfied with her life in Taiwan, which leads to arguments with her husband. An upside-down map and guidebooks are briefly glimpsed in the mother's box of treasured possessions, scattered among European LPs, music cassettes, franked letters, and a copy of *Le Cinéma Parlant*.[20] Travel and cinema sit inside the same box, with maps evoking memories of journeys previously taken, and kindling dreams of travel yet to come.

If the mother is drawn to Europe, then so is the film itself. Concluding his study of cosmopolitanism in Taiwanese cinema, Hu briefly observes that *Starry Starry Night*, like *Au Revoir Taipei* (Arvin Chen, 2010) and *Taipei Exchanges* (Hsiao Ya-Chuan, 2010), incorporates French and American artistic sensibilities to rework the concerns of 1970s melodrama for a more fickle, ironic generation.[21] The visual influence of German fairy tales is felt in the depiction of the grandfather's cabin, nestled in the dense green forest at night, its windows lit by a warm orange glow. This contrasts with the sterile rendering of the family's Taipei apartment, lined with mounted jigsaw puzzles of Impressionist paintings, completed by Mei and her parents in happier days. An elegant shot pans across the pictures as CGI enables these bygone moments to play out as reflections in the glass. But with the parents' divorce looming, the ubiquitous presence of European paintings has become oppressive, serving as a constant reminder that Mei's mother would rather be elsewhere. The apartment resembles an art gallery; even a bowl of apples, tastefully reflected in the polished surface of the dining table, gives the impression of careful curation. Symptomatic of the parents' malaise, the apartment is a space of empty pretence that leads Mei to become alienated, longing for the homely warmth of her grandfather's cabin.

As the family eat dinner, a synthetic white Christmas tree appears prominently in a wide shot. Another European import, its blatant artificiality feeds into the film's broader environmental critique, which initially seems to rest on an unconvincing dichotomy between urban superficiality and the authenticity of the forest. In the grandfather's cabin, the large workbench and shelves are cluttered with tools, wood carvings, books, postcards, ornaments, and rolled paper. He spends his time carving artisanal craft products and wooden toys; this is a place where objects are used rather than displayed, produced rather than exhibited. Given the sentimentality of this depiction, it might initially seem odd to conceive *Starry Starry Night* as a work of eco-cinema, which Tong defines in terms of its problematisation of the urban–rural binary.[22] However, the film gradually calls this dichotomy into question. If Mei's trip begins as a search for roots – for a childhood past, a family homestead – then her return to the forest does not yield any sense of wholeness. Instead, Mei is left feeling empty, a void the film emblematises as the missing piece of a jigsaw puzzle.

Initially, Mei's understanding of natural ecosystems is mediated through cultural forms such as European painting, animation, jigsaw puzzles, origami, and wooden handicrafts. Travelling by train to the forest, her imagination runs wild; CGI animation imposes Van Gogh's imagery onto the Taiwanese landscape, as Mei fantasises about the train taking off into the night sky, reminiscent of Kenji Miyazawa's 1927 story 'Night Train to the Stars'. Earlier in the film, she and Chieh are asked to create a classroom wall display featuring colourful rural scenery and representations of weather systems. The pair construct origami animals and add them to the display. Mei imagines a menagerie of these creatures following her and Chieh across the Tamsui bridge, and fantasises about an encounter with a life-size version of her toy wooden elephant, crafted by her grandfather. However, the destruction of the wall display by a jealous classmate signals the dismantling of this fantasy of prettified nature. This anticipates how Mei's experiences in the forest will imbue in her a more mature understanding of the natural world.

The pair's escape to the forest recalls the 1970s melodramas analysed by Hu, featuring sublime scenes of nature that 'capture the romantic spirit of defiance against the unyielding pressures of staying/going, inside/outside, and ethical/unethical', although the characters and the audience both know that this defiance is doomed.[23] Mei and Chieh's relationship is similarly romantic, with human experience depicted as merely one element in a broader natural tapestry – the functioning of a forest ecosystem, which contrasts starkly with Mei's childish fantasies. The animals here are not cute, but a source of food and infection. Dead foxes and racoons are strung up in hunting traps, while Mei becomes seriously ill with a fever, the result of an insect bite or exposure to rainfall and damp. The unpredictable weather is far removed from the cheerful paper clouds glued to the classroom display, or the festive snow that Mei imagines falling inside Taipei main station. The domesticated images of nature instilled in Mei leave her ill-equipped to survive in the forest, and to some degree, this reflects the filmmakers' own knowledge of the mountainous forest environment. The unreliable weather in Alishan, for example, played a significant role in determining what kinds of visualisations were possible, as Lin recalls:

> I remember that the second half of the script, where the children are lost in the forest, we had some setups but then we intentionally kept it loose also; just because when you're in the Ali mountains, you never really know what kind of weather you're going to get.[24]

For instance, on one day, it was so foggy that nothing more than five feet away could be filmed clearly, meaning that it was only possible to shoot close-ups for one of the scenes in which the kids walk through the forest.[25]

If the onscreen action reflects, to a certain degree, a credible experience of this environment, then more generally, *Starry Starry Night* seems reconciled to the inevitable mediation of the forest. When Mei and Chieh, drenched by the rain, take refuge in an abandoned church, there is no electricity, so they use a torch to illuminate a wall. Standing between the light source and the wall, Mei instructs Chieh to avert his eyes while she changes her clothes. So he watches her silhouette instead, a reverse close-up framing him like a spectator watching a screen. This disarmingly direct rendering of the male gaze recalls his own nude sketches, reminding us of his teacher's earlier remark that most students are too immature to understand the difference between art and pornography. Here, Lin connects sexual awakening to the experience of cinema itself, offering a direct depiction of *dianying* or 'electric shadows'. Even here, deep in the forest, cinema exerts its reach. The jigsaw also returns in the forest, in a manner that illuminates the formal relationship with mapping. When Mei is struck by fever, she experiences a delirious vision, in which CGI is used to show images of Chieh and the woods visually deconstructing before her eyes, in the form of jigsaw pieces dropping to the ground like leaves (Figure 3.2). She then finds herself in her parents' apartment, which again crumbles away like a collapsing jigsaw. Mei awakes in a hospital bed, back in the city. Having made the transition into womanhood, she must now come to terms with her grandfather's death, and accept the inevitability of her parents' divorce. Last seen in the disintegrating jigsaw, Chieh does not appear again onscreen.

The missing piece sought by Mei leaves a hole, an absence, the meaning of which is left unstated. Perhaps the incomplete jigsaw exposes the fragility of her broken family, or the void left by her deceased grandfather. Or perhaps it captures a more complicated set of emotions, as implied by the film's epilogue, set in Paris many years later, when older Mei (Gwei Lun-Mei, who also plays the protagonist in *Forêt Debussy*) visits her mother. She enters a shop, in which several jigsaws with missing pieces are on display, including *The Starry Night*. As an unseen person – possibly the older Chieh – ascends some stairs, the film concludes with Mei facing the camera directly, on the verge of cathartic tears. Perhaps her incomplete jigsaw makes sense to her only in hindsight, following her belated realisation that many years ago, she was attracted to Chieh, though not fully conscious of this. Without knowing

Figure 3.2 Chieh and the forest disintegrate in *Starry Starry Night* (Lin Shu-Yu, 2011).

it at the time, was she looking for *him* in the forest? The film ultimately leaves it up to the viewer to decide.

Conceived as a dissected map of the domestic, *The Starry Night* jigsaw motivates Mei's excursion from city to forest (a desire to view the night sky being her ostensible reason for undertaking the trip), while the void at its centre alludes to her emotional journey, her need for orientation. The collapsing jigsaw imagery, on the other hand, marks the disintegration of the domestic: the death of the grandfather, the parents' divorce, and Mei's separation from Chieh. These events are traumatic, especially for a young girl, and in this respect it is worth noting how the film uses landscape metaphors that at times border on pathetic fallacy. Take the scene in which Mei and Chieh emerge from the decrepit church in the morning sunlight. A wide shot reveals its location on the precipitous edge of a landslip; train tracks dangle precariously over the void. The church is in fact located on the Alishan railway, which at the time of shooting was not accessible to the public following Typhoon Morakot in 2009. This marks the intrusion of the realities that Lin had hitherto excluded from his fairy tale excursion to the forest, and that prompted an impulse to documentation:

> Before shooting, there was a big typhoon and there were landslides, there were mudslides, and then we had these tracks that were hanging there, which they hadn't come to fix yet. And when you see something like that, you're like: we've got to document this, we've got to shoot it, we've got to put this on celluloid.[26]

The scene further evokes indigenous presence, or rather absence, given the devastating effects of typhoon and earthquake damage on rural indigenous communities, many of whom had to be relocated.[27]

At this moment in the film, reality intrudes in the form of a scarred landscape, ruined infrastructure, and abandoned buildings. Narratively, all this appears when Mei is definitively making the transition into maturity, following the erotic frisson of the previous evening and a frank discussion with Chieh about his traumatic past experiences. It does not seem coincidental that at this point, the pair cease to be lost in the forest and are instead able to find their way, using the landmarks and following the train tracks. From this, we can draw out some allegorical possibilities, given that the film shows emotional and physical progress as intertwined, and that the processing of trauma is apparently central to this. The landslip is, after all, a topographical fissure, a geological void, suggesting that the environment is being depicted in a manner that reflects its protagonists' pain.

Karen Ya-Che Yang has written on these themes with reference to *Island Etude* (Chen Hwai-En, 2007), which she argues was significant in marking Taiwan's progress out of postcolonial traumas by telling stories memorialising postcolonial scars, rather than detailing processes of healing wounds.[28] These arguments seem too general to apply to Taiwanese cinema more broadly, while the fine distinction between wounds and scarring is theoretically rigorous, but relies largely on analogy. Can the forests in *Starry Starry Night* be seen to memorialise a postcolonial scar? Possibly, to the degree that the damaged tracks of the Alishan railway were a Japanese colonial construction, and the relocation of indigenous communities results from postcolonial dynamics. More persuasive and less political – but likely more in line with Lin's intentions – is that the environment is being used to allegorise characterisation in a traumatic narrative.

In *Starry Starry Night*, the landslide cuts open the landscape like Spilsbury's dissected map, later known as a jigsaw, the film's structuring metaphor. Moreover, this traumatic rupture is not merely geological, but finds a bodily parallel in a scene that appears shortly beforehand. Getting undressed in the church, Chieh removes his top, revealing a scar on the back of his shoulder, which the audience has not previously seen and which Mei touches. Chieh later explains that he was injured after his father beat him up in a drunken rage, having previously assaulted his mother. Through the scar tissue, reality intrudes: Mei comes to understand life's capacity for brutality, from which she has previously been sheltered. But her actions are also plainly erotic; she is drawn to Chieh's unclothed body and the scar holds a particular fascination for her. Provoking both fear and desire, scars – a fault line in a forest, a gap in a jigsaw, a void in a dissected map – help Mei come of age.

Spoilt Woods: *Soul* (2013) and *The Tag-Along* (2015) as Eco-cinematic Horror

In representing the woods as damaged or spoiled by human intervention, the horror films *Soul* and *The Tag-Along* can be said to share an ecological subtext, prompting this comparative analysis that assumes 'a pluralistic eco-aesthetic which can find value – cognitive, emotional, and affective – in a wide range of films' as David Ingram has argued.[29] Through a narrative and stylistic emphasis on animism, the films dramatise the place of the human in relation to what is considered natural. Questions of mediation are also central to both films. At the commercial end of the spectrum, *The Tag-Along* remediates a range of mythology and generic tropes, while *Soul*, inclined towards arthouse conventions, deploys self-reflexive screening devices. The effect in both cases is to undermine notions of the forest being pristine, in the sense that the environment is always depicted through the lens of existing forms.

In *Soul*, Chuan collapses at work in Taipei, and is taken to convalesce with his estranged father Wang (Wang Yu), who resides in an isolated house in the mountain forests. As Chuan's behaviour becomes increasingly erratic, it is unclear whether he has been possessed by a demon or is suffering from schizophrenia. When he kills his visiting sister (Chen Shiang-Chyi), it sets in motion a chain of violence that, disturbingly, begins to mend the rift between father and son. The film opens in the Japanese restaurant where Chuan works in the kitchen. Amidst glass and mirrored surfaces, the superficial trappings of traditional Japanese architecture are featured, including wood panel walls and a designer bamboo tap. The artifice of the urban façades initially seems to be contrasted with the authenticity of Wang's marginalised rural existence. The road is in a state of disrepair, while Wang lives precariously, his livelihood reliant on crop cycles and weather. A pallet truck is the only means of accessing his property, chugging slowly uphill and downhill through the woods.

Yet if there is a search for origins in the forest, then it is shown to be more authentic than the city only in the sense that cruelty is shockingly unrepressed. Chuan's killing of a live fish in the restaurant acts as the narrative's inciting incident, causing him to faint and provoking his breakdown. Chuan dismembers it behind a façade, a wall with a serving hatch that separates the tastefully decorated dining area from the gloomy kitchen. A wide shot shows him standing out of view of the customers, watching the death throes of the animal he has just slaughtered. This shot appears amidst a series of images, each cutting to black, depicting the creature's suffering: it gasps for oxygen; it writhes desperately; its flippers waggle as it is gutted; its head continues to twitch after its entrails have been removed. Finally, it lies frying on a barbeque, split in two, its mouth and eyes wide open in petrification. This is a grisly sequence routinely witnessed by Chuan, though typically of animal slaughter, it lies beyond the visibility of the consumers.

At the end of the film, Wang's sanatorium cell is lined with posters taxonomising fish and lobster species, reflecting the detached, observational aesthetics of scientific naturalism. Yet *Soul* has by this point suggested more profound interspecies connections. Ivy I-Chu Chang mentions the significance of fish heads within the oeuvre of Chung's films, while the association of fish with sex and fertility in Chinese mythology, and the appearance of this trope in eco-cinema, has been explored by critics including Jiayin Mi.[30] Chuan's killing of a fish suggests disruption to *qi* and may explain his apparent asexuality, while if we interpret this as a story of possession, then the soul of the fish has entered Chuan, as he alleges: 'I saw this body was empty, so I settled in.' Animism calls into question boundaries between humans, animals, and vegetation; for example a graphic match involving a leaf connects Chuan to the murder of his sister. As she walks in the woods, a close-up shows her examining a small leaf in her hand. This then cuts to Chuan's bloodied palm holding the same leaf; he has killed her, offscreen, in the interim. Later, as Wang murders his son-in-law, an insect is seen crawling across a red orchid. These edits suggest that given humans are *of* nature, then human violence must emanate from nature itself.

Animism is similarly prominent in *The Tag-Along*, which concerns a demonic girl dressed in red, who lures Taipei residents to the mountains, where their souls are captured by tree spirits. The story focuses on radio DJ Yi-Chun and her estate agent boyfriend Wei (Huang He), whose grandmother (Liu Yin-Shang) disappears after being led away by the spectral girl. When Wei himself then vanishes, Yi-Chun is compelled to investigate. *The Tag-Along* was inspired by some amateur camcorder footage taken in 1998 by hikers in the woodlands of Dakeng Mountain near Taichung. In the video, a disturbing girl in red appears whom nobody recalled seeing at the time. She was subsequently identified as a *moshenzi* or mountain demon, who was apparently responsible for tragedies that later befell some of the other people in the footage. Though there is some suggestion that the video may have been a hoax, it circulated widely on TV and became an urban legend.

Although mountain forests do not feature significantly until the final third of *The Tag-Along*, vegetation in the Taipei settings is used to dramatise the porous relationship between urban and rural environments. Tong argues that eco-cinema involves seeing urban space in an unfamiliar way; viewed differently, urban space is natural space without nature.[31] In *The Tag-Along*, this perspective is crucial to the construction of the narrative. One shot features a tree branch looming prominently and ominously in the foreground, while the housing estate in the background is kept out of focus. The leaves rustle menacingly, as if in league with the spirits that are preparing to wreak havoc on the humans. In the accompanying dialogue, a local resident remarks that the spirits have fewer places to live due to the destruction of their habitat, thus have ventured into the cities seeking to punish human beings. A mountain rescuer later relates a local legend: for every tree chopped down, the mountain will capture a person and plant their soul. The film incarnates a tradition of

Sinophone eco-cinema that conceives the supernatural as dependent on the preservation of natural ecosystems.[32]

If trees have emotional agency – and in *The Tag-Along*, they do – then the mountain is their home, their place, and their centre of 'felt value', as Tuan puts it.[33] The trees planted in Taipei, on the other hand, are away from home; they are out of place, incongruous. By planting humans in the woods, just as humans plant trees in the cities, the vexed spirits seek to enact a spatial revenge. This narrative motivation draws on complex cultural discourses. In fact forest cover, recorded at 60.9 per cent in 2012, has been stable in Taiwan for several decades; the island was not subject to severe deforestation except in the immediate decades following the KMT's acquisition of power, and levels have since recovered.[34] However, one of the most controversial aspects of deforestation was the loss of biodiversity, with activists from the late 1980s successfully campaigning for a ban on the logging of rare species such as native cypresses and old-growth forests.[35] Logging continues to take place illegally.[36] This is dramatised by the prologue to the film's sequel, in which a gang of loggers is terrorised by mountain demons.

Deforestation is emblematic of the film's broader concern with the ethics of land acquisition and use. Wei's real estate deals define place in terms of its financial, rather than emotional, value. In order to make money, he remortgages his grandmother's house without her knowledge. Later, when the elderly woman disappears, Wei feels remorse for his actions, and intriguingly, this is the very point at which he becomes vulnerable to the girl in red. Human guilt – whether over ecological or family matters – is what energises the mountain spirits, who apparently seek to punish deviations from the 'natural', conceived in a manner that overlaps with normativity. This is problematic in the depiction of Yi-Chun who, prior to the events of the film, had an abortion. The film deploys a range of imagery that connects her feelings of guilt to the supernatural threat. In a terrifying CGI sequence, Yi-Chun wakes up in bed at night, experiencing a vision in which blood leaks from her groin and becomes gruesomely intermingled with gnarled tree roots. Later, in the woods, a tree demon takes the form of her unborn child. Apparently, the gender politics of the woodland spirits are decidedly regressive, reminding us to exercise caution when referring to forests, female reproductive systems, or anything else as natural, if the term is somehow construed as being free of cultural value. The film aligns Yi-Chun's pro-choice beliefs with her independent lifestyle, but at the film's conclusion it is revealed that she is planning to marry Wei and have a baby. Charitably, one might argue that this is her choice; but viewed more critically, motherhood and matrimony here represent the restoration of the natural order.

Themes of parenthood are also central to *Soul*, which questions the ethics of maintaining family lineage at all costs. If *The Tag-Along* and *Starry Starry Night* mourn the loss of an older generation's values, then *Soul* conversely alleges the hereditary nature of violence: Chuan's behaviour has likely been caused by his father's capacity to kill. Wang's initial shock at the death of his daughter is quickly supplanted by ingenuity in disposing of her body, while he himself commits the second murder. Undoubtedly, there is a self-reflexive aspect to this genealogical emphasis. The presence of iconic *wuxia* star Wang Yu suggests the interrogation of a generational legacy, as does the use of the actors' own names (Chuan, Wang) for the characters. The gruesome, unjustified violence committed in the film seems at odds with the honourable codes of combat that typically define the *wuxia* hero. Yet paradoxically, a righteous kill motivates the narrative; we learn that years ago, Wang assisted his terminally ill wife in committing suicide. This ambivalence was typical of Wang's star image, which by no means offered an unquestioned affirmation of the martial arts ethos, as Tony Williams and Stephen Teo have demonstrated.[37]

Self-reflexivity occurs elsewhere in the film, with screening devices further undermining the woods as a realm of authenticity. The camera frequently shoots through surfaces such as glass, mirrors, and nets, with the cinematography making use of frames within frames. As Chuan lies silently in bed, his sister tries to communicate with him, but his emotional distance is visually captured by the mosquito net that separates them. The nets that Wang uses for orchid cultivation undermine notions of the pristine, given the obvious environmental damage they cause. The lights and heat lamps are always switched on, warming the air and using up energy, while the water sprinklers are wasteful and cause noise pollution. The machinery and energy consumption recall the craft of filmmaking itself, with the orchid farm even resembling a film set. Electric cables are plentiful; lamps are switched on during the daytime; nets reduce the density of the sunlight. When Chuan's sister converses with Wang among the orchids, they are apparently braving a rain shower. But suddenly the rain stops, revealing that sprinklers, rather than the weather, were responsible for the downpour. The effect recalls that of the rigs used to generate fake rain in film productions.

The window frame in the woodshed similarly serves to remind the viewer that even in the woods, cinema exerts its reach. In *Starry Starry Night*, Chieh watches Mei silhouetted by torchlight, like a film projection. Similarly in *Soul*, Chuan peers out from within the window frame of the woodshed, moving his hand rapidly in front of a torch, creating flashes of light. This is clearly intended to mimic the flickering rays that emanate from a cinema projection booth, and appropriately, prefaces Chuan's encounter with the Messenger, an entirely fantasised character whom he follows through a woodland dreamscape. Self-reflexivity of this type is not used in *The Tag-Along*. Yet the film similarly undermines notions of the pristine forest via its mediation, at a structural and formal level, of diverse mythology and generic tropes. Executive producer Tseng Han-Hsien explains that *The Tag-Along* is rooted in the taboos that result from collective fears. He suggests that superstition surrounding ghosts and death might have discouraged an earlier generation of filmmakers from dramatising these topics, while the lack of local industry expertise in genre filmmaking may also have been an issue.[38] Identifying a gap in the market, Tseng's ambition was to establish Taiwanese horror as a viable commercial genre, and he succeeded; *The Tag-Along* was exported to a range of Chinese-speaking territories, and spearheaded an explosion of Taiwanese horror films.

Bearing in mind the intention to reach an international audience, it was perhaps inevitable that local legends would be presented through the prism of universal myths and tropes – not to mention transnational industry practices. Tseng had, for instance, observed the success of Thai ghost films, and when working on the project, sought to learn from practitioners in Thailand, for example by inviting the post-production company Kantana to provide technical guidance.[39] The girl in red, meanwhile, owed her existence to mediation from the outset, while her later portrayal in the film further remediates some disparate cultural elements. Comparing the original camcorder footage with the filmic recreation, one notices that her trousers have been replaced by a dress, and she now bears more than a passing resemblance to Little Red Riding Hood, as popularised by the Brothers Grimm. Indeed the film's Chinese title, *Little Girl in Red*, would have been too similar for English-speaking audiences, and likely explains the title change. The girl's appearance owes much to the influence of Kantana, while her four-legged crawl was borrowed from earlier Japanese horror movies such as *Ringu* (Hideo Nakata, 1998) and *The Grudge* (Takashi Shimizu, 2002). The presence of an eerie child, moreover, has been a staple of the horror genre globally for many years.

Tracing a full historical genealogy of the local mythology depicted in the film is outside the scope of this book, and I would point the reader towards the work of Lin Mei-Mei, who has extensively researched how Taiwanese folk beliefs and myths relating to the supernatural have been culturally constructed.[40] Her research had a direct impact on *The Tag-Along*. The film's screenwriter Chien Shih-Keng attended Lin's class and also read the book she co-authored with Li Chia-Gai, *The Anthropological Imagination of the Demon God*, which inspired him to create the girl in red.[41] Local myths were then cinematically communicated to audiences through the adoption of generic forms and styles. More broadly, in the context of distribution, the reappearance of forests in Taiwanese cinema could be seen both as a guarantee of authenticity, and as part of a business strategy – the assertion of an allegedly unique Taiwanese identity in a changing transnational market.

THE FORMS OF THE FOREST: LOST IN *FORÊT DEBUSSY* (2016)

Forêt Debussy is a drama about an unnamed classical pianist and her mother (Lu Yi-Ching) who have fled to the forest following the murder of the woman's husband and child. Blaming herself for the killings, the woman undergoes an affective and physical journey, as the forest inflicts on her all manner of punishment. Directed by Kuo, a Taiwanese émigré living in Paris, and shot by French cinematographer Antoine Hérberlé, the film is aimed squarely at international arthouse audiences. The title alludes to Claude Debussy's practice of musically representing the sounds of nature, something there is no space to consider here. The film has minimal dialogue, withholds plot points and motivations, and favours shots of long duration. Strikingly, it is set entirely on location in the forest. Eighty-seven minutes elapse before the audience is given any sense of geographical orientation, when the woman stumbles upon an open hillside, encountering a sign that states, 'Land for sale – for multiple commercial uses'. This is incongruously surreal, given that symbols of human civilisation have been hitherto absent.

The film's depiction of the forest will be considered in relation to commentary from Kuo, as well as Lu Yen-Chiu, who was one of two location managers on the film. As the director had been living in France for many years, he was not very familiar with Taiwanese forests, thus the sourcing of appropriate landforms and landscapes became a collaborative endeavour.[42] Kuo's concept was that the protagonist would slowly immerse herself in the forest, and as she climbed to higher altitudes, would feel progressively less attached to the outside world.[43] However, open mountain views are not seen until the end of the film, meaning that the changes in altitude – and therefore the unfolding of the woman's affective journey – must be evoked by the vegetation. Lu explains that she began by scouting the outskirts of New Taipei City, then gradually extended her search to medium-altitude mountains in Yilan and Alishan before going to Mount Hehuan for the high altitudes.[44] She also notes that *Forêt Debussy* differed from standard practice in that it was shot entirely on location, thus did not incorporate artificial forest sets. However, the relatively low budget impacted on the choice of locations, which needed to be reasonably accessible, given the practicalities of travel, but also to appear isolated, in keeping with the script.[45] Alishan, for instance, was easy to reach. Lin Shu-Yu recalls that one of the benefits of filming *Starry Starry Night* on Alishan was that the terrain looked secluded, but at the same time, was easily accessible by road.[46]

Yet several of the other locations on *Forêt Debussy* were far less accessible, and the crew went further and deeper into the forests than on other productions. The rationale for this was that the environment needed to look remote and dangerous in order that the women's experiences could be depicted in a visceral manner. The characters live outside, exposed to the elements, sheltering only in makeshift constructions. They gather food, cook it on campfires, and wash in streams (for authenticity, Kuo consulted survival handbooks such as *Back to the Wild* by Alain Saury).[47] They become hungry and thirsty, and suffer from exposure. The woman eats poisonous berries, which give her a severe fever, while the mother dies after being bitten by a venomous snake. This kind of representation has a long genealogy, recalling tropes that Emma Jinhua Teng identifies in the work of Qing travel writers, in which mountain forests, 'especially the Taiwanese jungle with its tangled, dense, and thorny vegetation – were associated with qualities of impenetrability, darkness, and mystery'.[48] These themes endure in Forêt Debussy. Dense vegetation precludes clear views and impedes physical progress, while the forest is depicted as an eerie, primeval environment, devoid of people.

The forest is, in that sense, a construction, a fiction like any other, and hardly untouched by the filmmakers. Around 10 per cent of the vegetation that appears in the film was added to the location, although real plants rather than imitations were used, and none of the species was non-native.[49] Every single exterior location was filmed using lights.[50] It goes without saying that any film relies on a degree of fakery. Yet to an unusual degree, the cinematography strives to give the impression of immersion in a real environment, making extensive use of choreographed tracking shots that are long in duration, including several 360-degree pans. Mapping, meanwhile, is undertaken through the sequencing of vegetation types. Creative choices such as these suggest a particular impulse to authenticity, a concern with fidelity to the environment depicted. A pressing question, then, is to what degree the critic might accommodate the notion of a film location as having an existence in and of itself. Is it naïve to argue that there is something that the forest intrinsically gives, or affords, the filmmaker?

Kohn observes that ecologists often seek to counter myths of pristine nature by asserting that history permeates landscape, but he argues that 'instead, the history that gets caught in the forest is mediated and mutated by a form that is not exactly reducible to human events or landscape'.[51] The depiction of the Alishan railway in Starry Starry Night, or the forest trails in The Tag-Along, adhere to the former view, in that human history is shown to materially mark the landscape. By contrast, the approach on Forêt Debussy has more in common with Kohn's understanding of this environment. He argues that the tropical forest tends to amplify form, by which he means habits or regularities, such as patterns resulting from constraints on possibility, like the distribution of rivers or the recurrent circular shapes of whirlpools.[52] He contends that 'humans do not just impose form on the tropical forest; the forest proliferates it. One can think of coevolution as a reciprocal proliferation of regularities or habits among interacting species.'[53] To the degree that film poetics emphasises the study of patterns and form, and a forest as a film location might proliferate its own forms, it seems useful to consider these ideas.

On Forêt Debussy, while the filmmakers doubtless imposed their own cognitive schema onto an ecological system, there are also ways in which the forest imposed its own form onto the film – most noticeably, at the level of practice, which subsequently impacts on the aesthetic result. The density of vegetation in many of the forest locations, coupled with the topography of steep slopes and ravines, meant that much of the environment was inaccessible to the filmmakers in the first place; they were limited to accessing some of the places on foot, along routes and trails. Production assistant Wang Jen-You recalls that most of the locations were twenty to thirty minutes' walk from the base. The crew could take only limited equipment and had to carry heavy kit, all by hand, often uphill, which was tough work; the longest hike lasted one hour.[54] The locations on the border of Taroko and Nantou County were the trickiest areas in which to film; the shooting location on the Xiao Qilai trail involved a walk of 1.5 kilometres.[55] Production photos taken by Lu indicate the relatively small amount of kit that was carried to the locations, and also shows the uneven, rocky, and steep terrain that had to be negotiated as lighting, and rails for tracking shots, were set up (Figures 3.3a and 3.3b). Given that this is a film made by a Taiwanese director based in France, with some French crew and funding, these geographical challenges could be examined as restrictions placed on transnational flow. Shih remarks that notions of flow espoused by theorists of the transnational always need situating, because 'flow is always affected by topography', which can affect its speed, density, and direction.[56] That is literally the case here, and it has an aesthetic impact.

Lighting, for instance, was affected by the environment. First, natural light was limited because even in the summer, given the shade of the forest, there would not be enough light after 4 pm.[57] Second, the environment precluded filming at night owing to the risk of accidents resulting from low visibility and wild animals, and third, it was impossible to carry too much heavy equipment along steep hiking routes, especially given the limited time; only a few battery-powered lights and polyboards were taken to some locations.[58] An effect of all this, Kuo recalls, was that 'as we worked deeper and deeper in the forest, getting higher and higher, we used fewer and fewer lights'; however, these restrictions provoked creative responses, such as the decision to shoot many scenes day-for-night.[59]

The forest also imposed restrictions upon staging and performance. Once stepped upon, vegetation would become trampled and damaged. Therefore, when framing was being discussed prior to rolling the camera, the vegetation around the actors needed to be kept intact, meaning that the crew members had to be guided along alternative routes.[60] Given this, and the time constraints, rehearsals were impractical, so Kuo treated the first take as a rehearsal and completed most shots by the second or third take. Ironically, although the film was shot digitally, the workflows recalled those of celluloid filmmaking to which the director retains allegiance: 'I still retain the traditional spirit of working on film. I'm not a big fan of excessive takes.'[61] In these and various other respects, the activity of the filmmakers was constrained by the form of the

Figure 3.3a–b Production stills from *Forêt Debussy* (Kuo Cheng-Chui, 2016). Courtesy of Lu Yen-Chiu.

forest, but this was seen as a productive limitation. Other qualities of the forest did not shape the finished product, but certainly affected the practitioners. The locations were frequently situated too far away from bathroom facilities, making toilet trips unfeasible, and all waste, including human excrement, had to be returned to the base camp. So a tent was erected with a stack of nappies provided for the crew's use.[62]

Human waste could not stay in the forest for reasons of environmental protection, and one objective of regulations around this is the preservation of biodiversity. This is a major concern for green advocacy; in a recent study showing the percentage of environmental organisations engaging with specific issues in Taiwan, biodiversity was the most common area of focus.[63] This likely marks a difference with China, where substantial reforestation efforts have not tended to focus on improving biodiversity in the forest ecosystem.[64] But in *Forêt Debussy*, the rich variety of vegetation was important to visualising the narrative, as Lu explains:

> In terms of vegetation, there is an amazing diversity in Taiwanese forests; from low to high altitudes, we can see a significant difference in tree species, ferns, and vegetation. Although they all looked green to the layman's eyes, we were still stunned by the magnificence of Mother Nature when we were surrounded by it.[65]

These remarks raise several interesting points. First, while the suggestion of progress from low to high altitudes implies a coherent environment, it is worth stating the obvious: the forest we see onscreen is a composite that does not exist. The locations were scattered across central and northern Taiwan, and included Yangmingshan, the Pingxi mountain area, Mingchi at Yilan and the surrounding area, Alishan, and Hehuashan. There is no *Forêt Debussy*; it exists only in the film.

There is also the observation that for most people, the forest will look green. Kohn, drawing on Jorge Luis Borges' short story *Funes the Memorious*, argues that the dynamics of living and thinking are not built only from difference, but also on confusion – on forgetting to notice difference.[66] The same applies here, and is something that the film uses to its advantage. Unless a viewer is extremely familiar with the biodiversity of Taiwan's mountain forests – for example, if they were an indigenous inhabitant or a botanist – they would not be able to tell whether, say, a particular plant species that appears in one shot might credibly be found growing close to a different species in the next shot. This is because the forest appears to most viewers as 'the same'. As Lu concedes, the vegetation 'all looked green to the layman's eyes'. Hence the paradox: while biodiversity embodies narrative movement, the woman's affective journey through the forest, we may not actually recognise it.

Forests are often experienced by human beings, and characters in films, in terms of sameness. Indeed an inability to distinguish difference is the very essence of being lost in the woods, as Tuan elaborates:

> I follow a path into the forest, stray from the path, and all of a sudden feel completely disoriented. Space is still organized in conformity with the sides of my body. There are the regions to my front and back, to my right and left, but they are not geared to external reference points and hence are quite useless.[67]

This disorienting experience leads Tuan to consider whether a sense of spaciousness can be associated with this environment, given that 'from one viewpoint, the forest is a cluttered environment, the antithesis of open space' with distant views nonexistent.[68] This is how the forest is generally filmed in *Forêt Debussy*, as cluttered and claustrophobic. Kuo discusses this in relation to his earlier short film *Family Viewing* (2008), which featured the same actors and is

> a Taiwanese film in which you can't see any exteriors or street views. Everything is shot inside. On the contrary, *Forêt Debussy* is comprised of exterior locations, all shot in the mountains, but through my framing, I aim to make all the scenes look like they were shot in confined spaces.[69]

At the same time, as the film progresses, the woman's feelings of entrapment give way to a sense of liberation. She resolves to remain in the forest, affirming the film's utopian vision of freedom in an unspoilt environment. This is a place where she can escape society and leave her past behind.

The forest imposes visual confinement, but as such, provokes imaginative escape. Tuan observes a change in his perspective on the forest, when his initial disorientation gives way to a more subjective sense of spaciousness:

> The forest, no less than the bare plain, is a trackless region of possibility. Trees that clutter up space from one viewpoint are, from another, the means by which a special awareness of place is created, for the trees stand behind the other as far as the eyes can see, and they encourage the mind to extrapolate to infinity.[70]

These tensions are articulated visually in *Forêt Debussy*. Kuo notes his preference for 'a range of different types of framing within one shot or take' in which the viewer can 'see different kinds of space, which can be represented through camera movement, and sometimes the movement of the actors and their bodies'.[71] One choreographed shot, filmed in a single take of two minutes and twenty seconds, ends with the camera rising on a jib, moving away from the protagonist as it tilts up to focus on the towering treetops. This frame offers a direct rendering of what Tuan describes as the creation of a special awareness of place: the trees stand behind each other as far as the eyes can see, encouraging the mind 'to extrapolate to infinity'. This is a confined perspective, but one that offers the possibility of freedom, opening up an imaginative space.

Epilogue: A Structuring Absence

Absent from the films discussed in this chapter are any indigenous protagonists, despite the mountain forests being home to many tribes, historically and now. The filmmakers focus instead on how urban, ethnically Chinese characters experience these rural environments. Forest-set films in which the island's original inhabitants appear usually adopt indigenous experience as their subject matter; these include *Seediq Bale* (Wei Te-Sheng, 2011), *Finding Sayun* (Laha Mebow, 2011), and *Hidden Treasures in the Mountain* (Wang Tao-Nan, 2018). This argument can certainly be nuanced. The mountain rescue captain in *The Tag-Along*, for instance, is played by an indigenous actor, Yawei Basang, and demonstrates authority over the forest through his practical expertise and spiritual sensitivity. Yet while these traits code the character as indigenous, his ethnicity is never stated. In terms of conceptual perspective, meanwhile, *Forêt Debussy* pushes towards an alternative ontology of the forest, which aligns it to a certain extent with indigenous understandings of place, as suggested by my discussion of the work of Kohn, whose ideas draw on his ethnographic fieldwork with the Runa in Ecuador's Upper Amazon.

However, all the films considered in this chapter require the forests to be, if not pristine, then empty. Sometimes, this relates to issues of genre credibility; horror conventions dictate that characters must be isolated, in order to be vulnerable to threat. Yet however beautiful or powerful we consider these films to be, we need to remember that the depiction of Taiwan's forested mountain areas as being devoid of indigenous inhabitants has a problematic genealogy, especially in the context of historical mapping. Teng explains that in the late seventeenth century, the myth of empty lands facilitated the appropriation of tribal rights, and maps were used as a tool in this process, marking out Taiwan's mountainous regions as cartographically empty.[72] Qing writers alleged that monstrous people and demons resided in these areas. As one gazetteer attested in 1696, drawing an association between the horrifying and the indigenous, 'In the deep mountains where wheel tracks rarely reach, there live people with human bodies and animal faces … Hobgoblins of the trees and rocks, and spirits of the hills and water also come and go. It is truly another world.'[73] Horror, in this context, is not a genre without cultural baggage.

The lack of indigenous presence in these films deserves consideration as a structuring absence, in terms outlined by Berry as something that is noticeable by its absence, a topic that appears to have been avoided.[74] At some moments, reality intrudes, for instance in *Starry Starry Night*, when the scenes on the ruined Alishan railway and its church evoke the relocation of indigenous communities in the wake of Typhoon Morakot. Yet as Taiban Sasala and his co-researchers argue, even prior to natural disasters, colonialism and state hegemony had changed the local forest landscape, as well as the cultures, resources, and land ethics upon which the mainly indigenous inhabitants depend.[75] Questions around the ethics of land use are central to many films dramatising the experience of indigenous communities, and are taken up in the following chapter.

NOTES

1. Hu, *Worldly Desires*, 42–3.
2. Chang, *Place, Identity and National Imagination*, 9, 177.
3. Shih, *Visuality and Identity*, 190.
4. See Harrell, 'The eco-developmental state', 243.
5. Bettinson, *Sensuous Cinema*, 8–18.
6. Berry, 'Imagine there's no China', 119–20.
7. Ibid., 121.
8. Harrell, 'The eco-developmental state', 255.
9. Bettinson, *Sensuous Cinema*, 17–18, referring to the work of Wong Kar-Wai.
10. Chulphongsathorn, 'The cinematic forest', 186.
11. See, for example, Xuelin Zhou, *Youth Culture*, 105–12.
12. Yorke, *Into the Woods*, xviii.
13. Tong, 'Toward a Hong Kong ecocinema', 180.
14. Wu, *The Man with the Compound Eyes*, 220.
15. As defined by Tong in 'Toward a Hong Kong ecocinema', 180.
16. Bettinson, *Sensuous Cinema*, 18.
17. Tuan, *Space and Place*, 36, 56–7, 119–20. Kohn, *How Forests Think*, 153–90.
18. For colonial confusion over non-existent boundary lines, see Thongchai, *Siam Mapped*, 73.
19. Liao, *The Starry Starry Night*.
20. The text on the spine is too small to read. It is probably the 1966 book by René Jeanne and Charles Ford.
21. Hu, *Worldly Desires*, 180.
22. Tong, 'Toward a Hong Kong ecocinema', 180.
23. Hu, *Worldly Desires*, 42–3.
24. Lin, 'Director's Q&A, Taiwan Post New Wave Cinema Project'.
25. Ibid.
26. Ibid.
27. See Taiban et al., 'Indigenous conservation', 123.
28. Yang, 'Passionately documenting', 45–7.
29. Ingram, 'The aesthetics and ethics of eco-film criticism', 58.
30. See Chang, *Taiwan Cinema, Memory, and Modernity*, 200, 219, and Mi, 'Framing ambient *Unheimlich*', 27–8.
31. Tong, 'Toward a Hong Kong ecocinema', 181–2.
32. See Kaldis, 'Submerged ecology and depth psychology', 65.
33. Tuan, *Space and Place*, 3.

34. Harrell, 'The eco-developmental state', 254.
35. Lin, 'Politicizing nature', 89–92.
36. Huang, 'Taiwanese mountain and river literature', 34.
37. Williams, 'Wang Yu', 75–104; Teo, *Chinese Martial Arts Cinema*, 143–44.
38. Lin, 'If a society does not face its fears'.
39. Ibid.
40. See, for instance, Lin, *Taiwanese Ghost Stories*.
41. See Wang, 'Demon and ghost stories'.
42. Lu, Personal interview.
43. Lu, Personal interview, and Kuo, Personal interview.
44. Lu, Personal interview.
45. Ibid.
46. Lin, 'Director's Q&A, Taiwan Post New Wave Cinema Project'.
47. Kuo, Personal interview.
48. Teng, *Taiwan's Imagined Geography*, 132. Hsin-Tien Liao discusses how colonial Japanese landscape painters sought to 'subdue the untamed' in their work. Liao, 'The beauty of the untamed', 40.
49. Lu, Personal interview.
50. Kuo, Personal interview.
51. Kohn, *How Forests Think*, 183.
52. Ibid., 153–88.
53. Ibid., 182.
54. Wang, Personal interview.
55. Ibid.
56. Shih, 44.
57. Kuo, Personal interview.
58. Lu, Personal interview.
59. Kuo, Personal interview.
60. Lu, Personal interview, and Kuo, Personal interview.
61. Kuo, Personal interview.
62. Lu, Personal interview, and Wang, Personal interview.
63. Haddad, 'East Asian environmental advocacy', 34.
64. Harrell, 'Eco-developmental state', 256.
65. Lu, Personal interview.
66. Kohn, *How Forests Think*, 85.
67. Tuan, *Space and Place*, 36.
68. Ibid., 56.
69. Kuo, Personal interview.
70. Tuan, *Space and Place*, 56.
71. Kuo, Personal interview.
72. Teng, *Taiwan's Imagined Geography*, 86–8.
73. The *Gazetteer of Taiwan Prefecture*, cited in Teng, *Taiwan's Imagined Geography*, 132–3.
74. Berry, 'Imagine there's no China', 119–20.
75. Taiban et al., 'Indigenous conservation', 125.

4. INDIGENOUS LAND AND SEA

Introduction: Returning to the Village

A young man gazes ahead, the camera slowly tracking away from him. He is in a university seminar room, surrounded by a group of guys chatting about their plans for a summer vacation trip. Not paying any attention, he instead stares across the room at another classmate, a young woman. He is apparently smitten, but the soundtrack tells a slightly different story. As his friends discuss visits to Hsinchu and Taichung, the sound of the tide, with its ebbs and flows, rises out of nowhere. It is as if the camera is drawing the young man away, like the pull of the sea. The dreamlike mood of these opening shots from *Pakeriran* (2017), directed by Amis filmmaker Lekal Sumi Cilangasan, is abruptly broken as one of the guys asks Futing (Matam Hidaw) whether he is listening to anything they are saying. The sound of the waves subsides as the tracking shot brings into view a map of Taiwan. As the friends consult it, planning excursions to Kaohsiung and Kenting, it becomes clear that their itinerary spans the whole island. In fact, Futing will never take the trip, as shortly afterwards he is asked to return to his tribe's village on the east coast, which exasperates him at first. But over the course of the film, he develops an attachment to the village and a commitment to his ancestral community. And in retrospect, the map in the opening scene embodies a kind of visuality that seems to conflict with Futing's newfound understanding of place.

This chapter considers the body of fiction films that have emerged over the past decade about Taiwan's original inhabitants or *yuanzhumin*, the island's indigenous Austronesian peoples, who comprise ethnic groups known as tribes.[1] The case studies include the film that Lekal co-directed with Cheng Yu-Chieh, *Wawa No Cidal* (2015), *Lokah Laqi* (Laha Mebow, 2016), and *Long Time No Sea* (Tsui Yung-Hui, 2018), along with some additional analysis of *Pakeriran* and Mebow's earlier film *Finding Sayun* (2011). All these films dramatise the visiting or revisiting of a rural, tribal village by an urban character: either a non-indigenous outsider, or a member of the community returning home after a period of absence. This trope reflects the legacy of localist movements, and in particular the concept of tribalism (*buluo zhuyi*) proposed by the Rukai anthropologist Taiban Sasala, who urged indigenous activists to 'abandon the past mode of struggle in urban streets and return to our homeland; to carry out an aboriginal movement that puts the tribe as the centre in its resistance, the homeland as the point of departure in its struggle'.[2] Darryl Sterk, who has written widely on indigenous Taiwanese film and literature, argues that Mebow is among the cultural producers who have participated in a 'return to the village' movement, some of whom have started ethnic tourism ventures.[3]

For most of the twentieth century, indigenous culture was suppressed, first under Japanese colonial rule and later under the KMT, with cinematic depictions adhering to the prevailing ideology of the time. The Japanese film *Sayon's Bell* (Hiroshi Shimizu, 1943), for instance, fictionalised real-life events in order to portray tribespeople as loyal subjects of the Emperor, while the martial law-era *On Mount Hehuan* (Pan Lei, 1958) promoted an assimilatory message, alleging the triumphant sinicisation of Taiwan's mountainous frontier.[4] These racist depictions often reiterated tropes of the noble savage, which predated cinematic portrayals and were evident, for instance, in 1920s Japanese travel writing on colonial Taiwan.[5] With the transition to democracy, such stereotypes did not simply disappear overnight. Lee Hsing's *The Heroic Pioneers* (1986), a historical epic about Han Chinese settlers colonising northeast Taiwan, was blatantly neo-colonialist and excoriated by critics, ending his directing career.[6] Primitivist tropes linger in films such as *Fishing Luck* (Tseng Wen-Chen, 2005) and *Pongso No Tao* (Wang Chin-Kuei, 2008), even though these films intend to offer positive portrayals.[7] In 2009, Anita Wen-Shin Chang noted that 'the cinematic projection of the indigenous, especially by nonindigenous producers, is problematic and often wrought with exoticism and primitivism'.[8] Particularly controversial, given its cultural reach, was Wei Te-Sheng's epic *Seediq Bale* (2011), which was praised for dramatising a previously marginalised history, but criticised for its factual inaccuracies and presentation of tribal culture as a violent spectacle.[9]

In dramatising the return to the village, the filmmakers considered here are less preoccupied with probing urban malaise than those discussed in the previous chapter. If the films set in forests resemble mirrors in which ethnically

Chinese city-dwellers see themselves reflected, then Mebow, Cheng, and Tsui, who do not live among the communities they represent, are highly conscious of their status as outsiders. They are acutely aware of the troubling legacy of indigenous communities being gazed at by external forces – whether colonists, tourists, or filmmakers. Mebow's film *Finding Sayun* was the first feature-length fiction work to offer a sustained critique of these dynamics. Sterk refers to the film as 'an indigenous appropriation of primitivism' that ironically plays with audience expectations, self-consciously constructing an open-ended, modern indigenous identity.[10] Chris Berry argues that *Wawa No Cidal* was the first film to place indigenous identity centre screen, rather than conceiving it as subordinate to broader questions of Taiwanese identity.[11] Moreover the years after 2008 have witnessed the rise of an indigenous presence behind, as well as in front of, the camera, with filmmakers such as Mebow, Lekal, and Umin Boya achieving prominence. For Berry, this last point is critical, as it requires us to consider the films not simply in terms of their subject matter, but in relation to their production and reception by indigenous communities.[12] These dynamics need to be considered, I would suggest, in relation to the environment in which the filmmaking occurs.

Orientation: Mapping the East Coast

The films under consideration have focused attention on Taiwan's central mountain range and east coast, reflecting the contemporary concentration of tribal communities in these areas. While indigenous peoples comprise around 2.3 per cent of Taiwan's total population, they account for a far greater proportion of residents in eastern regions; around 28 per cent in Hualien, for instance, in 2014.[13] Referring to the reception of *Wawa No Cidal*, which was shot in Hualien and Taitung counties, Cheng remarks,

> When we screened this film in Taipei, many people considered it to be very remote, as if the story belonged to another country. Some people didn't even believe that what they saw had really happened. However, back in Hualien and Taitung, people responded to it very positively. This kind of feature film, that is, a commercial film shot from an east coast perspective, focusing on Hualien and Taitung, is rare. Other films have been shot there, but they are still from the perspective of Taipei; they do not offer a genuinely local perspective.[14]

Cheng and Lekal wanted to shoot a film that was not merely set on the east coast, but felt like it belonged to the residents of this region. The film was intended as a corrective to earlier representations by filmmakers from Taipei or other large urban areas, who had failed to challenge their own perspectives as outsiders.

As the Taipei audiences would have been predominately ethnic Chinese, when Cheng refers to an 'east coast perspective', it is fair to assume he is implying an indigenous viewpoint – especially given that his co-director is from the Amis tribe. If Taipei audiences found the events of the film remote, fictitious, literally outlandish, then there is clearly an ethnic dimension to this understanding of geography. For historically, the entire island of Taiwan was inhabited by indigenous tribes. The contemporary concentration of *yuanzhumin* communities in the island's central and eastern regions is a result of the gradual appropriation of tribal territory by external forces – the Dutch, southern Chinese immigrants, the Qing dynasty, the Japanese, and the KMT. Under the Qing, mapping played a central role in constructing ethnicity on the Taiwan frontier. The first 'savage boundary' was drawn in 1722 and underwent subsequent iterations, classifying the island's west and north as belonging to the Chinese population, with the area extending eastwards from the central mountains marked as indigenous territory.[15] It was not until 1879, however, that Xia Xianlun undertook the first comprehensive mapping of Taiwan's eastern regions.[16]

Mapping facilitated the appropriation of indigenous territory and can, along with the broader suppression of tribal cultures, be understood in terms of colonialism – though this is not uncontroversial. China's pro-unification stance is predicated on a denial of Qing imperialism, but as Emma Jinhua Teng argues, colonisers (whether Han Chinese, Dutch, or Japanese) were always experienced as external from the indigenous perspective.[17] Shu-Mei Shih similarly refers to the Sinophone as a product of colonial imposition, given the extent to which tribal cultures became sinicised over the centuries.[18] This process has been investigated by filmmakers such as Bauki Angaw in his 1997 documentary *Kavalan of Bird Stepping Stone Village*, which movingly traces the gradual disappearance of Kavalan territory and culture across several centuries.[19] He explains that when working at a TV station in 1994, his business card had a map of Taiwan with traditional tribal territories marked on the reverse, because most Taiwanese had little understanding of indigenous presence on the island.

Much has changed since the late 1990s, yet these cartographic legacies endure in Taiwan's contemporary imaginary. The very phrase 'east coast' bears witness to the legacy of historical, colonial mapping. It is positional, suggesting that the centre lies elsewhere, and implies verticality, with north conceived as upwards, which for a range of reasons (not least, the biases of Mercator projection) reinforces Western colonial dominance. In 2011, Jinn-Guey Lay and his co-researchers produced an alternative map of East Asia, with the southeast at the top, Taiwan in the centre, China below, and an oblique Mercator projection to reduce distortion.[20] Media coverage interpreted this variously as an assertion of Pacific interconnectedness, insular nationalism, and superiority to China.²¹ However, both conventional forms of mapping and this kind of imaginative remapping rely on abstraction. As such, they find themselves in tension with the indigenous tribes' traditional understandings of place. Some tribes, for instance, used cardinal directions historically (for example, 'Amis' means 'northerners' or 'people of the north'), while others did not; the Atayal language contains no words for north, south, east, and west, and used spatial reference systems based on orientation analogies including rivers, holy mountains, or historical places such as previous settlements.²²

Finding Sayun and *Lokah Laqi*, both of which are set in Atayal communities, capture the legacy of traditional orientation analogies in a hybrid, globalised context. The final section of *Finding Sayun*, shot in a fictionalised documentary format, shows the protagonist Yukan (Tsao Shih-Huei) and his grandfather (Chang Chin-Chen) returning to the tribe's previous settlement in the mountains, a gruelling trek that takes two days, in what is known as a 'root-tracing' event. For the community's older generations, to return to the mountain is to return home, back to the place where they were born. Geography is conceived in a manner that owes something to what James J. Fox terms 'topogeny', whereby placenames are indicated in spatial sequence as genealogy displays generations in time sequence, 'a projected externalization of memories' that figures prominently among Austronesian populations.²³ The root-tracing journey in *Finding Sayun* similarly aligns spatial with temporal movement. It is an affective route into the tribe's past, culminating in the grandfather reaching his childhood home and speaking to his deceased parents as if they were still present.

Mebow's filming of this journey can be understood as a challenge to abstract conceptions of land, emphasising instead the profound and affective, though diminishing, connection of tribes to their ancestral territory. In this respect, the experience of Taiwan's original inhabitants adheres to the broader trends identified by Thongchai Winichakul, who argues that as the regime of mapping became hegemonic, indigenous knowledge of political space was displaced by modern geography.²⁴ Faced with this legacy, the filmmakers considered in this chapter have set out to reassert indigenous conceptions of place, both narratively and through their practice, which taken in combination can be understood as a form of remapping or counter-mapping. Questions of land ownership and appropriation lie at the heart of many of these narratives, and the filmmakers share an interest, I will suggest, in the tools of mapping – in particular, what it means to 'survey' a territory.

Surveying the Terrain: Ambivalence, Desire, and the Aerial

'Land is the medium through which culture is passed from one generation to the next', asserts Omi Wilang, who heads the Indigenous People's Action

Coalition of Taiwan. 'When people's land rights are lost, their autonomy is also lost.'[25] Disagreements over the use and ownership of land are central to *Wawa No Cidal* and *Lokah Laqi*, in which land is both an ancestral legacy and a source of economic potential. In *Wawa No Cidal*, journalist Panay (Ado Kaliting Pacidal) quits her job in Taipei to return to her ailing father (Kaco Lekal) and two children Nakaw (Dongi Kacaw) and Sera (Rahic Gulas), who live in the Amis village of the Makudaai tribe on the east coast. Overseeing the restoration of the tribe's derelict paddy fields, Panay comes into conflict with developers who are seeking to build a hotel complex on the tribe's land. *Lokah Laqi* is about three Atayal boys growing up in a mountain village, who each face challenges resulting from their difficult family circumstances. A central focus of the drama is the relationship between Watan (Buya Watan) and his older brother Hu (Tsao Shih-Huei), who has recently returned to the village, having abandoned his studies in the city. Hu tries to persuade his grandmother to give him a plot of land, before resolving to farm cannabis covertly with a local gang instead.

To undermine indigenous land rights is to weaken what Kathryn W. Shanley observes as the 'long-standing place-based cultural identity from tenure in particular geographical locations', which represents 'the crux of difference between Indigenous people and other societies that have come to dominate in those places'.[26] Historically, the effacing of indigenous land rights was facilitated by mapping, which enabled colonisers both to claim ownership of territory, and to exercise power there – dynamics these films examine in a postcolonial context. *Wawa No Cidal* features several maps, and dramatises the tools of cartography at work. We see a land survey taking place on an elderly woman's paddy field that overseas developers have acquired with the assistance of corrupt officials. Distance and topography are measured using a Theodolite, providing the raw data that will be used to produce a map or an architectural plan of a tourist car park. While *Lokah Laqi* does not depict surveys or maps onscreen, Mebow can be said to share with Cheng and Lekal an interest in the act of surveying in its broadest sense, querying what it means to take a view, to examine, to appraise. There is sometimes a self-reflexive aspect to these depictions of the connections between visuality, land, and emotion; the tools of survey seen in *Wawa No Cidal* even bear a visual resemblance to those of film production, with digital devices mounted on tripods, and an operator checking a viewfinder.

These visual dynamics require consideration in the context of who is doing the surveying, and why. In *Lokah Laqi*, Mebow is notably ambivalent about the value of returning to the village. Homesick, Hu comes back only to promptly get embroiled in criminality, while the village schoolteacher Lawa (Huang Ching-I) would probably not have returned had it not been for a car accident that left her partly paralysed. If the village is shown to be an environment that attracts – affectively resonant as the tribe's home – then it simultaneously entraps. Watan, Hu, and Lawa are subjected to a repeated visualisation involving the metal bars that segment the windows of the school. At several moments, Mebow films the characters from outside the building, through the bars, implying their imprisonment. In one wide shot, Hu is shown walking the length of the classroom, as if entering a prison. Ironically this will be his literal fate, as he is ultimately arrested by the police.

This ambivalence towards the environment matters, because it attests to a situation in which outsiders are not the only threat to the tribe's place-based cultural identity. Insiders, feeling trapped, also seek change; Hu's economic frustrations lead him to cultivate an illegal crop on tribal land. In *Wawa No Cidal*, Cheng and Lekal similarly emphasise that the loss of ancestral land is not solely the responsibility of the developers. The estate agent Sheng (Bokeh Kosang) embodies these dynamics. He is a member of the tribe who is acting on behalf of Chinese clients, hoping that outside investment in tourist facilities will help to regenerate a disadvantaged community. He even undertakes his own informal survey, photographing Panay's land from multiple angles, making jokes about the value of the *yuan*. Cheng uses the character to question Manichean melodramatic conventions:

> There are a lot of people like Sheng, and they may be around you, they may be your own relatives. Even though they never intend to hurt you, you could have conflicts when it comes to land, due to contradictory values. In lots of movies, we have one bad guy, and we try to kill him in the end, in the hopes that the world will be peaceful. But in my opinion, reality isn't like this at all. So it boils down to a difference of values.[27]

The audience is similarly torn, given that Sheng is quite likeable, while the casting is canny. Truku actor Bokeh Kosang was already associated with a hybrid, ambiguous character of this type. He rose to prominence for his role in *Seediq Bale*, in which he played Hanaoka Ichiro, an indigenous tribesman who has opted for full assimilation into Japanese culture but later questions his loyalties.

Equally as ambivalent is the production design of Panay's living room. On the shelves in the background sits a globe, evocatively placed alongside a model of an old European galleon and a picture of Jesus. These objects – the map, the means, the message – allude to colonial travel and conquest, the historical effacing of local indigenous culture. But it also signals the integration of Christianity into tribal communities, where it remains a source of profound spiritual meaning. Religion has apparently shaped the outlook of Panay's family. Paul G. Pickowicz suggests that the climactic scene in which Nakaw stands in front of a digger with her arms outstretched reminds viewers of the 'tank man' from Tiananmen Square in 1989.²⁸ Equally if not more plausible, however, is that Nakaw's posture recalls Christian martyrdom iconography. Cultural hybridity is shown to have empowering possibilities. The viral YouTube video of Nakaw's protest, and the online campaign to sell the tribe's rice crop, reflect the real-life importance of social media in improving indigenous access to non-official information and building community bonds.²⁹

It is in this context that the films' controversies over land use must be understood – not solely as a conflict between those inside and outside the community, but also as an inner conflict within tribes and individuals. If we conceive of this context as a neo- or postcolonial one, then the character of Hu, for instance, can usefully be discussed in terms of mimicry, as articulated by Homi Bhabha – in the sense that he is shown to adopt culturally dominant forms of visuality that were earlier associated with colonialist mapping.³⁰ In one scene in *Lokah Laqi*, Hu is farming with his grandmother when, in close-up, he stops to look at something, which a reverse shot reveals to be his grandfather's plot of land. Hu is sizing up its potential, the actor's expression capturing conflicting emotions of guilt and longing. His gaze towards the landscape is not neutral but entails an appraisal of value; as the first stage of mapping, surveying is a practice that does not necessarily require tools. As Thongchai demonstrates in his classic study, mapping does not simply reflect reality, but seeks to bring it into being.³¹ In gazing at the land in an acquisitive manner and imagining a possible future for it, Hu is seeking to bring another reality into being.

Surveying is, furthermore, an affective process whereby characters must weigh their hopes for the future against the weakening of the tribe's identity, a tension that *Lokah Laqi* articulates visually. Hu decides to meet with a gang boss who is looking for land on which to grow cannabis. Their hideout is located at a high altitude, near the top of the mountain ridge. Hu enters an open-walled warehouse, a vantage point that offers a spectacular view of the valley below (Figure 4.1a). Inherent to any overview, however, is distance from lived detail, which here reflects how the boss conceives land in abstract terms of economic profitability, rather than human value. To affirm the point, the scene cuts directly to a shot of Hu farming in the valley with his grandmother, each crouched close to the ground as they plant cabbages (Figure 4.1b). This contrasting perspective emphasises proximity, identifying the land as terrain that is lived in, meaningful to inhabitants, and enables subsistence. Hu guiltily watches his grandmother. The editor, in cutting from the high edge of the mountain basin to the bottom of the valley, captures an ethical, as well as a geographic, movement.

This visualisation recurs later when Hu, seated in a makeshift cable-car that facilitates travel between hilly ridges, is granted an aerial overview of the secluded land where the gang plans to farm their illicit crop. This scene cuts to

Figure 4.1a–b A view from the mountain cuts to a shot of the valley in *Lokah Laqi* (Laha Mebow, 2016).

a ground-level view of the land as Hu's fingers run through the soil. The shot tilts up to reveal the other men preparing the field using markers. The editing again implies a tension between a vertical, aerial, distanced perspective on the land and a horizontal, grounded, proximate perspective. This captures the difference between conventional forms of mapping and indigenous conceptions of place, expressed for example in Wu Ming-Yi's novel *The Man with the Compound Eyes*. The protagonist Alice attempts to explain what a map is to Atile'i, an indigenous youth whom a trash vortex has washed up on Taiwan's shores. She projects a map onto the wall of a hunting hut, and uses a laser pointer to identify the location of Taiwan:

> 'This's the island we're on now. Can you point to the island where you come from? Wayo Wayo?' Atile'i smiled sadly.
> 'No, the earth, here.' Atile'i pointed at the ground, grasped a clump of dirt, and said, 'Not, there.'[32]

Atile'i is from a fictional tribe and an island apparently untouched by modernity; he is not intended to represent contemporary indigenous identity. Wu's point is rather to articulate the difference between the abstraction of mapping associated with dominant cultures and colonialism, and indigenous conceptions of place, which are rooted in the lived, material experience of ancestral land. This is not to imply an essentialised dichotomy. On the contrary, in *Lokah Laqi*, Hu's inner conflict attains its affective power precisely because he has grown up in a globalised environment, and is acutely aware of the tension between traditional, indigenous conceptions of land and the more abstract priorities of modernity, here epitomised by the aerial view.

Wawa No Cidal similarly critiques the distinction between aerial and ground-level views. When Panay applies for a subsidy to help reconstruct her community's paddy fields, she delivers a presentation to a group of funders and academics. On the slides behind her is an aerial photo of her village, including the jagged, rocky edges of the Fengbin coastline (Figure 4.2a). It is a photograph rather than an orthophoto-map, because the image has been shot from an angle that favours the foreground, and has not been adjusted to correct relief displacement. But Panay refers to it as a map, pointing to where the paddy fields were previously situated. As the scene concludes, there is a cut to a shot of the same rocky coast, but this time filmed from a horizontal, ground-level perspective, showing Panay's father looking out to sea (Figure 4.2b). This edit makes clear that aerial, map-like views are unable to express how land might be experienced, felt, and understood by those who inhabit it.

Counter-mapping: *Wawa No Cidal* (2015) against Abstraction

Aerial views, like maps, rely on a fiction of objectivity. While apparently detached, they conceal purpose, emotion, and bias. Take the example of the documentary *Beyond Beauty: Taiwan from Above* (Chi Po-Lin, 2013), comprised entirely of aerial shots filmed from a helicopter. Sang Eun Eunice Lee argues that this form of visuality helps demarcate a national territory, reinforcing the authority of the contemporary Taiwanese state and undermining indigenous claims to the land.[33] By contrast, in challenging the regime of the

Figure 4.2a–b An aerial photo of the coastline cuts to a horizontal view in *Wawa No Cidal* (Cheng Yu-Chieh, Lekal Sumi 2015).

aerial view, *Wawa No Cidal* focuses attention on traditions of community and counter-mapping. In her presentation to the subsidy funders, Panay puts her journalistic skills to good use by deploying imagery to which this audience is more likely to relate. By including an aerial photograph, she co-opts abstract forms of cartography for her own purposes. The film has previously aligned aerial maps with threats to the integrity of Panay's community; they are first seen when Nakaw visits Sheng's office, having resolved to sell her family's land. The estate agent tells her she is underage, but then finds a way to facilitate the transaction anyway. Their conversation is filmed in a series of shot-reverses in which a map appears on the wall behind each character. It is later revealed that the entire office is filled with cartography, the ownership and management of which is evidently how Sheng and the developers acquire power.

Behind Nakaw is an orthophoto-map of the village region, resembling that used by Panay in her presentation, though incorporating a wider area and adjusted for relief displacement. The map behind Sheng is a more conventional line rendering of Hualien County, which has been visually extracted from the rest of the island that surrounds it. This kind of visuality is potentially misleading. The eastern boundary of the county could easily be misinterpreted as marking the coastline, when in fact one-third of it is landlocked; a thin strip of terrain from neighbouring Taitung County extends up along the coast, but this is excluded. Moreover, aerial views are problematic in the context of the county's mountainous topography because, as Mark Monmonier explains, planimetric distance on maps ignores relief.[34] What appears aerially to be a 'small' area would, on the ground, be experienced as 'large', in the sense that it would take a long time to cross the terrain due to its steep inclines. Indigenous modes of orientation, which operate relative to natural features as they appear at ground level, account for this kind of lived experience – such as trekking up and down ravines – in conceiving such environments. Aerial renderings do not.

Robin Roth observes that a 'preference for relative versus metric distance and dynamic, multiple boundaries versus static, singular ones, are common characteristics revealed through cognitive mapping with indigenous people around the world'; the maps seen in Sheng's office conflict with this preference for multiple, overlapping, and flexibly bounded territories that defy easy representation in neatly delineated polygons.[35] Sheng's map of Hualien uses a predominantly green colour scheme, with territory divided into discrete administrative regions by bold yellow boundary lines. These allow for no sense of flexibility or overlap, and are entirely abstract in that they are not experienced as boundaries at ground level. This replicates cartographic forms that were earlier associated with Western colonialism; in the nineteenth century, for instance, the British preference for hard boundaries conflicted with the Chinese notion of a frontier with flexible zoning based on a native chieftain (*tusi*) system.[36] In a postcolonial context, the maps in the estate agent's office are instruments of power, deploying abstract notions of space in order to facilitate the underhand appropriation of indigenous land. This is, after all, exactly what happens in this scene. Taking advantage of a young girl's frustrations, Sheng facilitates the sale of her family's land to the developers.

Panay forces Sheng to return her land, and seeking to reclaim the community's initiative in such matters, proposes to renovate the tribe's derelict paddy fields. Partly she does this by engaging in community- and counter-mapping, activities that in real life have played an important role in enabling indigenous communities to reclaim their heritage. In 2001, for instance, Tsai Bor-Wen and Lo Yung-Ching were invited by the Council of Indigenous Peoples to assist on a project to map traditional territories; members of three tribes from the Atayal, Truku and Paiwan ethnic groups participated, and were asked to map their environments using GIS 3D virtual environment technology.[37] Community or counter-mapping of this type can be counterproductive.[38] Roth summarises that the unintended effects include increased conflict, the privatisation of land, and increased state regulation; however he does not see these effects as the inevitable outcome of mapping *per se*, but rather, the result of a dominant conception of space that frames cartographic representations of indigenous territories, whereby complex spatiality is rendered as abstract space.[39]

This tension between these two conceptions of space is central to *Wawa No Cidal*. Calling a meeting of the local tribespeople, Panay presents an irrigation plan for the restoration of the paddy fields, visualised using a geographic diagram (Figure 4.3). Her father makes the case for her proposal by asserting the ways in which postcolonial economics have reconfigured earlier colonial practices: 'The imperial soldiers chased us away with knives and guns. Now they use money to take our land away.' Panay directly challenges the abstract cartography that typically facilitates the appropriation of indigenous land, by counter-mapping in a way that emphasises the community's lived experience. This has much in common with Roth's advocacy of dwelling space, which has fluid and negotiated boundaries and is produced through practices related

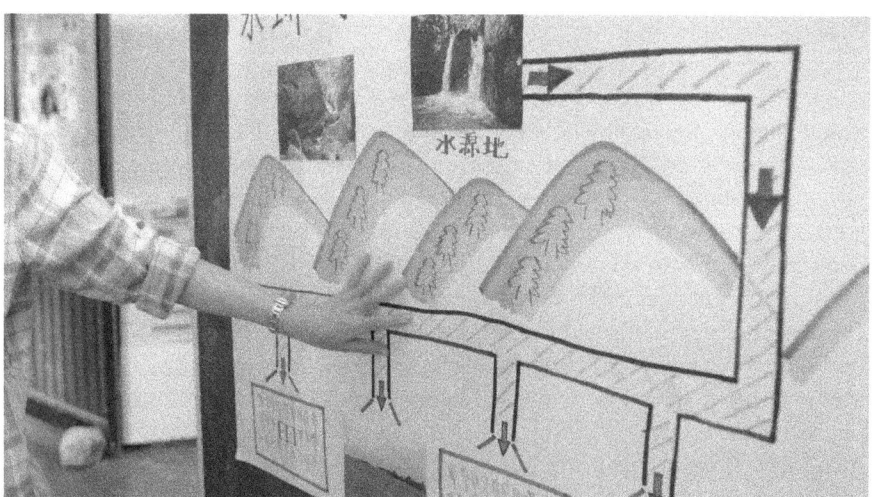

Figure 4.3 Panay's counter-map in *Wawa No Cidal* (Cheng Yu-Chieh, Lekal Sumi 2015).

to dwelling, procuring a livelihood, and interacting with the environment.[40] Panay's plan is informally drawn, not to scale, multi-perspectival, and affective. It is drawn using pens and paint, in bold colours resembling a child's drawing, thereby evoking familiarity and making it easy for non-specialists to understand. Locations are identified – a waterfall, a river, paddy fields – using pasted photographs shot from horizontal, ground-level perspectives, ensuring that the community feels connected to actual locations that they recognise and that provoke memories and emotions.

Panay's counter-map nonetheless draws on cartographic techniques that evidence her intention to persuade the community of the merits of her plan. The diagram evokes a balance between the natural, the curved lines indicating the mountains and trees, and human intervention, the straight lines and polygons denoting the system of irrigation channels. The colour scheme – shades of green for the mountains and woods, and blue for the water – uses landscape metaphors. Blue has connotations of life, purity, and renewal that are useful to Panay, even though the water in the stream and irrigation channels is at no point perceived as blue. Furthermore, as Monmonier notes, 'few map symbols are as forceful or suggestive as the arrow'.[41] Panay uses bold blue arrows to carefully to indicate the flow of the water, drawn thicker near the water source, and narrower in the irrigation channels. This suggests the equal – in other words, fair – distribution of water into what Panay terms 'our fields', while implying a natural, nourishing flow of water – when in fact the very point of the exercise is to irrigate fields using artificial means. Techniques such as these demonstrate the character's skill and knowledge of cartographic forms.

Panay's counter-map envisages a lived, rather than abstract, environment, encouraging the villagers to reclaim the heritage of their forebears. This fictional representation affirms the view of Taiban and his co-researchers that community mapping can help tribes better recognise ancestral knowledge and territories.[42] That said, it would be wrong to suggest that Panay's diagram represents, at this point in the film, a collaborative endeavour. Rather, it is a carefully conceived tool designed to persuade her audience, attesting to her own activist tendencies. With its dual ambitions of combatting neo-colonial cartography and encouraging allies to get on board, Panay's counter-map is an imaginative, empowering revisioning of what her community's land could be.

Everyday Acting: Place, Performance, and Non-professionals

A defining feature of the films discussed in this chapter is their use of non-professional actors, filmed on location. Aside from some of the protagonists and secondary characters, who are played by professionals, virtually none of the tribespeople we see onscreen ordinarily works as an actor. As such, the relationship between performance and environment requires consideration, not just as a mode of practice, but as a narrative theme. Performance is here understood, whether it occurs on or off screen, as everyday behaviour undertaken by people who are not actors – an activity with real resonance in this context, given the proclivity of external visitors to gaze at indigenous communities. In these films, members of those communities have the opportunity to acquire agency in their own representation, and an environment is created to facilitate this; the resulting staging has an aesthetic impact.

A defining context is the determination of Mebow, Cheng, and Lekal to ensure that their practices demonstrate respect for the indigenous communities involved. While there is a history of offensive portrayals at a representational level, patronising, exploitative, or disrespectful behaviour has also occurred at the level of practice. Dennis Lo suggests the two things are connected, arguing that the production practices adopted on *The Heroic Pioneers* directly impacted on the film's representation of place, thereby mythologising an expansionist mode of Han Chinese nation building.[43] Chang reports instances of Tao villagers resenting the intrusion of visiting filmmakers on Lanyu, with tensions overspilling in 2003, when one crew's vehicle was attacked by young residents throwing stones.[44] Although things have since improved, it is by no means a given that film crews will behave respectfully in indigenous communities – something that the directors discussed here have taken pains to ensure. If questions of externality are central to the narratives, in which someone visits the tribe or returns after a long absence, then these questions also preoccupy the filmmakers. Mebow is from the Atayal tribe but did not grow up in her ancestral village. She acknowledges that her experiences interviewing people in indigenous communities for TV projects informed her approach to filmmaking:

> Although I'm not external, there was, to be fair, a distance between myself and the tribe. ... Hence in *Finding Sayun*, the very beginning of the film features the audition sequences, an external point of view. *Lokah Laqi* approached the opening in the same way. I chose an outsider's, a journalist's point of view.[45]

Cheng, on the other hand, acknowledges his clearer status as an outsider. The main reference point for *Wawa No Cidal* was Lekal's documentary *Wish of the Ocean Rice* (2013), which was about his mother's role in restoring a village paddy field.[46] Cheng felt it was essential that he co-direct *Wawa No Cidal* with Lekal, in part to ensure that the film authentically depicted indigenous life, but also to make certain that the production operated in a way that was respectful to the community:

> If there were any disagreements, I obeyed his decision. Because it's his home. He knows what is best for his village. For me, it's a film. But for

him, it's his real life ... I leave the village after shooting, but he lives there. So we can't do anything that harms the village.[47]

Cheng explains that as he was filming in one of the more traditional Amis villages, he needed to get permissions in line with customary practices. The village had an age-grade hierarchy of management, and the filmmakers needed to gain permission from the villager whose role was the 'Mama No Kapah', or Father of the Youth. While making the film, even during pre-production, for anything related to the tribe, permits had to be acquired through the Mama No Kapah.[48]

Aside from a community's specific rules and systems, Mebow emphasises the need to establish informal relationships based on trust, and to negotiate these with sensitivity:

I tried to build up a close relationship with my tribe, and the other tribes, because I knew I'd be back. So when our producer arrived, I found some important figures in the tribe and informed them that if they saw something inappropriate, they should let the producer know straightaway. After the production, the crew leave, but I still need to maintain a relationship with the tribes.[49]

Mebow stresses the importance of maintaining relationships of mutual trust. The filmmakers' mode of directing and staging must similarly be understood as involving intense dynamics of trust. The use of indigenous actors to play *yuanzhumin* is itself a fairly recent development; Berry observes that this first occurred in *Man from Island West* (Huang Ming-Chuan, 1991), and prior to that, ethnically Chinese actors would play the roles.[50] By contrast, the films considered here use indigenous actors and non-professionals both to authenticate the drama, and to affirm the directors' ethical approach by giving often marginalised communities agency in their own representation. In *Wawa No Cidal*, some of the cast members re-enacted fictionalised versions of events such as the protest in which they themselves had participated.[51] That said, it is rare for people to literally play themselves, while the cast do not necessarily live in the same villages where the films were shot. The three youngsters in *Lokah Laqi* each came from different villages, while the children in *Wawa No Cidal* came from a neighbouring village, because the Makudaai school authority would not allow children to have time away from the classroom.[52]

In general, the amateur performers had no acting experience, so strategies had to be developed for preparing and directing them. On *Wawa No Cidal*, Cheng had responsibility for the professional actors Ado Kaliting Pacidal and Bokeh Kosang, while the non-professionals were directed by Lekal; Cheng felt this was necessary because Lekal knew them better and they would be able to confide in him.⁵³ Mebow directed all her actors, and in developing methods for training non-professionals, she was particularly conscious of how mainstream techniques might be unsuitable, and even actively damaging, for indigenous representation:

> I didn't hire an acting coach, because I was worried that this kind of preparation would result in indigenous people learning how to play indigenous people. Since non-professionals have no clue what acting really is, I'd rather train them on my own, using an approach of you-trust-me-and-I-trust-you.⁵⁴

To avoid the actors performing an outsider's view of indigeneity, with all the problematic implications that entails, Mebow favoured training through the building of relationships and trust. On *Finding Sayun*, she went to visit the actors playing Yukan and the grandfather every Saturday of the six months prior to the shoot. For most of that period, they did nothing related to the script, but instead chatted and tended the vegetable farm. The rehearsals started quite late, about one or two weeks before the shoot. Observing them, Mebow would adjust the script, for example adapting the role of Yukan to fit with the actor's personality, meaning that when filming started, 'you just play yourself, in a sense'.⁵⁵

Performance is also crafted through staging and cinematography, which when combined, create a space that enables a particular kind of acting to occur. All the films under consideration were shot mainly in one village location, rather than in studios or across multiple locations. Some locations were adapted to fit the narrative, however. In *Lokah Laqi*, Watan's family home was in fact a local resident's *gongliao* – a type of working accommodation, usually intended as a temporary structure where people stay for work purposes – to which some set dressing was added.⁵⁶ The staging in this location is typical of how Mebow tends to deploy longer takes, in which the performances play out in full, even if the footage is subsequently edited. In an early scene, a long take commences in the kitchen area, in which the grandmother greets a social worker. As this occurs, the shot pans to the left, bringing into view another room, in which Watan can be seen playing on a computer. The next shot simply reverses the view, with Watan now in the foreground. The drama is covered from just two angles, with the performances in each take presumably playing out in full.

Other scenes are edited even less. In *Finding Sayun*, Mebow uses a stationary, wide shot, fifty seconds in duration, as a dispute plays out in Yukan's home. Staging within unbroken takes is often used to underscore thematic points, as occurs in a scene in *Lokah Laqi*. It is shot from within Watan's bedroom area, curtained off from the main living area, as he sits chatting with his brother Hu. The take lasts one minute fifteen seconds before a cut occurs, but makes dynamic use of offscreen space, with the grandmother eavesdropping and occasionally interjecting. This is used to poke fun at Watan's gendering of the space. He idolises his brother and complains that his grandmother, by listening in and peering through the curtain, is interfering in 'man's talk' – a precocious affectation that is amusing to Hu and the grandmother. This realm of masculine chitchat is shown to have porous boundaries and to Watan's exasperation, is easily breached by the feminine: a curtain hardly serves to delineate the space.

Wawa No Cidal makes use of similar forms of staging and cinematography, intended to make the non-professional actors feel at ease. Cheng initially wanted to shoot the film on a BlackMagic camera, which is relatively small, portable, and unintrusive. However, after successfully applying to the Film Subsidiary Fund, he felt a responsibility to raise the camera specification in line with the increased budget, in order that the film could be screened in any commercial cinema. So a RED Epic was used, a much larger piece of kit that necessitated the development of different approaches to performance. The cast felt less at ease in front of a large camera, and so as a result, 'we spent a very long time waiting, letting people get familiar with us, so they would forget about our existence'.[57] Mebow similarly reports that the non-professional actors were sometimes bothered by the size of the camera, the volume of camera and lighting equipment, and the presence of a large crew. She recalls that one of the adult actors was very extroverted during rehearsals, but once the camera was set up, she was unable to perform, to the point where Mebow had to make adjustments, such as turning the camera away from her, or allowing her to say nothing.[58]

Situations like these required a response, such as minimising the number of camera setups, or allowing takes to play out in full, or both – thereby reducing interventions on the part of the filmmaker, and helping the actors to forget, as far as possible, about the presence of the camera. Unlike an earlier generation of Taiwanese *auteurs* such as Hou Hsiao-Hsien or Tsai Ming-Liang, the directors considered here demonstrate no aesthetic allegiance to visual forms such as unbroken takes. These are not necessarily preserved in the edit room, while even material that was shot economically is sometimes edited at a snappy pace. Where devices such as the unbroken take are adopted, they are undertaken for practical reasons; to facilitate shooting on location with non-professionals. It should be said that the aesthetics associated with the Taiwan New Cinema were shaped, at least initially, by similar concerns. Hou used long takes and static camerawork to put his inexperienced casts at ease.[59] When directing *A Borrowed Life* (1994), Wu Nien-Jen similarly filmed the non-professional actors when they thought they were only rehearsing, as he wanted to capture their most natural behaviour and to avoid them being self-conscious.[60] We see Cheng doing something similar two decades later:

There is one scene at the end of the film, for example, in which a lot of people have a barbeque under the shade of the trees. On set we allowed them to have a real barbeque, and they did! They just started eating, and when they'd forgotten about us being there, we sent the actor in. I didn't shout 'action' or anything like that.[61]

These approaches have something in common with the modes and workflows of documentary. This is perhaps unsurprising given that earlier representations of the tribes in the democratic era were, with a few exceptions, confined to television documentaries. Certain types of visualisations recall observational documentary forms, such as the use of locked-off camerawork and long takes, intended to help people feel comfortable in front of the camera. The emphasis on rigorous ethical standards when working with non-professionals also owes more to documentary practices than to those of fiction filmmaking. The finished films, on the other hand, do not generally resemble documentaries, despite the appearance of visual tropes here and there. An exception is the final section of *Finding Sayun*, which Mebow filmed six months after the completion of principal photography because she felt something was missing from the film: 'What should I call it – a fake documentary? It's a semi-documentary, I guess.'[62] Taking the actors playing Yukan, his grandfather, and journalist Hsiao-Ju (Fang Chih-Yu), and guided along the mountain route by a group of local hunters, Mebow filmed these scenes herself on a small DV camera. Shooting from a first-person perspective, she performed as Hsiao-Ju from behind the camera, her voice later replaced in Automated Dialogue Replacement (ADR) by the actor.

If this marks Mebow's performative intervention in the world of the film, then her approach here is not typical of these films more generally, which are instead preoccupied by the performative capacity of everyday people. This can be understood as a mode of filmmaking, but as a theme, it is also intrinsic to the narratives. Cheng is himself an actor as well as a director, and when questioned about his films' focus on performance, explains: 'it's because it's part of real life. Everyone is basically pretending. The difference is whether you do it consciously or not.'[63] This distinguishes between performativity, understood by Judith Butler as the unconscious acting out of a culturally conditioned role, and performance, conscious pretence, or theatrical role-play.[64] I have argued elsewhere that in Cheng's earlier film *Yang Yang* (2009), the two are not necessarily easy to distinguish, and the same is often true here.[65]

Certainly, the indigenous characters are repeatedly shown to be performing consciously, especially in the context of the touristic gaze. In *Wawa No Cidal*, for example, the tribespeople are shown dressed in traditional costume, performing dance shows for coachloads of visitors. This is a deliberate display of self-exoticisation, like when the children attempt to sell fruit to tourists in *Lokah Laqi*. Performance is also central to the coming-of-age dynamics of *Pakeriran*, although here, even when Futing is consciously acting out tribal rituals, it is unclear whether he is always aware of his own gender performativity. Forced to return home for the summer, he initially has no interest in his tribe's culture, much of which is centred around the ocean and fishing. He fails to perform the role expected of him as a young member of the community, because he has become so distanced from it. In one excruciating scene, Futing is asked to serve the older tribesmen a drink, but oblivious to the customary etiquette, and barely able to communicate in the local dialect, he humiliates himself. This scene is staged in almost theatrical terms, with the unimpressed older men seated in a row, watching Futing, who stands facing them.

If the film's first half is framed as a failure of performance, then in the second half, Futing begins to integrate himself into the community, learning how to fish and gaining respect for its traditions. Lekal dramatises the youngster's increasing success in engaging with the performative rituals that sustain the tribe's identity, which are often closely connected to constructions of gender. In one scene, Futing's mentor Kacaw (Apo' Kofid Talo) points across the water to the small, rocky island of Pakeriran, explaining its significance to the tribe: that those who can swim there will become men. The film's title thus connects masculinity to geography, and the rocky island is central to a climactic scene that ultimately, in its wry perspective on male coming-of-age, plays out like an extended topographical joke. Near the end of the film, Futing wants to prove to himself that has acquired the skills to undergo this test of masculinity, and resolves to swim across the bay to Pakeriran. The currents are strong and make the task difficult and dangerous, but Futing perseveres and after much effort, reaches the island, exhausted. He has passed his test of manhood.

But this self-satisfaction is soon supplanted by confusion. He hears voices nearby, and the camera tracks him walking to the other side of the island, settling on a frame in which Futing discovers a group of women collecting shellfish. 'How did you get here?' he repeatedly asks one of them, somewhat exasperated. 'From over there', the woman replies, pointing behind her. This cuts to a wide shot, in which we can observe that the other side of the island is, in fact, readily accessible, via rocks and shallow water, from the shore, where other women are busily gathering shellfish. Futing's difficult swim across the bay has been utterly pointless, geographically, and again he feels humiliated – his achievement of manhood awkwardly undermined by the feminine presence. He is, however, able to see the funny side. In exploring the performative qualities of gender, *Pakeriran* affirms the importance of ritual in sustaining community identity, while implying that the hapless Futing is perhaps taking the implications for his masculinity a little too seriously.

ISLAND OUTLOOK: BEYOND THE MAP IN *LONG TIME NO SEA* (2018)

Long Time No Sea is set on Lanyu – Orchid Island – which is inhabited by the Tao indigenous people. It is a drama about a boy named Manawei (Pangoyod Si) who lives with his grandmother; his father, working as a taxi driver in Kaohsiung, is largely absent from his life. The film's other main character is Chung-Hsun (Huang Shang-Ho), a teacher from the mainland who is posted to the island, and gradually forms a bond with the boy. Like the other films discussed above, *Long Time No Sea* used a mainly non-professional cast, something director Tsui has discussed at length in various interviews; for example, she ran drama workshops on the island for the local communities, from which actors for the film were eventually sourced. Having a strong conviction that the actors must themselves be from Lanyu, she opposed the cross-ethnic casting of actors from other Taiwanese indigenous groups.[66]

My focus here is on the film's representation of the island's geography in relation to the surrounding ocean. Lanyu is around forty-five square kilometres in size, and located around sixty kilometres from Taiwan's mainland. It is not represented on a map within *Long Time No Sea*, although in the school classroom, a large painting shows the island viewed frontally. Green peaks rise out of the water in a homely, inviting manner. The canoe in the foreground and the positioning of the viewpoint, from the ocean, affirm that the Tao are a seafaring people. This situated, affectionate perspective on Lanyu is shared by the film's indigenous characters, who conversely refer to Taiwan as somewhere external. Manawei's uncle, for example, tells him to wear his new shoes 'when you go to Taiwan', leaving it ambiguous whether this is conceived as a larger island, or a nation. Chang Hsi-Wen observes that Tao people do not identify as Taiwanese indigenous people, but instead emphasise their ethnic relationship with islanders of the Batanes, the northern islands of the Philippines, who have a similar culture and language.[67] The Tao originally emigrated to Lanyu from the Batanes 800 years ago, and their language, Yami, is part of the dialect group of Ivatan, an Austronesian language spoken on the northern Philippine islands. Recently, scholars from various disciplines have sought to challenge the dominant prism through which Taiwanese identity is examined, namely the cross-strait relationship with China, and to instead explore Taiwan's connection with other countries and environments.[68] Reconsidering Wu Chuo-Liu's novel *Orphan of Asia*, Adam Lifshey argues for a critical shift southward; referring figuratively to the waters that circulate between Taiwan and the Philippines, he argues that 'the transarchipelago could be viewed not as a weak, peripheral, parochial space of absence but as a powerful, central place of global production'.[69] While the Philippines are not directly referenced in *Long Time No Sea*, the notion of trans-archipelagic ocean waters as productive deserves further consideration.

Ninety per cent of Tao people have not registered their land because to them, Chang suggests, relationships between people and the land and ocean are self-evident. Land is not conceived as a commodity that can be traded using money, and territorial boundaries are flexible.[70] This understanding of terrain conflicts with that promulgated by dominant forms of mapping, which moreover conceives water using aesthetics borrowed from representations of land. Philip Steinberg refers to 'a series of latitude–longitude points that can be characterised by certain constant values across key variables', which fails to account for the complexity of the ocean as a mobile space whose very essence is constituted by fluidity.[71] Taiwan claims a substantial body of water as well as land, its baseline cartographic boundaries defined by its incorporation of islands including the Pescadores in the west, Peng-Chia in the north, and Lanyu in the southeast. By this measure, Taiwan is remapped as a straight-edged pentagon, with islands the frontier outposts of the territory. This is a perspective reflected in much popular media, in which Lanyu is portrayed as remote – indeed, this is the essence of its appeal for tourists. But remoteness, like size, is relative, and always implies a centre: remote from what? In this context, to adopt a perspective on space that emphasises centre and periphery is to privilege ethnically Chinese over indigenous experience. It is also to confirm the connotations of this alleged remoteness, that Lanyu is an idyllic paradise, distant from civilisation and so on – the touristic tropes that underline the stereotyping and misrepresentation of indigenous communities.

These tensions are evident in the opening credits sequence of *Long Time No Sea*, which further demonstrates the set of geographical restrictions that Lanyu places on the filmmaker. Chung-Hsun and Manawei ride a scooter after the teacher arrives on the island, in a sequence evidently designed to showcase the stunning scenery to an external audience. Yet to those who are familiar with Lanyu, the presentation of the environment may seem jarring. Chung-Hsun is apparently making his way from Kaiyuan Harbour to his accommodation in one of the island's villages. Initially, this entails a scooter ride along the western coast of the island, with the locations depicted sequentially, in the order they would appear along the actual route. But the editing then incorporates footage of places scattered elsewhere on the island, with the sea located on the left-hand side of the frame in some shots, but on the right-hand side in other shots. As a continuous journey, this is geographically impossible, as Lanyu has only one coastal road around its circumference. Thus if the camera remains in the same position in relation to the characters, as it does here (facing them frontally), the sea will either be on the left or the right, but never both. Evidently, the actor was filmed travelling in different directions in different shots. The spatial restrictions of the island environment immediately undermine any idea that this is a credible journey from harbour to accommodation.

What commences as an excursion along an actual route evolves into a montage of scenic views. The sequence is strongly reminiscent of the opening of *Wawa No Cidal*, in which Nakaw also rides a scooter along the coastline of Hualien and Taitung counties. This is perhaps unsurprising given that both films were shot by the same Director of Photography, Liao Ching-Yao, who impressed Tsui with his proficiency in responding to and capturing the non-professional performances as they unfolded.[72] In the opening scene of *Wawa No Cidal*, however, the real-life locations on Nakaw's route appear sequentially, and are spatially and temporally consistent. Of course, many viewers watching *Long Time No Sea* will not be familiar with Lanyu, or notice the spatial inconsistencies. For them, the opening montage will function rather like a trailer, enticing them into the story by presenting the island from a familiar, comfortable, commercial viewpoint: that of the tourist. Yet this is probably ironic; for subsequent scenes dramatise the island's geography in a manner that is spatially accurate, and mirrors Chung-Hsun's transition from an aloof, arrogant outsider to someone worthy of being accepted by the community.

Early in the film, there is a cut from a village harbour, where Chung-Hsun sits in the evening, to a shot of him walking towards a shack where Chin-Yi (Ling Chang) is serving drinks. He has apparently strolled over to a local establishment. His visit becomes embarrassing, however, when he realises that he has no money to pay for his drink and must head to a cashpoint. Chung-Hsun is then shown riding his scooter along the coast, at which point it becomes clear that the film has deliberately been toying with constructions of cinematic space. For the bar is not in the immediate vicinity of the harbour. In contrast to the credits sequence, this lightly comic scene is rooted in a credible depiction of the island's geography, with the real-life bar located around a kilometre from the nearest village. Furthermore, there is only one cashpoint on Lanyu, in a different village even further away. Narratively, this knowledge heightens our sense of Chung-Hsun's embarrassment. He is not simply popping out to a nearby cashpoint, but creating a massive inconvenience for Chin-Yi by making her wait for him to complete a lengthy round trip. He then cringe-worthily fails to return, because he has a traffic accident.

The viewer is led to question their assumptions about convenience, activity facilitated by easy economic and geographical access. Fittingly, Chung-Hsun's trip to the bar is sandwiched between scenes involving Manawei, who is sulking after a dispute with his grandmother. She prepared him fish for dinner, a local dish, when he had demanded fried chicken, a Taiwanese import. As a peace offering, she brings him a pre-prepared ready meal, which alludes to another geographic fact about the island: this would have been purchased in one of the two 7-Eleven stores on Lanyu. While this suggests the more limited material reach of global capitalism, these scenes nonetheless attest to its internalised impact: Manawei fantasises about capitalist convenience, while Chung-Hsun mindlessly adheres to it. The absence of banknotes in his wallet evidences a credit-card mentality but also thoughtlessness, Chung-Hsun's initial unwillingness to adapt to the island environment; it seems likely that he has been posted in Lanyu against his will, as part of a fee subsidy scheme. When arriving at his homestay, he rudely requests a change of room, then complains about the lack of air conditioning. In school, he demonstrates ignorance of his privilege, chastising Manawei for wearing slippers rather than shoes, when the boy has no choice and is, in fact, desperate for his father to bring him a new pair of trainers from Kaohsiung. Ultimately, Chung-Hsun is changed for the better by spending time on Lanyu, and primitivist tropes endure insofar as indigenous culture prompts moral change in a non-indigenous character. Yet these tropes are simultaneously challenged by Manawei's parallel story. Anita Wen-Shin Chang suggests that the narrative and characterisation in *Fishing Luck* signify the problematic notion that Lanyu remains a stable entity against which the rest of Taiwan can define itself.[73] This is certainly not the case in *Long Time No Sea*, in which Manawei's dramatic arc is left ambivalently unresolved. There is no sense that his father will be returning any time soon, nor is it clear how long his teacher will remain on the island. His grandmother is saving money for his future education on the mainland, but this is under threat from his father, who is eyeing up the funds for a potential business venture.

At the end of the film, a map is mentioned in the song *Tears in the Sea* that appears over the end credits, performed by the Puyuma singer Chen Chien-Nien. The lyrics connect maritime geography with an emotional journey that has gone 'beyond the map', evoking both protagonists' yearning for someone who is absent on the Taiwanese mainland. Chung-Hsun misses his girlfriend, while Manawei pines for his father, who left Lanyu in order to support his family financially, but in doing so, lost all meaningful ties with them. The film is structured in terms of trans-archipelagic longing, placing emphasis on affective connections between islands; this recalls recent attempts by indigenous cultural producers to explore the ties between Austronesian peoples based in different Pacific island locations. Mebow's documentary *Ça fait si longtemps* (2017), for instance, instigates an encounter between indigenous musicians from New Caledonia and Taiwan.

Long Time No Sea occupies an interesting position in relation to critical perspectives on the ontologies produced by the ocean. On the one hand, the film shares what Steinberg argues is the tendency of poststructuralist theorists to present water as a metaphor; a spatial signifier for a world of shifting, fragmented identities and connections.[74] Yet the film moves beyond metaphor in certain respects, as suggested by the film's Chinese title *Only the Sea Would Know*, which positions the sea as a source of knowledge. The film depicts water in a way that draws a contrast between its two protagonists' conceptions of space and materiality. Chung-Hsun's trans-archipelagic longing is dramatised in terms of measurable distances, phone reception, and internet access. He sees himself as situated somewhere tiny and remote; water is a barrier to where he wants to be. By contrast, Manawei's understanding of geography is 'beyond the map', in that it is framed in terms that are affective, fluid, and relative – and as such, his understanding of space owes much to the sea itself. It is unsurprising that the boy comprehends water in these terms, given the importance of the ocean to Tao culture and economic activity; as Hsi-Wen Chang elaborates, the Tao have defended their core values on the basis of an intimate, intersubjective relationship between people, land, and ocean.[75] Manawei is shown to be particularly at ease with water, while Chung-Hsun's initial incompatibility with Tao culture is suggested by his aversion to it; he is first introduced vomiting in the harbour, due to seasickness (in *Pakeriran*, Futing is similarly apprehensive around water). In structural terms, the sea is used to align the film with Manawei's perspective. Near the beginning, he waits at Kaiyuan Harbour, hoping that his father might disembark, but instead witnesses Chung-Hsun's arrival. The harbour serves as an entry point to the island, but also as an entry point into the narrative – characters cross the sea and enter the boy's world, the harbour serving as a portal.

Water shapes Manawei's understanding of space. When asking his father about Kaohsiung, his immediate questions relate to whether the city is located near the sea. Affirming this, the father offers an idealised description of Kaohsiung, waxing lyrical about swimming in the beautiful Love River at night, to avoid discussing the more prosaic reality. Manawei is thus led to connect Lanyu to Kaohsiung through water, conceiving his distance from his father in fluid emotional terms, rather than measurable distance. This is visualised literally when the action shifts to Kaohsiung, where the schoolchildren must perform a traditional tribal dance in a competition. None of the characters is shown travelling to mainland Taiwan. Rather, the transition is made in a single edit, which cuts from footage of Lanyu to a downward-tilted shot of rippling water. The camera tilts up to reveal Kaohsiung's harbour and skyline, a deliberately disorienting edit that again disrupts our assumptions about cinematic space: the presence of water leads us to assume that we are still in Lanyu, but we are not. Visually, this edit connects the two environments through the ocean, reflecting Manawei's more relative conception of the relationship between island and city.

Water is portrayed not as an abstract space of absence, but as a realm in which emotion is produced. Later in the film, distraught after being rejected by his father, Manawei dives into the Love River at night, apparently taking the man's earlier yarn at face value. As he breaks the surface of the water, there is a cut to underwater footage shot in Lanyu in daylight, in which Manawei swims with his father. The boy seems not to register the river as an entity distinct from the sea, instead diving into a watery realm that is fluid both spatially and temporally (given that the boy's idyllic activity with his father may be remembered, fantasised, or both). Scholars developing ontologies derived from water have suggested that the sea requires us to think about time in a different way, as nonlinear and non-measurable.[76] This is what seems to have been intuited in this artistic decision, with the film again drawing a distinction between Manawei's perspective on water and that of Chung-Hsun. The teacher rushes to the police in search of the missing boy, and worries about the immediate health and safety concerns, while the viewer similarly registers the potentially fatal consequences of the father's well-intentioned lie. Manawei, however, conceives of water in affective terms. 'All my tears have fallen into the Love River', he tells Chung-Hsun, rather poetically, as they drive through the city afterwards. In emphasising that the boy's voyage has 'gone beyond the map', the film suggests the limitations of abstract notions of cartography, instead demonstrating an allegiance to affective mapping.

Epilogue: Pop Art Is for Everyone?

A brief discussion of the costumes worn by actor Huang Shang-Ho in *Long Time No Sea* anticipates the next chapter, which turns to questions of urban design. The various T-Shirts that Chung-Hsun wears throughout the film feature international brands, trademarks such as Mickey Mouse, and boutique designs. He is evidently able to afford this clothing, attesting to his roots as an urban mainlander. Brands are identified as the products of the city, with a Louis Vuitton sign very prominent in one shot of Kaohsiung. Manawei, on the other hand, wears second-hand clothes, and must wait several months for a single pair of Nike trainers that represent a significant expense for his father. 'Pop Art is for everyone', announces the text on the T-shirt that Chung-Hsun arrives wearing, with Andy Warhol visible among the graphics. The film demonstrates this to be patently untrue, given the teacher's relative privilege.

Clothing is often used by filmmakers to underscore the relative economic hardship faced by indigenous communities. In *Finding Sayun*, Hsiao-Ju browses a fashion website, thoughtlessly explaining to a young Atayal girl how to purchase products online. The girl informs Hsiao-Ju that she receives hand-me-down clothes from her sister. In *Lokah Laqi*, Watan covets the clothing that his friend receives from his mother – again including Nike trainers. His brother Hu eventually gifts him some new clothes, yet this generosity is shown to be unsustainable, given that it is funded by illegal activity. Designer clothes connote disposable income that is out of these characters' reach – as well as urban lifestyles and desire, depicted and invented in the films considered in the next chapter.

NOTES

1. In English translation within Taiwan, and in popular and critical literature, the communities discussed in this chapter are sometimes referred to as 'aboriginal'. I do not use this terminology here as it has a problematic lineage and connotations, especially in the context of white Western and colonial perspectives on indigenous people and environments.
2. Chen, 'Building a new society on the base of locality', 297.
3. Sterk, 'Ironic indigenous primitivism', 211.
4. See Berry, 'Taiwan's indigenous peoples and cinema', 229–33, and Sterk, 'Romancing the Formosan Aborigine', 49–62.
5. Shimazu, 'Colonial encounters', 33.
6. Lo, *The Authorship of Place*, 56.
7. Berry, 'Taiwan's indigenous peoples and cinema', 234–5.
8. Chang, 'In the realm of the indigenous', 646.
9. See Wu, 'Re-examining extreme violence' and several contributors in Chiu et al. (eds), *Taiwan Cinema*.
10. Sterk, 'Ironic indigenous primitivism', 209–10.
11. Berry, 'Taiwan's indigenous peoples and cinema', 239.
12. Ibid., 229.
13. Executive Yuan, *Republic of China Yearbook 2014*, 49, and Yu and Pan, 'Aborigines now make up 28% of Hualien County', 3.
14. Brown, 'Even if you have nothing'.
15. Teng, *Taiwan's Imagined Geography*, 120, 134.
16. Ibid., 233.
17. Ibid., 250–2.
18. Shih, *Visuality and Identity*, 119.
19. Sometimes known by the alternative English title *The Kavalan: Past and Present*.
20. Lay et al., 'Mapping Taiwan from an alternative angle', 245–6.
21. Ibid., 247.
22. Tsai and Lo, 'The spatial knowledge of indigenous people', 401–3.
23. Fox, 'Place and landscape in comparative Austronesian perspective', 8–12.
24. Thonghai, *Siam Mapped*, 129.
25. Cited in Wu, 'Re-examining extreme violence', 27.
26. Shanley, '"Mapping" indigenous presence', 12.
27. Brown, 'Even if you have nothing'.
28. Pickowicz, 'The protest film genre', 127–28.
29. Chang, 'Indigenous attitudes toward nuclear waste', 210–11.
30. Bhabha, *The Location of Culture*, 121–31.
31. Thongchai, *Siam Mapped*, 129–31.
32. Wu, *The Man with the Compound Eyes*, 244.
33. Lee, 'Taiwan from below', 133–4, 141.
34. Monmonier, *How to Lie with Maps*, 35.
35. Roth, 'The challenges of mapping', 209–10.
36. See Chang, *Place, Identity and National Imagination*, 102–3.
37. Tsai and Lo, 'The spatial knowledge of indigenous people', 392–4.
38. Chi and Chin, 'Knowledge, power, and tribal mapping', 733–40.
39. Roth, 'The challenges of mapping', 207–8.
40. Ibid., 211.
41. Monmonier, *How to Lie with Maps*, 118–19.
42. Taiban et al., 'Indigenous conservation', 122.
43. Lo, *The Authorship of Place*, 55–63.

44. Chang, 'In the realm of the indigenous', 648.
45. Brown, 'By introducing my culture', 297.
46. Cheng, Personal interview.
47. Brown, 'Even if you have nothing'.
48. Ibid.
49. Brown, 'By introducing my culture', 298.
50. Berry, 'Taiwan's indigenous peoples and cinema', 236–7.
51. Brown, 'Even if you have nothing'.
52. Brown, 'By introducing my culture', 298, and Brown, 'Even if you have nothing'.
53. Cheng, Personal interview.
54. Brown, 'By introducing my culture', 297.
55. Ibid., 297–8.
56. Mebow, Personal interview.
57. Brown, 'Even if you have nothing'.
58. Mebow, Personal interview.
59. Lu, *Confronting Modernity*, 109.
60. Davis and Wu, 'A new Taiwan person?', 726.
61. Brown, 'Even if you have nothing'.
62. Mebow, Personal interview.
63. Brown, 'Even if you have nothing'.
64. Butler, 'Performative acts', 527–28.
65. Brown, 'Performance enhancement', 28.
66. See, for example, Yan, 'One island'.
67. Chang, 'Indigenous attitudes toward nuclear waste', 201.
68. See contributions in Chang and Lin (eds), *Positioning Taiwan in a Global Context*, and Shih and Liao (eds), *Comparatizing Taiwan*.
69. Lifshey, 'Translating Taiwan southward', 39.
70. Chang, 'Indigenous attitudes toward nuclear waste', 201–2.
71. Steinberg, 'Of other seas', 159–60.
72. Yan, 'One island'.
73. Chang, 'In the realm of the indigenous', 650.
74. Steinberg, 'Of other seas', 158.
75. Chang, 'Indigenous attitudes toward nuclear waste', 212.
76. Steinberg and Peters, 'Wet ontologies', 255–6.

5. LOVE IN A DESIGNER CITY

Introduction: Remixing Taipei

Design 7 Love (Chen Hung-I, 2014) tracks the fraught interpersonal relations at a Taipei design agency, while at a formal level, experimenting self-reflexively with what it means *to design*. Through the choice of locations, production design, and lighting, complemented by costume, hair, and make-up decisions, a fictitious urban space is constructed that tends to exclude Taipei's older or historic architecture. Instead, the film generates an alternative city, comprised largely of new plazas, bars, hotels, boutiques, restaurants, and shops. The plot centres on the employees of a design agency named Remix. Pa-Tzu (Mo Tzu-Yi) helps his ex-girlfriend Doris (Hsu Wei-Ning) get a job there, but fails to tell his colleagues about their previous relationship. Meanwhile their client Mark (Thomas Price) seeks to redesign his family's traditional hotel as a boutique venture, and gets embroiled in the conflict.

Design 7 Love is divided into seven sections, each commencing with an onscreen quotation from a designer: Marcel Wanders, Kazuyo Sejima, Dieter Rams, Philippe Starck, Harry Bertoia, Kenya Hara, and Anthony Dunne. Each quotation encapsulates a particular philosophy of design, while laying out the narrative focus for each section. The remark from Sejima, for instance – 'It's very difficult to create, but very easy to destroy' – resonates with the subsequent depiction of urban demolition, while narratively reflecting how Pa-Tzu unwittingly sets in motion the destruction of his professional and personal relationships. As this implies, the film is about the act of designing in its broadest sense, provoking questions that enable us to consider some wider trends in recent representations of Taipei. A range of films produced in the years after 2008 may not feature design as a narrative subject, but arguably share with *Design 7 Love* an impulse to construct Taipei as a designer city. Notably these include *Love* (Niu Cheng-Tse, 2012), *The Mad King of Taipei* (Yeh Tien-Lun, 2017), *52Hz I Love You* (Wei Te-Sheng, 2017), *The Story of the Stone* (Wu Hsing-Hsiang, 2018), along with Chen's other features, and the portmanteau film *L-O-V-E* (various, 2009), while aspects of *Young Dudes* (Chen Yin-Jung, 2012) and *Zone Pro Site* (Chen Yu-Hsun, 2013) also adhere to this trend.

Strikingly, none of these films have a single person as the protagonist. Those with the most sustained interest in design utilise ensemble casts (*Design 7 Love, Love, 52Hz I Love You, The Story of the Stone*), while the other films have two or three lead characters. This pattern recurs despite the diversity in genre, subject, production scale and target audience, and the shared Taipei setting is central to this. The use of ensemble casts signals an attempt by the filmmakers to represent a collective experience of the city, and particularly to examine how its residents are shaped by a designer experience. A publicity photo for *Design 7 Love* shows the ensemble cast dressed in multicoloured designer outfits, complementing the vividly decorated backdrop of the design agency (Figure 5.1). To some degree, this focus on design reflects the real-life growth of the sector in Taiwan, which occurred around the same time as a new kind of cinema emerged. Between 2010 and 2015, the design market, and employment in this sector, grew dramatically in Taiwan, both almost doubling.[1] As *Design 7 Love* opens, the narrator informs us that Taipei was chosen as the 2016 World Design Capital by the International Council of Societies of Industrial Design (now the World Design Organization), which led to embarrassment among city councillors when it emerged that no other cities had been shortlisted for the designation. Ironically paying homage to the then-upcoming honour, the voiceover nonetheless acknowledges that there is something about Taipei that both attracts and proliferates design. This is borne out by statistics; the city accounted for 56 per cent of turnover in Taiwan's design sector by 2015.[2]

Colour Schemes: Decorating the City

To design, or *sheji* 設計 in Chinese, entails both intention and practice. It is to sketch or plan the formal elements of a proposed object, decorative scheme, or work of art. It is also the artistic fashioning, the organisation and structuring, of these formal elements in line with a stylistic approach. Design incorporates disciplines that, in the West, were previously categorised as applied arts: architecture, interior design, fashion, mass-produced products, ceramics, calligraphy, and also cartography. Ostensibly these differ from the fine arts in

Figure 5.1 Publicity photo for *Design 7 Love* (Chen Hung-I, 2014). Courtesy of Chen Hung-I.

that what they produce has a function. Yet design frequently operates beyond utility, and overlaps with art to the extent that it encompasses not solely an object's formal and structural qualities, but also what decorates its surface, such as patterns or motifs, which might be painted or drawn. For Hara, the central difference lies less in practice than intent: while art is fundamentally 'the act of discovering a fresh human spirit', the essence of design 'lies in the process of discovering a problem shared by many people and trying to solve it'.[3] While it is true that art cannot really be understood as problem solving, Hara's description of what motivates design – 'the will to interpret the meaning of human life and existence through the process of making things' – certainly sounds a lot like filmmaking.

In this chapter I want to consider this overlap, focusing on the interconnections between design and film mapping, and how these relate to what David Bordwell identifies as the three objects of study in film poetics: thematics, large-scale form, and stylistics.[4] Production design facilitates cinematic placemaking, and is an element of stylistics. Mapping could be considered a large-scale form, and its principles arguably have much in common with those of design.[5] Thematically, it is my contention that in these films, Taipei is presented as a 'designer city': a filmic environment that is creatively designed; where developments in contemporary architecture, interior design, decorative arts, and fashion mutually shape one another. Something is 'designer' if it bears the mark of the person or organisation that designed it – whether literally, for example via branding or in terms of the object having forms, structures, and patterns that identify it as their work. In these films, the city's spaces and their visual appearance have moved well beyond functionality. Instead they are creatively structured and decorated in a manner that is strongly influenced by contemporary artistic practice and, crucially, evidences the intention to design. The viewer is meant to notice that these Taipei environments are designed.

While many of the locations exist outside the world of the film, this onscreen Taipei is simultaneously the imaginative construction of filmmakers, and in this sense, the designer city can usefully be defined by what it is not. Significantly, it is Taipei, rather than other cities in Taiwan, that has been the focus of this aesthetic preoccupation; no comparable trend can be identified in, say, films set in Taichung or Kaohsiung. Moreover, the designer approach can be contrasted with depictions of Taipei in which traditions of realism endure. *When a Wolf Falls in Love with a Sheep* (Hou Chi-Jan, 2012) is a teen romcom that offers a visually naturalistic rendering of the Nanyang Street area and its cram schools. The film certainly stylises reality by incorporating stop-motion photography montages, animated sequences, and surreal set-pieces. Yet despite all this, the locations appear largely unadorned and ordinary; the environment is not aestheticised in line with a designer vision. A similar conception of authenticity shapes *White Ant* (Chu Hsien-Che, 2016). Both Hou and Chu are noted documentary-makers, which perhaps explains their propensity for more naturalistic portrayals of Taipei. In contrast, the films considered here present Taipei as an overtly designed city, and central to this is the use of multicoloured palettes. Referring in passing to the 'radically different aesthetic look' of post-2000 Taiwanese cinema, Yingjin Zhang notes filmmakers' predilection for 'gorgeous colors'.[6] This is particularly evident in these films, whose colour schemes differ enormously from those of previous representations of Taipei. Fran Martin notes that in his 1990s work, Tsai Ming-Liang shared with Edward Yang a tendency to 'emphasize the repetitively grey, worn, concrete surfaces' familiar to the residents of Taiwan's cities.[7]

Love opens in the Songshou Square Park in Xinyi, which has been designed in a bold red and pink colour scheme. A banner on a wall features an enormous scribbled design of a pink heart, along with text querying what love is, with some possibilities broken down in acrostic. The trunks of the palm trees have been wrapped with patterned material, that is pink with white polka dots. The menus and serviettes on the tables are pink. All this achieves what any good production design should, in that it articulates the film's theme, love. Yet the approach here differs from typical practice, in that the viewer is meant to notice the ways in which the park has been designed within the world of the film itself. This is also the case in *The Mad King of Taipei*. When Hsiao-Hu

(Kuo Shu-Yao) begins working at her pop-up stall, located on the veranda outside the fashion boutique owned by her friend, a series of reverse shots captures her interactions with customers. In the medium-close-ups of Hsiao-Hu, shot frontally, a multicoloured graffiti display can be seen on the buildings behind her, along with a red neon sign. In the reverse shots of the customers, some different but equally colourful graffiti appears in the background, accompanied by a blue neon sign, while the red neon is here reflected in a mirror.

While these multicoloured compositions evoke the garish colour schemes and street art of Ximending, the production design also strongly embellishes reality. Evidently, many of the graffiti displays have been designed for the film itself, and even by the characters within the story world. The Ximen-King (Lee Lee-Zen) is shown with a paintbrush next to a Banksy-like image of a young girl, attaching her hand to that of an adult man. This imagery assists character development, capturing the man's anguish at losing his daughter. A slow-motion scene in which the Ximen-King arranges for banknotes to fall from the sky is accompanied by an accordion soundtrack that strongly recalls Yann Tiersen's score for *Amélie* (Jean-Pierre Jeunet, 2001). Yet while Jeunet's film famously airbrushed out the Montmartre graffiti, Yeh's film amplifies the street art of Ximending. The result, however, is not dissimilar: an air of whimsical unreality. All this is consistent with the film's Chinese title, *West Side City Tale*, which foregrounds the western districts of central Taipei as central to the narrative (unlike the misleading English title, which focuses on a single character and the city as a whole), and frames the film as a *tonghua*, understood as a fairy tale.

Design 7 Love demonstrates the importance of coloured lighting in shaping the depiction of Taipei. In one scene, Emma (Huang Lu), Chiang (Wang Ta-Lu), and Chi-Tzu (Chen Kai-Ting) visit a bar located on an upper floor of a high-rise building in Xinyi. The interior is designed using a complementary colour scheme of purple and yellow – situated at opposite sides of the colour wheel – offset against black. Much of the furniture and the area around the drinks counter is black, while the ceiling-to-floor windows showcase a nighttime view of the city. This gives the overall impression of a dark background, and the far planes of the shots are not brightly lit. However, distinct from this are the numerous yellow lamps that hang from the ceiling, the yellow fabric of the stools and seats, purple strip-lights, and the white wall panels that have been illuminated purple using up-lighting. Yellow and purple are highlighted against the dark backdrop, and reflect in the glass. The impression of artifice, of this being a designed space, is reinforced by the use of contrasting complementary colours.

As Chiang and Emma head onto the balcony, the camera pans right but does not immediately cut to a closer shot as they begin conversing outside. Instead, the camera remains within the interior of the restaurant; Emma and

Chiang stand on the balcony in the background, behind glass, while inside the restaurant, other guests eat their meals in the foreground. This shot is composed to showcase a multicoloured city view, and is intersected by four vertical window bars (Figure 5.2). Inside each segment of the shot, the architecture is illuminated with lighting that has been colour-graded differently: green in the lower-right, blue in the bottom-right, yellow in the top-right, white in the centre, purple in the top-left, red in the centre-left, and orange in the bottom-left and upper-right. The composition captures all six primary and secondary colours, along with white and black. Strikingly, the colour of the lighting in the bottom-left panel changes rapidly throughout the shot, displaying all the above tones in kaleidoscopic rotation. Here, *Design 7 Love* showcases the possibilities of multicoloured palettes, the creative potential of using the full range of the colour wheel as a design tool.

In this shot, the boundary between interior and exterior colour schemes and lighting is shown to be porous, which is also the case in several of the other films considered here. In *The Mad King of Taipei,* Hsiao-Hu's apartment is decorated in a congruent colour scheme, utilising reds, yellows, and oranges across the furniture and wall coverings. The space is lit warmly, including by several onscreen lamps, some of which have red shades. Notably an enormous neon lamp, in the shape of the letter G, is of the size that would typically appear on the exterior signage of businesses, here integrated into the domestic sphere. An enormous 4K sign on the wall of the cinema opposite, its text also red, can be seen prominently through the window, emphasising the interpenetration of house and filmhouse, appropriate given the prevalence of cinemas in Ximending. There may also be a reference here to *The Dream of the Red Chamber* by Cao Xueqin.[8] The literary classic has been adapted for the screen on multiple occasions, and Chin Han's 1978 version starring Ivy

Figure 5.2 Multicoloured palette in *Design 7 Love* (Chen Hung-I, 2014).

Ling Po is mentioned by the gangster Fei Mao-Chiang (Chiang Kuo-Pin), an enthusiastic film buff, when he first appears. The red palette of Hsiao-Hu's apartment seems to derive from popular understandings of the title as depicting an interior red chamber. A mansion with a red exterior is evoked here by the frequent background presence of the Red House, the Japanese colonial construction built in 1908 that is now a cultural and commercial venue in Ximen. More generally, Cao's influence is felt in the film's integration of the dreamlike into reality; the percolation of the cinematic into everyday environments.

The Story of the Stone – an alternative title for *The Dream of the Red Chamber* and released as *Hongloumeng* in Chinese – is a more direct reimagining of Cao's work, set amidst Taipei's gay subculture, that explores issues relating to chemsex and HIV. The film is set in the Red House, where the fictitious 'Stone' bar is located, although the building itself barely features at all. Indeed red is almost entirely excised from the film's colour palette, which is cool and washed-out. Blues, greys, and purples feature strongly, with ultraviolet lighting accompanying the scenes of drugs parties and orgies. Given the title of the source material, the absence of red is an audacious choice, but matches the iconoclastic approach to the literary classic (Bao-Yu's jade is reimagined as a cock ring). While multicoloured, saturated palettes tend to dominate in the post-2008 films considered here, the shared feature of these films is not any colour scheme, but rather the overall impression that spaces have been deliberately designed. *52Hz I Love You*, for instance, favours pastels over saturation, its colourful embellishment of mundane environments evidently influenced by *The Umbrellas of Cherbourg* (Jacques Demy, 1964).

Boutiques: Fashioning the Creative City

The preceding analysis suggests some ways in which filmmakers look to the past, mining existing artistic traditions as part of their effort to represent contemporary Taipei. Yet they undertake this with an eye on the future, a characteristic they share with designers. To design something is, after all, to plan it: to intend and envisage it. As Damon Taylor puts it, 'design, if it means anything at all, describes an activity that attempts to control circumstances through the act of imaginatively inhabiting the future'.[9] In *Design 7 Love*, Chen sought to satirise what this might mean:

> I think both design and love are a kind of deception. The deception may be well-intentioned. The government tells us what our city and our future life will be, and what we need to achieve that. All this has been planned. It may be well-intentioned deception, telling you that the old things need to go, so that the new things will make your future life better.[10]

In the films considered here, Taipei is visualised in a manner that both amplifies contemporary design trends, and speculates on the city's potential or emergent futures. This is most literally the case in *Design 7 Love*, which includes CGI animations in its wide shots of the urban landscape, in which futuristic architecture magically constructs itself on rooftops and walls.

In this respect, it is hardly accidental that most of these films include significant scenes set in Xinyi, visually the city's most futuristic district. Comprising contemporary architecture including the iconic skyscraper Taipei 101, it is the only central area in Taipei to be entirely designed from scratch, and furthermore, as a commercial and financial hub it is readily recognisable as a globalised space. *Love* opens in Xinyi, in the Songshou Square Park located next to the Shinkong Mitsukoshi department store, before moving to the W Taipei hotel next to the Eslite department store. The climactic scenes of *52Hz I Love You* take place in the Lawry's rib restaurant situated in the next block. *Design 7 Love* opens in the Taipei World Trade Center Square. International and transnational activity is, moreover, dramatised within the films. *Love* is set partly in Beijing, with one storyline relating the experiences of a Taipei businessman who shuttles between the two cities. In *Design 7 Love*, we learn that Emma has previously worked in Shanghai, New York, and Hong Kong, while the mix of Chinese and English character names (Doris, Pa-Tzu, Emma, Chiang, Andrew, Mark, Chi-Tzu) and the casting of two mixed-race actors (Hsu, Price) attest to the transnational realities that exist beyond the world of the film. The kinds of spaces frequented by the characters in *The Story of the Stone*, meanwhile, recall what Hongwei Bao identifies as 'transnational and commercial queer spaces' in China.[11]

Quite evidently, this recent trend of Taipei films could, from the outset, be analysed with reference to theories of globalisation, although these would need to be contextualised in relation to the island's specific geopolitical situation. Tom Conley argues that a consideration of film mapping can illuminate the history of strategies that inform a film's construction.[12] In this context, the efforts to promote Taipei as cultural and creative hub, and in particular as a design capital, can be understood as what Kristina Karvelyte terms the 'making' of a creative city, which in East Asia is seen by policymakers as 'a means for economic growth, but also as a strategic national policy device'.[13] She argues that in the case of Taipei, it has mainly been the ambiguous international status of Taiwan and its relationship with China that has driven this process.[14] Yi-Kai Juan, Yu-Ching Cheng, and Yeng-Horng Perng interpret this in less directly political terms, but nonetheless suggest that it was a desire to synergise soft power (culture, creativity, design) with hard power (information and other technologies) that stimulated Taipei's application to be the World Design Capital in 2016.[15] These films certainly help 'make' a creative city, in the sense of cinematically constructing it, although the degree to which filmmakers are consciously engaged in political strategising is debatable. Sometimes – as with Chen – they actively satirise political pretensions.

Considering that design is an international discipline and a globalised practice, can a case even be made for the uniqueness of Taipei as a designer city? This is a question thematised in the films themselves, with the depiction of boutique and independent stores – where many of the characters work – a focal point. On the one hand, these recurring narrative spaces are shown to enable individual creative expression and self-fashioning. For instance, in *The Mad King of Taipei*, Hsiao-Hu acquires a reputation as a fashion stylist. She displays her wares outside a boutique store, where her customers use a makeshift changing cubicle. The street is literally the place where their appearances are transformed, in line with the aesthetic of the street: Hsiao-Hu's makeovers are bold, brash, and colourful. Such depictions of Taipei shape a similar kind of impression to that which Agnès Rocamora argues helped consolidate Paris as a fashion capital, a belief in 'the symbolic value of fashion as that which originates outside the world of commerce. Fashion is not the outcome of astute strategists and businessmen but that of the intangible creative spirit of the city'.[16]

Yet while city branding is a factor in some of these films, it is not undertaken unanimously or uncritically. The boutique store is at once small, exclusive, and independent, but also a speciality version of a broader business model. It emblematises the tension between individual creativity and globalised, assembly-line consumerism that is a defining feature of design. The films adopt different perspectives on this. *52Hz I Love You* offers the most idealised vision, presenting its characters as craftspeople; An (Lin Chung-Yu) works in an artisan bakery where he designs each cake decoration by hand. More cynical is *Design 7 Love*, in which Chiang and Chi-Tzu are dismayed to encounter another couple wearing the same clothes as them, confirming them all as unwitting subjects of mass culture. Utopian visions of design also tend to ignore the supply side, acknowledged in *The Mad King of Taipei*, in which Hsiao-Hu's designing and making of fashionable clothes is shown to involve repetitive, exhausting labour.[17] *The Story of the Stone*, meanwhile, is critical of demand. The characters' social lives are overtly transactional, with younger men treated to high-end designer attire by older men expecting sexual favours in return. Sean (Chi Yan-Kai) ultimately leaves for the UK in order to study interior design, an interest apparent earlier in the film: he owns an upmarket fashion boutique that he has decorated in a chic industrial style, décor that is replicated in clothes stores across the world.

Yet to interpret these films primarily as allegories or embodiments of global economic flows would ultimately tell us everything and nothing. More productive would be to ask how design and film, both international practices, interact aesthetically in this context. In 2007, James Tweedie argued that when examining cinematic depictions of Taipei, it was necessary to supplement the narrative of globalisation that had taken hold in scholarly discussions of city films with 'a competing narrative of cities in the confines of space'.[18] Analysing post-2008 portrayals of Taipei as representations of globalisation would be similarly reductive and entail an odd shift in critical emphasis, focusing on what the filmmakers do not prioritise, rather than what they do. The directors considered here may be interested in global flows, but they hardly seem preoccupied by them. They are, however, engrossed in depicting Taipei specifically; *Design 7 Love* was the third film in Chen's 'Taipei Trilogy', while Yeh had been executive producer on *MRT Love*, a series of seven films inspired by the city's metro stations.[19] They are also very interested in experimenting with colour, as I have shown. And they are creatively drawn to designer greenery, and the redesign of disused structures, as I will shortly demonstrate.

Above all, however, these filmmakers are interested in love. That is what these films are all about. It features in the title of many of them: *Love*, *L-O-V-E*, *Design 7 Love*, *52Hz I Love You*.[20] But it is where love leads us that is interesting. What can love tell us about how Taipei is designed onscreen at the historical moment that is post-2008 cinema? Can love enhance our understanding of the connection between design, space, and narrative? Can love map? In these films, characters want each other just as they desire certain fashions and accessories, or the lifestyles afforded by designer spaces. This is even the subject of a pun in *Design 7 Love*. As Emma rides in a cab, the driver (played by *Wawa No Cidal* director Cheng Yu-Chieh) asks what her job is. Emma replies, in English, that she works in 'design' but he mishears her, and queries 'Desire?' The scene is played for laughs – he concludes that she must work for an escort agency – but attests to a serious point, that both narrative and design are motivated by desire. To design is, after all, to plot.

Random Hookups? Design, Desire, and Narrative

Designing as plotting often has negative connotations – to 'have designs' on something is to desire it in a manner that involves scheming and intrigue. This meaning is also conveyed in Chinese; the *ji* in *sheji* can mean a plan, but can also refer to a plot, stratagem, or scheme. This understanding of the terminology is taken up in *Design 7 Love*, in which one storyline concerns the execution of a plan through plotting and strategising. Doris pits younger members of the Remix team against one another, manipulating them into sharing ideas that she then steals and pitches as her own. Having realised what is going on, Pa-Tzu confronts her at the film's climax by exclaiming: 'You are designing us!', translated more passively in English as 'We're all players in your grand design'. The way that Doris responds is intriguing – not with an admission or apology, but indifference. It doesn't matter, she suggests, because they are all part of a broader scheme anyway: 'We all think we're designers. But often we're the ones being designed.' The dialogue signals metanarrative recognition that an unknown power – the filmmaker – is asserting itself over the characters, confirmed in the film's concluding section. The film here acknowledges that storytelling is itself an act of design, an idea neatly articulated in the film's poster, which depicts actors Mo and Hsu embracing (Figure 5.3). Instead of kissing each other, however, they are making out with a pentahedron – specifically, a square pyramid. The space between lips anticipating a kiss is filled with 3D geometry. Where there is desire, there is design.

The construction of a plot, undertaken by a screenwriter, entails planning and craft, while the visual fashioning of Taipei examined in the previous sections similarly focuses our attention on the etymology of the colour *scheme*: a plan, and as such, something fundamentally forward-looking (in Chinese this is expressed as 'colour design' or *secai sheji*). The city's designer appearance is a declaration of decorative intent; not Taipei as it exists, but as it is imagined to look in the future. In his fictionalised archaeology of an imaginary Hong Kong, Dung Kai-Cheung reflects on the nature of the 'plan' as understood in the context of cartography:

> A 'plan' is a plane figure but also a design, a present visualisation of future form. On the one hand it does not yet exist and is unreal, but on the other hand it is being designed and will be constructed. A plan is thus a kind of fiction, and the meaning of this fiction is inseparable from the design and blueprint. A fiction is not the same as something completely lacking any connection with reality.[21]

Fiction films also have a blueprint for their mapping of space, and that is the script. In the overtly self-reflexive *Design 7 Love*, the film's screenplay appears onscreen during the opening credits, with the narrator reading out dialogue that the actors then proceed to deliver in the first scene. This was done, Chen explains, in order to highlight that 'a film is also a kind of design'.[22]

The script anticipates future action, and thus provides a structural plan for the onscreen mapping of narrative space – a process that arguably has a genealogical basis in cartography, itself an applied art or design practice. The films considered in this chapter share a defining structural feature: they all lack a single protagonist, and instead utilise an ensemble cast. As a result, narrative movement must be designed in a particular way. What occurs is a choreography in which each character (or subset of characters) takes a journey around Taipei that sometimes intersects with the journeys of other characters. These itineraries and their intersections are spatial and temporal, but also sentimental; characters might cross paths at different locations and moments in time, but also at emotional thresholds, thereby heightening the affective stakes of the ensuing encounter. Exactly how this is structurally undertaken

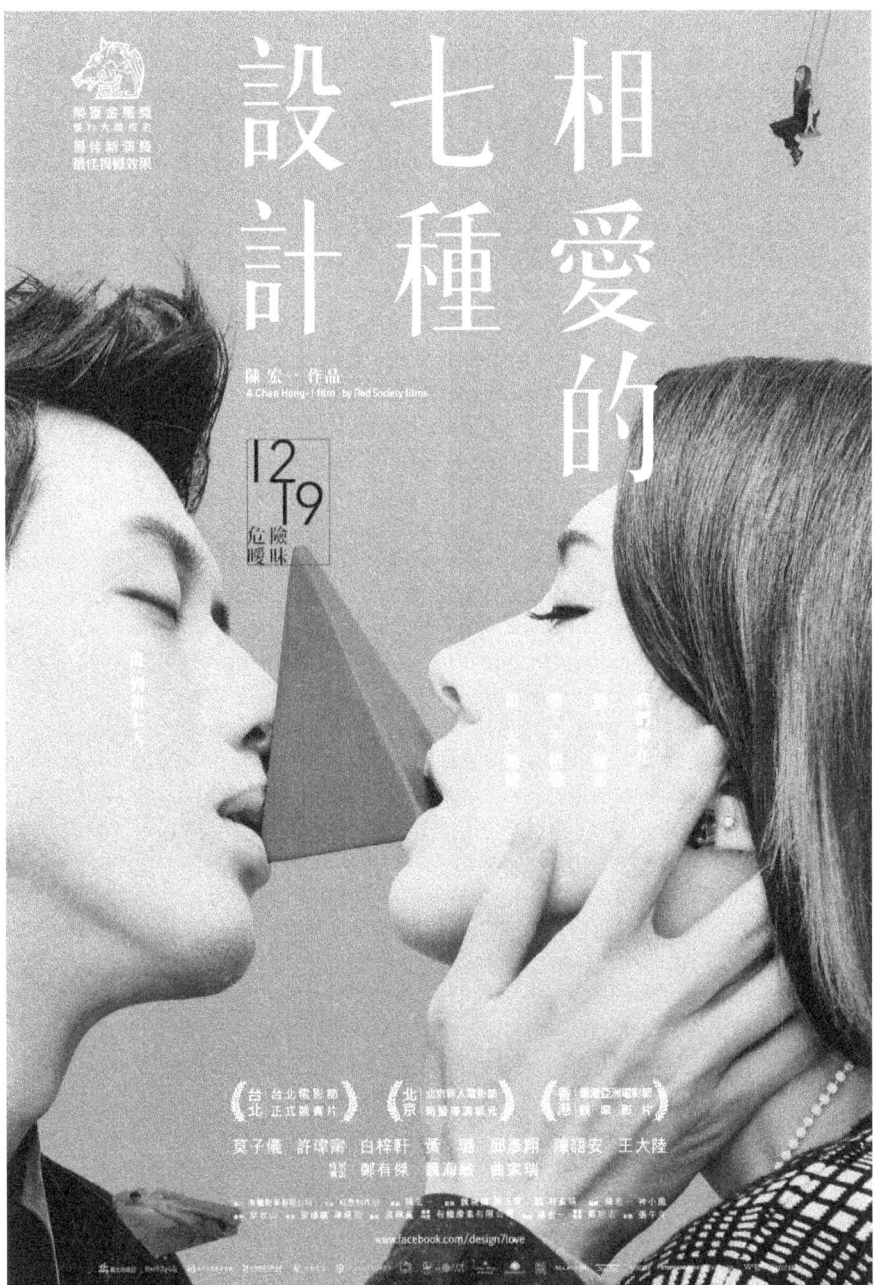

Figure 5.3 Poster for *Design 7 Love* (Chen Hung-I, 2014). Courtesy of Chen Hung-I.

varies from film to film. Characters might meet regularly (*The Mad King of Taipei*), only at certain points (*52Hz I Love You*), not at all (*Love*), or they might congregate around a shared location from which they depart on separate excursions (*Design 7 Love*).

The basic rules of classical storytelling emphasise that characters should want and need something, which in turn provokes action. Here, this is articulated in more specifically spatial terms; acting demands movement from one place in Taipei to another, and desire is shown to be the force that engineers this movement. In *Love*, Jou-Yi (Shu Qi) ultimately abandons the mansion she occupies with her boyfriend Lu (Niu Cheng-Tse), in favour of the modest roof terrace inhabited by love interest Hsiao-Kuan (Juan Ching-Tien). In *The Story of the Stone*, Josh (Lu Chin-Hsiang) moves between bars, clubs, saunas, and boutiques in search of sex. *52Hz I Love You* initially conceives romantic movement from a business angle. Hsin (Chuang Juan-Ying) and An are both 'delivering love', as she puts it, working as couriers who transport flowers and chocolates across the city on Valentine's Day. Chance encounters are crucial to the design of these films' narratives, given their reliance on discrete plotlines that must intersect at node points, temporally but also spatially, at locations scattered across Taipei. This might involve moments of serendipity, when characters have the good fortune to meet by accident, moments of misfortune, or both.

The screenwriter designs contingency; in *Love*, for instance, Hsiao-Kuan just happens to be leaving his local 7-Eleven store at the precise moment that Jou-Yi gets out of a nearby car. One scene in *The Story of the Stone* depicts Josh in a designer boutique store, flirting with the owner, Sean, while in the background, through the ceiling-to-floor glass window, Josh's love interest Lin (Chen Yan-Ming) walks by. He stops to watch the pair, then continues on his way, unseen. This brief visualisation of a chance encounter is subtle to the point of being missed, but captures a defining moment, for Lin henceforth refuses to countenance a romance with the carefree Josh. This reminds us that there is narrative intent in meetings that do not happen, and in connections that are ignored. In *Love*, the characters are ultimately all shown to be interconnected, making it peculiar, for instance, that Hsiao-Kuan never discusses with Jou-Yi his pre-existing connection with Lu by virtue of his sister being best friends with Lu's daughter. Here, if characters do not meet in a space, they tend not to express knowledge of those outside the space. Whether or not we accept the inclusion of random encounters, or the exclusion of likely encounters, as credible depends on our assessment of the screenwriter and director's skill.

The apparently contingent intersection of mapped routes is fundamentally forward looking; these characters encounter one another because narratively, something needs to happen between them in the future (and that something is usually love). Random encounters involving vehicles abound in these films, with driven journeys readily facilitating movement around the city. In *Design 7*

Love, the characters are constantly driving around Taipei; Emma ultimately hooks up with a cab driver. Traffic accidents are a prominent device. In *Love*, Kai (Peng Yu-Yan) is riding a bike and collides with the car driven by Mark (Chao Yu-Ting), thereby connecting the pair in the opening tracking shot. In *Story of the Stone*, Josh almost rides his bike into the car driven by Sean – a missed encounter, as the pair will not meet again until later in the story. In *52Hz I Love You*, Hsin and An first meet when her van and his scooter collide. Each accident or near-miss takes place at a road junction, the transport network at these moments materialising the intersection of narrative routes.

The filmmakers seek to *contrive* these vehicular encounters – that is, to plan or plot them – without making them appear *contrived*, that is, artificial through being too obviously plotted. It is a tricky balancing act, and *Design 7 Love* mocks the strained devices that screenwriters sometimes indulge in order to expedite such encounters. The scene in which Mark just happens to be driving around the East District, where Doris just happens to be walking, is intended to be comic. Their over-convenient rendezvous generates amusement precisely because it anticipates the future a little too transparently; as Doris gets into Mark's car, we know that a romance is on the cards. But any residual sense of credibility is blown away when Pa-Tzu then arrives out of nowhere and gets into the car, jealously squeezing next to the flirtatious pair. The double coincidence mocks the narrative contrivance of contingency: in keeping with the designer aesthetic that percolates the film more generally, this scene is very obviously and deliberately *fashioned*.

The final section of *Design 7 Love* abandons diegetic realism altogether, as the actors come out of character and begin playing themselves, discussing the making of the film and how the story should conclude, themselves contemplating the future design of the narrative. This recalls processes associated with 'design thinking' that became increasingly prominent in the early twenty-first century, examined in the documentary *Design & Thinking* (Tsai Mu-Ming, 2012), produced by the Taipei-based creative studio Muris. Paul Pangaro, one of the interviewees in the film, explains that the term arose

> in order to distinguish between what others think of as design, which is usually just the surface, to the *thinking behind* – thinking is something you do first, and then you make. And it's also a couple of processes: begin from where the user is and understand human needs, through a kind of ethnography and observation; then to brainstorm and diverge, and understand what all the possibilities might be; and then to prototype, and to improve the prototype through iteration.

In its portrayal of the Remix agency, *Design 7 Love* dramatises the brainstorming, prototyping, and iteration that are typical of design thinking. Yet Tsai's documentary argues for the broader applicability of the term across disciplines, including in filmmaking; in this sense, could the final mockumentary section of *Design 7 Love* itself be considered an example of design thinking – a practice of thinking through the rationale for, and possibilities of, film narrative?

The film's onscreen workshopping is not market driven, however, nor is it motivated by a real-world problem (not, at least, unless we see the endurance of classical film narrative as a problem). Instead the film's final section embodies the overlap of design thinking with what Anthony Dunne and Fiona Raby refer to as conceptual design, which 'deals, by definition, with unreality', with outputs conceptual not 'because they haven't yet been realized or are waiting to be realized but out of choice. They celebrate their unreality and take full advantage of being made from ideas.'[23] After the self-reflexive brainstorming in *Design 7 Love*, an offscreen fire occurs, in which Doris suffers burn injuries and is hospitalised, another Act of God on the part of the filmmaker. As she recovers, the same concluding scene is filmed twice, with each of her love interests alluding to the apparently arbitrary nature of the plot device. In their respective scenes, Mark and Pa-Tzu both query, 'Can love be designed?' Chen's answer is evidently affirmative, and over the credits, the actors discuss which of the endings they prefer: should Doris opt for the ordinary but devoted Pa-Tzu or the arrogant but dynamic Mark? This closing section of *Design 7 Love*, which an onscreen title states is devoted to 'nihilistic love', evidences a cynicism about classical narrative to the degree that it is driven by design. This is encapsulated by the final onscreen quotation from Dunne, which states that 'art exists because design has failed'.

The other films considered here are not as self-reflexive, or as cynical. But their narratives are nonetheless designed with spatial precision, sometimes incorporating allusions to the principles of their own construction. *52Hz I Love You* focuses on two pairs of characters who coalesce just once, at the film's climax. Earlier in the story, Ta-Ho (Suming) ambles through a thunderstorm singing, in an homage to *Singin' in the Rain* (Gene Kelly and Stanley Donen, 1952), 'How can the two parallels meet at some point?', one means by which the future encounter between the two sets of characters is teased. All the films considered here fuse some diverse traditions of multi-character storytelling. *The Dream of the Red Chamber* is a reference point for two of them; Cao's text features around thirty main characters and several hundred minor ones, whose trajectories nonetheless intersect around two main locations. Global filmic traditions of ensemble drama are also important. *Love* draws on the structure and themes of *Love Actually* (Richard Curtis, 2003), while the plot structure of *Design 7 Love* was inspired by a multi-character novel by Chinese author Bi Feiyu, *Massage*, that was adapted as a film by Lou Ye.[24] Sylvia Chang's *20:30:40* (2004) was structured as what Zhang Zhen terms 'multidirectional narrative lines crisscrossing Taipei's urban geography', reconfiguring melodramatic coincidence as 'haphazard proximity'.[25] One might also look to the ensemble dramas of certain *auteur* directors such as Robert Altman, or Edward Yang – notably *A Brighter Summer Day*, although Yang's earlier classic *Terrorizers* might also inform the preoccupation of *Love* with the mapping of contingent encounters.

Some readers may raise their eyebrows at this point. Is it too far-fetched to look for *Terrorizers* in *Love*? I began this chapter by asking whether love can map, and in this case, it can, and in more complicated ways than might initially be apparent. *Love* opens with a Steadicam shot that lasts just under twelve minutes, introducing all the characters and their differing levels of wealth, as they circulate around Xinyi. There is a cut concealed in post-production, when the camera exits a hotel window and ascends to the floor above, yet the opening take is still five-and-a-half minutes long. The camera commences in the Songshou Square Park, then moves north up the Songzhi Road, east along the Songgao Road, then north again towards Zhongxiao East Road. We then arrive at the W Taipei hotel, enter the lobby, ascend in an elevator, move along a hall, and finally enter a bedroom. This unbroken take visually maps an actual route in Xinyi, while the following scene shows Mark visiting Beijing on a business trip, looking to buy property. He visits an historic part of the city, just north of the Forbidden City, speaking to estate agent Xiao-Ye (Zhao Wei) on the phone as he gives his exact location, at the intersection of the Gongjian Lane and the Beihai North Alley, which we see indicated on street signs.

Love immediately locates itself in very specific districts of Taipei and Beijing; both are shown to be impacted by the soaring value of real estate, which threatens to exclude locals. Through mapping comparatively, the film establishes a contrast between the sleek, contemporary look of Taipei, and the traditional brick courtyard architecture of Beijing (the film largely excludes Beijing's contemporary buildings). Taipei is the designer capital, whereas Beijing is the ancestral home – a theme directly reflected in the plot. Mark and Xiao-Ye initially hate one another, but ultimately end up in a relationship, an overt metaphor for cross-strait relations – the dialogue refers to the couple's shared Manchu roots and Mark's family having left China in 1949. Co-produced by the Huayi Brothers and released in China, *Love* ultimately facilitates a reconciliation between the bickering pair. A map that appears very briefly near the end of the film seems relevant in this respect. In a twenty-second scene that forms part of a montage, Hsiao-Ni (Kuo Tsai-Chieh) sits in a university lecture theatre. Lots of writing and diagrams can briefly be glimpsed on the chalkboard (Figure 5.4). In the centre, a map of the world is drawn, identifying the location of various ethnic groups. The lecturer explains, 'Behind any idea that indicates separation lies a great crisis. Once what's good and bad is defined, there will be conflicts and wars.'

Figure 5.4 Lecture map and annotations in *Love* (Niu Cheng-Tse, 2012).

The map appears in close-up for only a few seconds, but the eagle-eyed viewer will see, chalked next to it on the left, the question 'What is the meaning of love?'. This is followed by the same responses that appeared at the beginning of the film, on the banner in the Songshou Square Park, here written both in Chinese and English. The English text reads 'Listen, Obligate, Valued, Excuse', but this translation has been skewed to accommodate the LOVE acrostic. In fact, the four meanings of love translate in English as: listen, appreciate, respect, forgive. These symbolise the theme of each of the film's four storylines. Evidently, this is not the topic of a real lecture but a meta-filmic intervention, sneakily inserted into a montage sequence. By placing this text onto a lecturer's chalkboard, the film incorporates knowledge of its own narrative design into the production design.

Furthermore, by placing this text alongside a map, the film connects romantic conflict to global divisions that – as the lecturer explains – are indicative of underlying crisis. In the Mark/Xiao-Ye storyline, the crisis of separation is both romantic and geopolitical, and the film proposes to solve this through reconciliation. Additional scribblings on the chalkboard give a sense of how this might proceed narratively, though the mutual working out of a paradox: 'Love, Contradiction, Forgiveness.' Released in a period of relative calm in PRC-ROC relations, *Love* is very much a film of its moment, with a conciliatory tone that would not find a place in Taiwanese cinema later in the decade. The scene also involves a cameo appearance. For the lecturer is played by Hsiao Yeh, the novelist and screenwriter known for co-writing *Terrorizers* with Edward Yang. It is questionable whether his appearance is intended to signify anything too precise, given the volume of other cameos in *Love*; what it does demonstrate is the film's awareness of the design principles of its own screenplay. A noted writer appears in the context of an annotated map, with dialogue evoking a principle of classical storytelling – the resolution of a crisis that plays out in each of the film's four storylines. This is facilitated by the characters' movement around Taipei, a pattern evident more broadly across the films considered in this chapter. The following sections will explore two kinds of environment in which the characters are narratively set on the path to conflict resolution: green spaces and repurposed spaces, reimagined in line with a designer vision.

Flower Arranging: Green Spaces and Designer Vegetation

Urban vegetation features in all the films considered here. Pre-2008 visualisations of Taipei tended not to feature green spaces – in part, because fewer of them existed. Some films captured transitional moments in the redevelopment of the city in the 1990s, which entailed the designing of new parks.[26] Notably, *Vive L'Amour* (Tsai Ming-Liang, 1994) featured scenes shot on the construction site that would become the Daan Forest Park, where an informal residential district, hosting the veterans' village of Jianhua Xincun, had been controversially demolished in 1992, forcing the relocation of 12,000 people.[27] Environmentalist rhetoric was used to justify the construction of this and other parks, which some have argued was a cover-up for rampant demolition, intended to drive up the value of adjacent real estate.[28] Tsai's film would seem to associate the emergent park with profound alienation, emblematised by the final scene in which May Lin (Yang Kuei-Mei) traverses a landscape of barren earthworks punctuated by young saplings before breaking down in tears. Martin, however, draws on the work of Chang Hsiao-Hung to suggest that Tsai might well be imagining the new park as a possible site of queer desire, constructed upon the ruins of the *jia*.[29]

Eighteen years later, in *Love*, the Daan Forest Park is indeed a space of possibility, although there is nothing queer about this. The vegetation has grown lush, and the environment is depicted as a tranquil, leafy spot, where Jou-Yi and Hsiao-Kuan enjoy a walk the morning after they meet. *Love* is typical of the films considered here, in which green spaces are depicted as realms of authenticity, where characters experience genuine emotion that they are less able to express elsewhere. In this, they have something in common with other narrative spaces that are not subject to the designer aesthetic otherwise pervading these films. In *Design 7 Love*, the kitchen in the design agency is cluttered, cramped, and hidden from public view. It is poorly designed with no room for anyone to move. Yet it is here, behind the façade, where truths are revealed; where Pa-Tzu speaks openly with Doris about his feelings, for instance. If the depiction of designer spaces enables an exploration of artifice and insincerity, then apparently undesigned spaces are conceived as realms of truth.

In *The Mad King of Taipei*, the homeless Ximen-King resides in what appears to be a derelict courtyard. Hidden from public view, it is accessible only via a staircase in a decrepit building. Hsiao-Hu discovers that he has created a makeshift dwelling in the courtyard, in which greenery has sprung up: trees, plants, and grass. The character enjoys the solitude of a secret garden, audaciously positioned in a ruined structure amidst one of Taipei's most densely developed and least vegetated districts. This recalls the aesthetics of the Ruin Academy, a research centre in Taipei conceptualised by the Finnish architect Marco Casagrande, who advocates a 'third generation city', an organic ruin of the industrial city that promotes alternative ways of living.[30] The Academy itself is housed in a decaying structure within which vegetation grows freely.[31] In contrast with, say, the trees planted on the Daan avenues in *The Tag-Along* (Cheng Wei-Hao, 2015), the vegetation in *The Mad King of Taipei* has emerged spontaneously and organically, unintended by urban planners, lending connotations of natural purity and authenticity that serve plot and characterisation. In one scene, Hsiao-Hu falls asleep, after expressing a wish to visit a hot spring. When she awakes, the Ximen-King has built one for her: a bathtub with a hot shower, in the middle of the garden, in which she proceeds to bathe. Narratively, this instigates emotional cleansing and honesty; as Hsiao-Hu admits, 'If I don't stop lying to myself, nobody will be happy.' At the same time, the incongruous appearance of a bathtub among ferns – recalling the conventions of a shampoo commercial – marks this out as a fantasised, patently artificial space.

These tensions play out as the film progresses, and more of the large, atrium-like space is gradually revealed. Eagle-eyed viewers might note that the Ximen-King's salvaged furniture is stacked on staggered rows, and just over an hour into the film, when gangster Fei arrives to threaten the squatter, a pan from the street reveals the exact location of the courtyard. It is situated opposite the Taipei Sun cinema, an IMAX theatre owned by Vieshow Cinemas. Consulting a historic map will reveal that the Ximen-King's residence is not, in fact, a courtyard: it is the former Taipei Xiyuan cinema. Reminiscing about the past, Fei explains that *The Swordsman* (King Hu and others, 1990) was the highest-grossing film to screen there. Discussing the character of Fei, director Yeh explains that 'his previous aura no longer exists, which is a metaphor for Taiwan's film industry ... I wanted to use this character to talk about the transformation of the domestic film market', noting the decline in national production since the heyday of popular filmmaking.[32] As the former function of the space is revealed, it is visually framed for the first time from what would have been the perspective of the audience in the back row, giving an overview. Urban greenery now emanates from where the screen would have been located, suggesting the emergence of authenticity from artifice.

This trope relies on the supposition that nature is authentic because it cannot be designed. Vegetation might be patterned, decorated, and structured, but crucially, it is not designed because these characteristics lack intent or planning

LOVE IN A DESIGNER CITY

(assuming, of course, the absence of divine intent). While set dressing was added and likely some fake vegetation too, this secret garden did actually exist, as Yeh recalls:

> From the outside, it looks like an abandoned site. It was originally on the third floor of the movie theatre, but a whole forest has grown and is thriving. The natural light shines in. It's so beautiful and wonderful![33]

This location is unusual because more generally, in urban contexts, natural vegetation requires anthropologically designed parameters in which to grow and flourish; similarly in these films, while urban greenery is narratively aligned with the natural, its placement is often carefully curated by the filmmaker. The broader paradox is that spaces apparently exempted from the designer aesthetic are, in fact, designed – and how this is undertaken in the ruined cinema setting will be discussed below.

Some films show the design of urban greenery to be undertaken by the characters themselves. In *52Hz I Love You*, An is first introduced on the apartment rooftop where he lives in a smart, shed-like extension. The terrace is beautifully lined with potted plants and hanging baskets, indicating that he is a keen gardener. As he sings, sad that his girlfriend doesn't reciprocate his feelings, An wanders past the plants, checking their leaves. Narratively, his sensitivity and interest in greenery anticipates his compatibility with florist Hsin, even though the pair will not meet for almost an hour of the running time. Contextually, the downward-tilted angle of one wide shot reveals that An's terrace garden resembles a miniature version of the local park situated in the lower-right of the frame; both are green areas contained within straight-edged polygons (Figure 5.5). Moreover, vegetation emanates from several nearby rooftops and balconies. *52Hz I Love You* offers a utopian imagining of a future, greener Taipei. The warm orange lighting

Figure 5.5 An's rooftop terrace in *52Hz I Love You* (Wei Te-Sheng, 2017).

129

and idyllic CGI backdrop sentimentalise what would ordinarily be considered an illegal rooftop construction, which can often provide poor living standards. If the affordability of rent in central Taipei is a subtext, then Wei envisions An's modest terrace as a designer green space. A T-shirt on the clothes line, with the logo BRKLYN, suggests that inspiration may have come from Brooklyn's lofts and terraces, reconstituted through gentrification.

The cinematic appearance of green rooftops occurred in the context of Taipei's 'Garden City Initiative', which supported the establishment of urban gardens including community, rooftop, and school gardens. Introduced as a policy in 2015 by newly elected mayor Ko Wen-Je, the initiative drew on developments in the urban agriculture movement that were gaining traction at the time.[34] The urban gardens discussed by Jeffrey Hou, in his study of the policy and its implementation, are generally spaces open to the public in which food is grown, whereas the rooftop gardens in these films are private and not agricultural. Nonetheless, the utopian vision of *52Hz I Love You* would seem to owe something to the popular discourses instigated by groups such as the Farming Urbanism Network, whose white paper was adopted by Ko's campaign team to promote 'a vision of a green and healthy city'.[35] Hou discusses urban gardening as a 'placemaking activity' that can have a positive impact on social interactions.[36] There is arguably conceptual overlap between this, and the cinematic placemaking observable in these films, in which narrative emphasis is placed on the capacity of rooftop terraces to generate positive relationships.

In *Love*, Hsiao-Kuan also lives in an extension constructed on the top floor of an apartment block. The roof has been lined with wooden decking, and Hsiao-Kuan is also a gardener, having filled his terrace with potted plants and vines (Figure 5.6). The space is used to trace the development of Jou-Yi and Hsiao-Kuan's relationship and appears in four scenes. In the first, Hsiao-Kuan returns from the bathroom to find Jou-Yi asleep in a deckchair, surrounded by the

Figure 5.6 Hsiao-Kuan's rooftop terrace in *Love* (Niu Cheng-Tse, 2012).

greenery; this is a place where she can rest and unself-consciously be herself. The contrast with Jou-Yi's patently superficial, loveless existence in a sleek but soulless mansion could not be starker; similarly to *52Hz I Love You*, the environment helps the viewer anticipate the pair's compatibility. The second time the location appears, Jou-Yi opens up to Hsiao-Kuan, questioning her life choices. Her fear of being without money has over time evolved into dependence: 'Someone pays my credit bills, buys me designer handbags, and keeps me in a mansion. Why should I leave?' The implication is that commencing a relationship with the impoverished Hsiao-Kuan would be a psychologically healthy move (although ironically, the implicit criticism of consumer culture is accompanied by some rather overt product placement, as Jou-Yi munches on a Häagen Dazs ice cream). When the garden terrace next appears, the pair embrace and kiss for the first time, an experience Jou-Yi intriguingly associates with a place:

Jou-Yi: Have you realised?
Hsiao-Kuan: Realised what?
Jou-Yi: We're holding each other.
Hsiao-Kuan: What about it?
Jou-Yi: It feels like home.

This confirms what the production design, dialogue, and performances have hitherto implied; that Hsiao-Kuan represents the virtues of domesticity. Home entails an affective attachment to place that is here associated less with nostalgia for an abode previously inhabited (Jou-Yi's childhood sounds less than happy) than with anticipation of a future one, materially sensed through an intimate act in a green space.

Hsiao-Kuan and An incorporate greenery into their terraces by buying it, of course, reminding us that urban gardening is also an economy. The florist where Hsin works is a central narrative space in *52Hz I Love You*, first appearing immediately after the scene on An's roof terrace. The pair finally meet in a minor traffic collision involving the bright yellow van that Hsin uses to deliver flowers to customers. In a film plentiful in allusion, Wei's choice of the business and its vehicle may well be a nod to *20:30:40*, in which director Sylvia Chang similarly played a Taipei florist who delivers her flowers in a van. Visually, the correlation between the vehicles is striking; both are yellow, featuring a stencilled design of plant stems and flowers. *20:30:40* takes a typically gendered role and activities – the florist and flower arranging – and utilises these in a narrative of female empowerment. This suggests a trajectory that connects post-2008 depictions of Taipei with an earlier tradition of 'middlebrow' melodrama.[37] While neglected by film scholars, Chang's films in various respects anticipate forms and styles that would later become commonplace after 2008; in this case, the symbolism of flowers and their arrangement amidst urban environments.

A far less empowering view of flower arranging pervades *The Story of the Stone*. Lin works as a florist in the Jade flower shop, where in addition to live plants and bouquets, he sells dried and pressed flowers that are incorporated into designer products and arrangements. Bunches of dried flowers can be seen hanging from the ceiling in the Stone bar. The film mostly depicts vegetation as being distanced from its original state – dead, dried, and carefully curated within designer environments – thereby assisting a narrative of decay and decline. Even living plants have their green hue desaturated as a result of the film's washed-out palette. *Design 7 Love* depicts an equally ambivalent kind of urban vegetation: the green walls used to conceal construction sites. In one scene, Pa-Tzu and Doris walk along a street, captured in a wide lateral tracking shot. They pass by some small commercial stands, which give way to a covered walkway with a green wall; a construction company logo then comes into view. The shot suggests temporal movement from past to future, the inevitability of the old commercial units being demolished and replaced. The appearance of a green wall suggests the irony of organic growth being used to mask destruction.

Urban Installations: Curated Waste, Repurposing, and Narrative Value

The design of new architecture often results in the demolition of existing structures, made apparent in *Design 7 Love*, in which construction projects and roadworks are ubiquitous. Pa-Tzu is unhappy to witness the bulldozing of his neighbourhood soya milk shop, asking why 'we keep inventing new stuff' when 'old things are being erased, levelled, and gutted'. This scene possibly references a real-life incident in Taipei, in which an elderly woman died the same day as her soya milk shop was demolished; she was one of many residents of informal settlements re-categorised as squatters in 2006, a designation that enabled land redevelopment.[38] In *Design 7 Love*, a title card ironically refers to Pa-Tzu as a 'social poet', capturing his contradictory perspective on Taipei: he mourns the passing of the old, while himself designing the new. More generally, while envisioning the future design of the city, the films under consideration simultaneously locate narrative authenticity in older or disused architecture. In some ways, this is the latest incarnation of what Yomi Braester terms a 'poetics of demolition', visible in several Taiwanese films made since the mid-1980s.[39] These 'foreground spaces that contain the signs of their recent or imminent erasure', he argues, challenging gentrification and the engineering of memory, in order to 'reclaim the ruins of the past'.[40] The difference in these post-2008 films is that design, as a discipline, is shown to be partly complicit in this urban erasure. Underlying the designer aesthetic, at times paradoxically, is a fear that traditional values are facing dissolution – and a scepticism that the values embodied by contemporary design are up to the job of replacing them. Almost despite himself, Pa-Tzu misses 'the taste of old love and soya milk'.

The repurposing of old architecture, furniture, appliances, and products is one means through which a designer might reconcile the values of the past with a vision for the future; the films considered here embody this tendency. A recurring trope is the appearance of salvaged material in narratively significant locations, overtly aestheticised to the extent that it comes to resemble the forms of art installation. In *The Mad King of Taipei*, the Ximen-King spends his days collecting plastic bottles, paper, and other items for recycling. His makeshift home in the ruin of the former cinema is crammed full of discarded furniture, storage units, appliances, and items stored in crates, baskets, bags, and shopping trolleys: fans, televisions, traffic cones, mannequin legs, tennis rackets, signage, gas canisters, and so on. Comprised of cultural detritus, the Ximen-King's dwelling comes to resemble a reconstituted home, in which he and Hsiao-Hu develop a substitute father–daughter relationship.

At night, the space is illuminated by pink light emanating from the street, plus several reclaimed neon signs that have been incorporated into the living space. The appearance of coloured lighting makes no logical sense, but credibility is not the point. What matters is the filmmakers' impulse to present the salvaged objects as aesthetically arranged, as designed for contemplation. An old bicycle, for instance, has apparently been repurposed by the Ximen-King as a storage stand, with items now affixed to it. But when examined in detail, its functionality is questionable. Why, for instance, has a paper coffee cup been attached to a tennis ball, then hung from the handlebars with the aid of a textile bow? Even for a character committed to recycling, this arrangement serves no purpose other than to attract a gaze. The way the material is arranged onscreen recalls the curation of installation art, with the site designed as an experience that requires a guest to enter, explore, and view: both inside the story world (Hsiao-Hu), and outside it (the viewer).

This is a paradoxical space. On the one hand, it may appear to be a mess: a derelict, cluttered, junk-filled courtyard that is apparently excluded from the designer aesthetic that elsewhere pervades the film. Yet this can itself be considered a designer environment, given how urban detritus is presented in terms that suggest its future potential. David Trotter explains that waste matter, unlike mess, 'remains for ever potentially in circulation because circulation is its defining quality' and thus 'however foul it may have become, it still gleams with efficiency'.[41] What we see in the Ximen-King's home is not mess; it is curated waste. The strategically arranged, salvaged objects gleam with efficiency; discarded rubbish is already beginning to take on the qualities associated with designer goods. Some items have potential in themselves, as vintage or retro merchandise. Others may acquire value through upcycling or repurposing. The bottle crates that hang upside-down from the ceiling, with light bulbs fitted in the manner of lanterns, would suit a bar or restaurant designed in a shabby-chic or post-industrial style. The production design captures a process described by theorists of waste, whereby rubbish provides a channel for durable objects to increase in value with time, a change that is rooted not in their intrinsic properties, but in emerging judgements of taste.[42]

The environment primes us to consider the waste generated by design, and the futurity of the objects represented. The emphasis on the potential of creative salvage has a narrative parallel, for the Ximen-King is viewed by others as worthless, owing to his apparent destitution, while Hsiao-Hu lacks a sense of self-worth. In the dilapidated courtyard they develop a relationship that is meaningful and durable, and structurally facilitates the resolution of conflicts. This is character salvage, underscored at the film's cathartic climax, when Hsiao-Hu's old home videos are screened on the site of the ruined cinema, the Ximen-King pedalling on an exercise bike to generate a power supply. Narratively, this facilitates a reconciliation between Hsiao-Hu and her estranged mother (Yang Kuei-Mei). With the cinema screen long since dismantled, the format of the screening recalls that of video art installation. Hsiao-Hu and her mother sit on a sofa watching their videos play on discarded television sets – around sixteen or so monitors, that are stacked on top of one another (Figure 5.7). This recalls the exhibition format of a range of installations, notably works by the pioneering video artist Nam June Paik, such as TV Eyeglasses (1971) and TV Garden (1974–7).

A similar kind of space appears in *Zone Pro Site*, in which Hsiao-Wan (Hsia Yu-Chiao) competes in a cookery contest in Taipei, where she finds legendary

Figure 5.7 TV installation in *The Mad King of Taipei* (Yeh Tien-Lun, 2017).

chef Master Silly Mortal (Wu Nien-Jen) residing in a disused railway tunnel. As the MRT trains rattle past on an adjacent track, Hsiao-Wan approaches the location in the darkness. It is suddenly illuminated by white lighting along the tunnel wall, and coloured lights within the space, revealing living quarters and seating areas, full of miscellaneous furniture and multicoloured recycled and repurposed objects. The Master cooks with a wok, surrounded by illuminated banners and paper umbrellas. Comprised of strategically placed and lit salvaged objects, the tunnel resembles partly an art installation and partly a pop-up designer bar. It effectively functions as the latter, as Master Silly Mortal dishes out food to the local homeless population, who congregate at mealtimes. The walls of the tunnel have been decorated with multicoloured pictures, drawn in the style of indigenous painting. They illustrate folklore relating how, in bygone days, the great catering masters moved between villages carrying only their utensils. This is presented in proto-cinematic form, as the Master guides Hsiao-Wan from right to left, narrating the contents of the pictures, which he illuminates with a torch while soundtracks of the painted scenes are heard. He concludes by wistfully remarking that the traditional values of cookery, where chefs sought only appreciation and affection, are long gone. This myth of the artisan chef, narrated by a socially conscious Master who has forsaken wealth in favour of integrity, is lent a self-reflexive air by the casting of Wu, a key figure of the New Cinema. As with the other green and repurposed spaces discussed in this chapter, the tunnel is shown to be a realm of authenticity and moral improvement, where Hsiao-Wan learns the essential value of her craft.

These installation-like environments whimsically imagine the creative redesign of Taipei's disused sites and infrastructure. Here there are parallels with the preoccupations of Taiwanese urban design more generally, for instance the proliferation of Cultural and Creative Parks, a trend that first took off in Taipei with the opening of sites at Huashan and Songshan. In these parks, former industrial buildings – disused factories, warehouses, and offices – were renovated and repurposed, rather than being demolished. Blending creative, commercial, and heritage agendas, the sites were transformed into trendy designer spaces that house art galleries, exhibitions, boutique shops, and eateries. The Taiwan Design Museum is itself located at the Songshan park, and more generally these environments sit at the intersection of art, design, and urban lifestyles. For example, in 2014, the Urban Regeneration Office sponsored an art installation at Huashan entitled 'Next Play: Green Factory', in which city residents were invited to plant vegetables in portable containers. The event helped consolidate the urban gardening movement in Taipei.[43]

The Huashan Cultural and Creative Park also features as a location in *Love*. Hsiao-Ni displays her artworks there, and in a climactic scene, finally agrees to forgive her unfaithful boyfriend, Kai. The colonial red brick architecture is decorated by the filmmakers using a pink colour scheme, with Hsiao-Ni framed in medium close-up against a fluorescent fuchsia background, while Kai wears a pink shirt. Repurposed through offscreen and onscreen design, Huashan becomes an environment in which desire is set free. A similar aesthetic was previously evident in *L-O-V-E* (2009), a portmanteau feature comprised of four short films set in Taipei, starring teen idols in romantic plots. One of these, *Huashan 24'*, directed by Fang Wen-Shan, is set entirely in the former winery at a point when it was midway through renovation; much of the architecture was still in ruins, overgrown with vegetation and weeds. A map appears prominently in one shot, indicating which zones have been restored and which are yet to be completed. The director tends to focus on the latter areas, presumably aware of their pending redesign and keen to document them. The plot concerns a film crew making a music video, using the dilapidated parts of the site as a backdrop, with tour guide Hsin-Yu (Liu Hsin-Yu) roped into performing. Hsin-Yu experiences *déjà-vu* when walking around Huashan; it is ultimately revealed that she is suffering from amnesia and has forgotten about her previous relationship with the music video director (Lan Cheng-Lung). Material proof is provided in the form of a message the lovers wrote on the reverse of an old roof tile, which lies buried in the rubble, their romance inscribed on the architecture itself.

This dramatisation of memory in a Japanese colonial construction evidently offers allegorical possibilities: letters and post-boxes, plus a cameo by Chie Tanaka, suggest *Cape No. 7*, released a year earlier, was an influence. But what concerns me here is the way that Huashan itself is shown to unleash desire: not just through the remembering of love in ruined structures, but also, crucially, through the renewing of love in redesigned structures. The office in which Hsin-Yu and her colleagues work anticipates several of the designer tendencies that would later become commonplace in filmic depictions of Taipei. Bold colours are noticeable; the interiors have been filled with fluorescent-coloured postcards, signs, and stationery. Recovered historic objects (such as a red British-style telephone box) are scattered around, while other salvaged material has been informally curated on shelf displays. Much is made of Hsin-Yu's interest in collecting old toys, and it emerges that one of these was given to her by the director, prior to the onset of her amnesia, connecting love with recycled objects. *Huashan 24'* draws narrative power from the filmmakers' knowledge that these dilapidated environments will soon be given a new lease of life by designers. Salvaging the past leads to romance in the present, as the characters experience love, in all its futurity.

Epilogue: Undesigning

While the above films imagine the creative redesign of Taipei through the repurposing of its older structures, *Thanatos, Drunk* (Chang Tso-Chi, 2015) serves as a brief counterexample, in that it deliberately avoids the designer connotations of its location. A drama about marginalised characters living in a shabby, liminal tenements, the film was shot at Baozangyan – Treasure Hill – near Gongguan, a former veterans' village hastily constructed in the early nationalist period. Unlike similar developments in Taipei (such as the informal residences razed to make way for the Daan Forest Park), it was saved from demolition following an agreement to transform it into an art district under the auspices of the city government's Department of Cultural Affairs.[44] Yet in *Thanatos, Drunk*, Chang films Baozangyan through a lens of grungy naturalism, completely excising the artisan workshops, cafés, art and design studios, and exhibition spaces that today characterise this corner of the city. This is fundamentally different to the designer aesthetic explored in this chapter, which requires the audience to notice the ways in which Taipei as an environment attracts and proliferates design.

Nonetheless, *Thanatos, Drunk* reminds us that any depiction of the real, authentic, or unadorned is itself an act of design, entailing intent, fashioning, and structuring. The difference is that we are not meant to notice it, something generally true of the films considered in the next chapter, although designer tropes occasionally surface. The climactic theatre performance in *Dear Ex* (Hsu Yu-Ting and Hsu Chih-Yen, 2018) features a collection of household appliances and other domestic junk, colourfully lit, and carefully arranged on stage. This again suggests a broader preoccupation among filmmakers with repurposing as a visual spectacle, recalling the forms of art installation. The onstage set design in *Dear Ex* assists its directors in questioning what is understood by the domestic – in remapping the home, the focus of the next chapter.

NOTES

1. Lin, 'Local and trans-local dynamics of innovation practices', 1420.
2. Juan et al., 'Preparations for developing a world design capital', 3.
3. Hara, *Designing Design*, 24.
4. Bordwell, *Poetics of Cinema*, 17.
5. Ibid., 18.
6. Zhang, 'Taiwan film market', 29.
7. Martin, *Situating Sexualities*, 166.
8. Cao, *The Story of the Stone*.
9. Taylor, 'Design futures', 51.
10. Hsieh and Hung, 'Design Game of City and Love'.
11. Bao, *Queer Comrades*, 47–53. He discusses, for example, Shanghai bars and clubs where Chinese gay men in their twenties and thirties 'proudly command both economic and cultural capital and are active participants in the transnational queer scene' (51).
12. Conley, *Cartographic Cinema*, 14.
13. Karvelyte, 'Shifting meanings in changing contexts', 168.
14. Ibid., 175.

15. Juan et al., 'Preparations for developing a world design capital', 2.
16. Rocamora, *Fashioning the City*, 74–5.
17. Textile and clothing manufacturing were major industrial sectors in Taiwan from the 1970s to the 1990s, but Hsiao-Hu is working well after the point when they went into decline, from the mid-1990s. See Hu and Chen, 'Creative talent drive', 1091.
18. Tweedie, 'Morning in the new metropolis', 120–1.
19. Maple, 'Interview with Yeh Tien-lun'.
20. Similarly in Chinese: 愛, 愛到底, 相愛的七種設計, 52赫茲我愛你.
21. Dung, *Atlas*, 56.
22. Hsieh and Hung, 'Design Game of City and Love'.
23. Dunne and Raby, *Speculative Everything*, 12.
24. Yang, 'Interview with director Chen Hung-I'.
25. Zhang, 'Migrating hearts', 104.
26. Braester, *Painting the City Red*, 189.
27. Jou et al., 'Gentrification and revanchist urbanism in Taipei?', 560–61.
28. Braester, *Painting the City Red*, 210.
29. Martin, *Situating Sexualities*, 167.
30. Harrison, 'Ruin Academy', 309–10.
31. Ibid., 310–11.
32. Weng, 'See a ruin amidst the bustle'.
33. Maple, 'Interview with Yeh Tien-lun'.
34. Hou, 'Governing urban gardens', 1403.
35. Ibid., 1405.
36. Ibid., 1400, 1408.
37. Zhen Zhang has argued that Chang's films have attracted limited scholarly interest because her work did not conform to masculinist, modernist traditions of *auteur* criticism. 'Migrating hearts', 89–90, 107–8.
38. Jou et al., 'Gentrification and revanchist urbanism in Taipei?', 570.
39. Braester, *Painting the City Red*, 192–3.
40. Ibid., 192.
41. Trotter, *Cooking with Mud*, 20.
42. Thompson, *Rubbish Theory*, 1–18, 112–37, and Frow, 'Invidious distinction', 34–6.
43. Hou, 'Governing urban gardens', 1404–5.
44. Braester, *Painting the City Red*, 211–13.

6. HOUSE STYLE

Introduction: Staying Indoors

A map appears in Bon An's film *Sen Sen* (2018), hanging on the dining room wall in the home of the elderly protagonist, Lili (Paw Hee-Ching). It is a county map of Taichung City that serves to reinforce the film's setting – she resides in a suburb of the city – while alluding to character information. The reason Lili has a map displayed so prominently, we can surmise, is that she works as a taxi driver, thus can consult it when taking bookings and planning her routes. It might also serve to underscore the shooting location from a funding perspective, given that *Sen Sen* was made with the involvement of the Taichung Film Development Foundation and the Taichung City Government Information Bureau. However, from a narrative standpoint, this map of Taichung serves another important function: it disappears. Along with all the other contents of Lili's home, the map is cleared away and removed from her home after she dies, leaving a blank wall where it hung previously.

The rearrangement of domestic material is a central concern of this chapter, which investigates the mapping of interior space in a range of post-2008 films that have opted to situate significant portions of their dramas in relatively confined living quarters: flats, apartments, and houses. At stake in films such as *Exit* (Chienn Hsiang, 2014), *Black Sheep* (Bon An, 2016), *Sen Sen* (Bon An, 2018), *More than Blue* (Lin Hsiao-Chien, 2018) and *Dear Ex* (Hsu Yu-Ting and Hsu Chih-Yen, 2018) are commonly accepted notions of what the domestic and the familial entail. Placing issues of gender and sexuality centre stage, all these films feature characters who do not conform to stereotypes of what a conventional family should be: a lone woman experiencing the menopause; a father and son in a toxic relationship; a young boy seeking solace with an elderly woman; two soulmates with a relationship that resists definition; and a teenager who moves in with his deceased father's gay partner.

The decision to stay indoors can sometimes be explained by budgetary limitations impacting on logistics, as is the case with *Black Sheep*, which was made on a shoestring budget of 2 million NTD.[1] Yet filmmakers working with higher budgets have similarly opted to focus on the interior space of the home, as is the case with *More than Blue*. For these films arguably share several thematic tropes and aesthetic preoccupations, despite vast differences in the type and scale of production and the intended audience. *Exit, Black Sheep* and *Sen Sen* were small, independent dramas geared towards festival audiences. *Dear Ex* was an unexpected hit and picked up for distribution through Netflix. *More than Blue* was a commercial production aimed at mainstream audiences and was the highest-grossing domestic film of the year, reaching number 14 at the local box office in 2018.[2] It remains one of the top twenty domestic films of all time, spawned a 2021 TV adaptation, and set a ten-year record for overseas sales.[3] Yet budgetary and box office differences aside, the films are all intimate domestic dramas. Discussing these films from the perspective of cinematic cartography partly entails a consideration of how they seek to situate the domestic in relation to the outside world. But the interior geography of a house or apartment can, in and of itself, be mapped cinematically, and this chapter will look at some ways in which the filmmakers go about this.

Mapping Alternatives: Themes, Strategies, and Domestic Critique

Thongchai Winichakul argues that in constructing nationhood, 'a map anticipated spatial reality, not vice versa', that it was 'a model for, rather than a model of, what it purported to represent'.[4] Counter-mapping challenges hegemonic power, but also adopts its forms to the extent that a counter-mapper similarly seeks to propose a desired future. There is something of that aesthetic at work in the films considered here, in which the filmmakers cinematically map interior geographies. Querying popular idealisations of gender and sexuality, they implicitly propose alternative ways of understanding domesticity. This speculative reimagining of that most ambiguous of territories – the home – might have implications for the construction of nationhood, given the intertwined relationship between concepts of home and nation in Sinophone cultures.[5] Yet while associations between home and nation have animated much critical discussion of Taiwanese films made under martial law and in the 1980s and 1990s – quite rightly given the historical contexts – I would question whether this can be sustained when analysing post-2008 depictions of domestic life. That is not to say that connections between home and national identity cannot be made, but to approach the films in these terms from the outset risks oversimplification. There is also a more general question regarding the way post-2008 depictions of the home in Taiwanese cinema are understood as making a political intervention, and how we avoid effect being confused with intention.

The films discussed in this chapter are not, after all, activist films. They do not openly advocate for a political cause or a particular policy, but to the extent that their protagonists are all marginalised in some way, they are driven by a common strategy: a desire to legitimise alternative understandings of domesticity, to accommodate people whose experience does not match idealised conceptions of family life. Sometimes this is undertaken tacitly, by diagnosing the inadequate conditions of the present. In *Exit*, for example, Ling (Chen Shiang-Chyi) experiences early-onset menopause in addition to other pressures. She is divorced and lives alone in her apartment in Kaohsiung, working as a seamstress for a small clothing manufacturer, undertaking repetitive, tiring work that she is forced to take home. Her elderly mother-in-law is terminally ill in hospital and Ling is left with the responsibility of visiting her. Ling's daughter rarely sees her. Her exhausting routine is thankless enough, but made worse by the onset of menopausal symptoms including dizziness, cold sweats, and feeling overheated. Ling spends most of her time in her apartment, suffering from deteriorating mental health.

Other films query typical formulations of what a family should be, such as *Black Sheep* and *Sen Sen*, both directed by Bon An. *Black Sheep* examines the relationship between Lu Ming (Han Chang) and his teenage son Chi-Ping (Pan Chin-Yu), who are forced to live together in the same small apartment in New Taipei City. Divorced by his wife, Lu Ming lives on the brink of destitution: he struggles to make money, is pursued for debts, cannot hold down a job, and his apartment utilities are cut off. These pressures lead him to drink heavily and become aggressive, while Chi-Ping, who has recently returned from a spell in juvenile detention, is tempted to follow his best friend into a life of petty crime. *Sen Sen* is about the elderly Lili, who lives alone in Taichung. Her daughter Yi-An (Yen Yi-Wen) lives in Taipei and is unable to visit frequently; however the sprightly Lili maintains a busy lifestyle by working as a taxi driver, attending dance classes, and hosting a popular webcast. She is terminally ill with Stage 4 lung cancer, and her life-affirming webcast attracts the attention of Yu-Sheng (Wu Chih-Hsuan), a boy whose brother died recently in a car accident. The pair develop a close friendship, each facing death in their own way. The two films offer divergent portrayals of family and domestic life. *Black Sheep* dissects a relationship between a father and his biological son, and finds it barely fit for purpose, while *Sen Sen* explores a relationship between two strangers, who develop a friendship so close that it comes to resemble the familial ideal.

Dear Ex relates the conflict between the two partners of a middle-aged man who has recently died of cancer. His wife, Liu San-Lien (Hsieh Ying-Hsuan), is shocked to discover that his life insurance policy cuts out his son, Cheng-Hsi (Huang Sheng-Chiu), and instead names his male lover Chieh (Chiu Tse) as the beneficiary. San-Lien feels that her son deserves the payout and vows to reclaim the money. Yet as the story unfolds, it emerges that her husband Sung Cheng-Yuan (Chu Shan) was in a relationship with Chieh long before he met his wife, calling into question who has the moral entitlement, a dilemma captured by the film's Chinese title *Who fell in love with him first?* Things become more complicated when Cheng-Hsi, sick of bickering with his mother, moves into Chieh's apartment, thereby provoking further conflict between the warring exes. A brief consideration of the film's reception allows us to consider some broader questions regarding how we conceive (or indeed whether we conceive) of filmmakers having a political agenda.

Dear Ex achieved widespread acclaim in the context of nationwide debates over the legalisation of same-sex marriage in Taiwan. In May 2017, it was ruled that gay and lesbian couples had the constitutional right to marry, and same-sex marriage was ultimately legalised in May 2019. In the interim, however, there was a divisive public debate on the issue that encompassed broader discussion about the place of LGBT rights in Taiwanese society more generally. This culminated in a referendum that also asked voters whether LGBT issues should be taught in school sex education classes; both this, and the recognition of same-sex marriage in the civil code were rejected. Existing marriage laws were therefore left intact, and the government instead passed a separate law for same-sex couples. *Dear Ex* was released at a propitious moment, on 2 November 2018, three weeks before the referendum was held on 24 November. A drama about the entitlements of a deceased gay man's partner, with a child at the centre of the narrative, *Dear Ex* resonated strongly in the political context.

When considered in composite, the strategies deployed by such films could, at a macro level, be conceived in terms of soft power as understood by Song Hwee Lim in his account of Taiwan cinema.[6] Taiwanese films about LGBT characters proliferated in the years after 2008; more recent examples include *Alifu, the Prince/ss* (Wang Yu-Lin, 2017), *Dear Tenant* (Cheng Yu-Chieh, 2020), and *Your Name Engraved Herein* (Liu Kuang-Hui, 2020). Often involving themes of family and domesticity, these films can be understood in terms of Taiwan asserting its liberal credentials internationally, distinguishing itself from the social conservatism that is alleged to predominate elsewhere in East Asia. At the level of funding, this may well be a consideration for filmmakers. The implied social liberalism is of course contentious; after all, two-thirds of Taiwanese voters rejected, rather than endorsed, the proposed changes to the civil code and sex education.[7] However, given this context, it is not hyperbolical to suggest that a film like *Dear Ex* certainly has the capacity to challenge much of the population's assumptions regarding what should, or should not, constitute domestic life.

Yet the relationship between intention and reception is rarely straightforward. While not initially marketed as an LGBT film, unfolding political events led to a change in promotional strategy, as co-director Hsu Yu-Ting explains:

> With the gay marriage march and protest and related events unfolding, we did make two promotional videos for LGBT communities. One of them had more of a comedy style, and one was very touching. The touching one went viral and was shared by hundreds of thousands; we were really surprised by the impact. We uploaded it the night before the march. It reached many people, and was shared amongst mothers of gay people, or families with gay children.[8]

Events such as this march helped make the case for marriage equality, which had already been advanced significantly by diverse social movements having formed alliances during the years of the Ma Ying-Jeou presidency.[9] The *Dear Ex* videos contributed to this cause. However, the irony is that the film was never intended as an intervention in the same-sex marriage debate. 'It was a coincidence', Hsu remarks, noting that the script, by Lu Shih-Yuan and redrafted by Hsu, was written a few years earlier.[10] While cinematic mappings of the home can be seen as strategic in terms of the filmmaker's desire to promote a particular vision of domesticity, *Dear Ex* reminds us that it can be far more difficult to conceive of this as strategy in the harder political sense. Nonetheless, the film's topicality helped ensure its success; *Dear Ex* won major awards, propelled its lead actors Chiu and Hsieh to film stardom, and made around 65 million NTD at the domestic box office, three times the initial forecast.[11]

By far the most commercially successful film under consideration, however, is *More than Blue*. A remake of the 2009 South Korean film of the same name, it is a melodrama about soulmates Chang Che-Kai (Liu Yi-Hao), known as K, and Sung Yuan-Yuan (Chen Yi-Han), known as Cream, who have lived together since high school. But when K is diagnosed with terminal leukaemia, he decides to conceal this from Cream, and resolves to ensure her future happiness by setting her up with dentist Yu-Hsien (Chang Shu-Hao). The film's central relationship resists conventional definition; Cream says that K is like a mother, father, and brother rolled into one, a family member who is also a lover. While they have lived together for ten years and sleep in the same bed, they have never had sex (though they confess to having kissed and hugged). On the one hand, the lack of sexual consummation aligns the film with the chaste ideals of teen melodrama, with ambiguities depicted merely as an extended state of confusion before the inevitable shift to wedlock. But while the script increasingly looks in that direction, in truth marriage is an uneasy fit. *More than Blue* raises challenging questions about why relationships tend always to require definition. Heteronormativity relies on cultural prescriptions of domestic and conjugal life to which K and Cream do not adhere. In their shared household routine, the pair are happy, and until events force things, they feel no need to define what their relationship is, or is not.

Unhealthy Realism? Performance and the Ailing Home

In alleging that there is something wrong with popular idealisations of domestic life, all the films considered here demonstrate a preoccupation with the home as an unhealthy, ailing space. In narrative terms, what incites change within the domestic sphere is the onset of health problems (experienced either by the protagonist, or someone close to them), while all these films have hospitals as a second setting. In *Exit*, Ling is fatigued by menopausal symptoms, while witnessing her mother-in-law slowly dying and comforting a man with burns injuries. In *Sen Sen*, Lili is hospitalised with cancer, which ultimately takes her life; the same is true of the father in *Dear Ex*. In *More than Blue*, K is faced with a terminal leukaemia diagnosis. The alcoholic Lu Ming in *Black Sheep* ends up in an accident and emergency ward following his suicide attempt. As this last example suggests, mental health is as much a concern in these films as physical conditions. It is evident that all the protagonists in these films are suffering from worsening conditions including depression, stress, and anxiety. This is explained by grief (*Dear Ex*, *Sen Sen*, *More than Blue*) or despondency over cumulative psychological pressures (*Black Sheep*, *Exit*), with diverse symptoms, although obsessive–compulsive disorder is a common trope.

Often, physical ailments or disease ironically provide the catalyst for an improvement in the mental health of the main character, resulting in narrative closure and resolution. Thus in certain respects, these films rework a Taiwanese tradition of recuperative family melodrama. The healthy realist films of the 1960s and 1970s, for instance, extolled traditional Confucian values and family enterprise, idealised the rural as a space of social harmony, and emphasised the importance of labour and perseverance in contributing to national progress.[12] At first sight, healthy realism would not seem to have much in common with the films considered here; however Meng-Hsin C. Horng has argued that directors such as Pai Ching-Jui and Lee Hsing responded to the gradual dissolution of the KMT's ideological claims 'by projecting the home as a tenuous space which must be dismantled, relocated, and otherwise recuperated'.[13] On the one hand, the films examined here tackle issues with distinct contemporary relevance in Taiwan, pinpointing them as unique to the post-2008 context. Yet the interest in recuperation remains. The home is shown to require reconfiguration in the light of changing cultural attitudes towards care for the elderly in the context of an ageing population, same-sex partnerships, toxic masculinity, cohabiting millennials, and the experience of the menopause.

However, recuperation is as much a form as a theme. Many of the narrative characteristics of post-2008 Taiwanese cinema – classical structure, clear plot points, the building of tension and suspense, and the resolution of conflict and crisis – have much in common with earlier popular modes of filmmaking, such as healthy realism and the contemporaneous Qiong Yao melodramas. Taiwan New Cinema and its second wave marked a departure from these modes, but also had an influence. When discussing films shot predominantly in domestic interiors, it is difficult not to think of Tsai Ming-Liang, whose earlier films are dominated by 'a variety of relatively nondescript and interchangeable apartments', as James Tweedie puts it.[14] Tsai's legacy looms large in some of the films considered in this chapter. Numerous critics have discussed the ways he reworks the family ethical drama or melodrama, through a focus on reconfiguring the *jia* (house, family) both materially and figuratively – something we also see at work in these recent films.[15] Yet there are important differences, structurally and stylistically. Tsai's films do not adopt the forms of classical narrative, and rarely offer resolution to their domestic dilemmas; when they do, this generally occurs in a shocking or subversive manner.[16]

By contrast, the films considered here, even when they have a sad ending, continue to hold out hope for the recuperation of the home, through the resolution of narrative conflict and character redemption. Lin Hsiao-Chien, the director of *More than Blue*, has been dubbed 'a *liaoyu* director'; the word derives from Japanese pop culture and literally means to be cured or healed, but here refers to a story that uplifts the audience, not in the sense of being feelgood, but by having therapeutic qualities.[17] Intended effects of this kind, achieved through narrative construction, have something in common with pre-New Cinema traditions of popular filmmaking. With a little irony, Emilie Yueh-Yu Yeh and Darrell William Davis refer to Pai as an 'unhealthy realist', given his propensity for social critique and ambiguous ideological commitments.[18] But perhaps unhealthy realism is not a bad way to categorise this recent trend of otherwise diverse films that share a preoccupation with sickness and disease as symptoms of figurative trouble within the home. In suggesting this, I am not merely acknowledging, but actively foregrounding, the ways in which melodrama has been intrinsic to realist practices across Sinophone cinema, as Chris Berry, Mary Farquhar, and others have argued.[19] Melodramatic styles (theatricality, exaggeration, sentimentality) are prominent in these films, while in structural terms, all adopt narratives of victimhood, a defining feature of the melodramatic mode.[20] Lin has defended melodrama as a form, arguing for its importance as a means of communicating with a mass audience.[21]

Crucially, however, these films are very much *about* performance, with the melodramatic mode enacted structurally and stylistically to varying degrees, but also dramatised as a theme. Take the example of *Dear Ex*. Upon discovering that she has been deceived her whole life, San-Lien begins to question, 'was all of it a lie?'. Her fear is less about performativity in the sense defined by Judith Butler, as a series of acts that reinforce dominant social norms, outside of the individual's control.[22] San-Lien seems instead more concerned with performance, suspicious that her husband deliberately and consciously faked it. The theatre is both a site and the subject matter of *Dear Ex*, which in exploring questions of gender and sexuality looks at performativity in the context of theatrical role-playing. Chieh is a professional actor, but outside the theatre he stumbles around in his pyjamas, drunk or stoned, not caring what people think; this helps distinguish his behaviour from the banal, socially conditioned performativity of San-Lien. Yet she too comes to engage in conscious theatricality. After her husband finally reveals his secret, her immediate instinct is to maintain the public deception: 'We can still be the happy family people envy', she tells him. But Sung has grown weary of acting out a role and has resolved to leave, retorting: 'It's not up to others to define a happy family'.

Crucially, these revelations occur in flashback, while the film's main events occur after the point at which San-Lien's family life has already been upended. This is also true of the other films considered here, which commence post-crisis, when norms of family and gender have already proven inadequate to the task of sustaining domestic life. In other words, the filmmakers dramatise what happens after the mask slips – after performativity has been shown to fail. Perhaps for this reason, the films place significant emphasis on performance in the more conventional sense: on people acting out a role, putting on a show, engaging in deception, or being overtly theatrical. The films sit on a broad spectrum in this respect. *Dear Ex* literally depicts actors in a theatre, while *Black Sheep* retains perhaps the greatest interest in performativity, ruthlessly chronicling a father and son's failure to adhere to masculine ideals, with theatrically inflected performance occurring instead at the level of practice.

Journeys in a Material World

The construction of domestic atmosphere is important in these films. Graig Uhlin writes that atmosphere entails 'both the mood of an artistic production and the experience of an environment, whether natural or built', and discusses how the two are connected in films about environmental crisis.[23] The films considered here are not works of eco-cinema, but they certainly dramatise crisis within the environment that is the home. Writing from the perspective of design studies, Lois Weinthal observes that the meteorological, planetary use of the term is rooted in science, measurement, and objectivity, whereas designers tend to frame discussions of interior atmosphere subjectively and emotively.[24] She argues conversely that atmosphere in design practice can, and should, be measured, and that emotion should be a post-design reflection rather than a starting point.[25] On the critical side, this arguably finds a parallel in the constructivist methods of film poetics. The elements of interior design that are vital to the construction of atmosphere – curtains, doors, and light fixtures – are not simply components of a backdrop in these films, but objects with which the characters interact.[26] This is narrative infrastructure, and it is very prominent in all of these films, which dramatise journeys that are, in both senses of the word, interior: characters who move physically within the home, but who also undertake affective travel.

The films considered here place great emphasis on the sheer materiality of the home: its shell, fixtures, and fittings; the furniture and objects it contains. This tangible, physical stuff of the home – what I will refer to as 'domestic material' – is sometimes shown to entrap the characters. This is certainly the case in *Exit*, which marked Chienn's debut as a feature director; he had previously worked as a Director of Photography on films including *Blue Gate Crossing* (Yee Chih-Yen, 2002), *20:30:40* (Sylvia Chang, 2004), and *Zone Pro Site* (Chen Yu-Hsun, 2013).[27] He also shot *Exit* and frequently films Ling in wider shots, in which she is situated in the background planes of the image, with furniture, shelves, and other objects in the foreground. Ling is thereby visually enclosed, her material significance within the composition depreciated. On the roof and stairwell of the apartment block, features such as metal bars, grating, and wire mesh further emphasise the theme of imprisonment. Shots of the architecture extend for a significant amount of time after the character has departed the frame, underscoring the endurance and permanence of these structures, their indifference to fleeting human appearance.

Exit is structured as a showcase for the performance of Chen, a regular in Tsai's films, and the influence of the *auteur* seems to percolate the film, even if Chienn considers the films of Yee and Wu Nien-Jen to be better reference points.[28] The story focuses on the psychological deterioration of a character within a confined domestic setting, while locked-off, unedited takes of extended duration are occasionally used. But *Exit* most strongly recalls Tsai's work in the connections it makes between material and psychological dissolution. If, in the context of the film's medical themes, good health connotes integrity, functionality, and wholeness, then Ling's apartment is an unhealthy space. Filmed as one object among many, Ling is overwhelmed by architecture, fixtures, and fittings that torment her psychologically. In one scene, the corner of some wallpaper comes loose as a result of damp, and she sellotapes it back in place, an action she later repeats. The material shortcomings of the apartment come to figuratively emblematise Ling's more general dissatisfaction, her attempts to fix the recalcitrant wallpaper an obsessive-compulsive displacement activity.

The wall itself is also an annoyance; through the thin walls, Ling overhears the sound of a neighbour having sex, a reminder of her own frustrations.

The tension between the character and her domestic infrastructure reaches its climax in the film's bold final scene, a locked-off wide shot of four minutes and thirty seconds in duration, in which Ling struggles to exit her apartment via the broken front door (Figure 6.1). The lock has been temperamental throughout the film, but at this point, the door will not budge. This subject matter again recalls that of Tsai, whom Fran Martin argues has 'an obsession with doors', as well as gates, windows, and other framing thresholds.[29] In the last scene of *Exit*, Ling repeatedly tries to open the door. Failing, she slumps to the floor and cries, before summoning a final burst of energy, pounding the door with her fists, and finally managing to release it. The scene offers an unedited showcase for Chen's physical performance, and was not in the original script but derived from the actor herself. Chen recalled having accidentally become locked in her own home, evidently alive to the allegorical possibilities of this predicament:

> I think at some time in your life, there is always a door that you need to break down in order to find your own way. Six months before we started shooting, I discussed this with director Chienn, and he agreed this was something we should put in the film. I think it is such a powerful scene to see a woman locked in a house and then break through the door.[30]

Chienn explains that this was one of the last shots they filmed, as both he and Chen understood its importance: 'she could only have one take to achieve the

Figure 6.1 Breaking down the door in *Exit* (Chienn Hsiang, 2014).

maximum level of engagement in her performance. I did consider composing this scene using several shots but it would not have been as powerful as one long shot.'[31] Ling's battle with the door epitomises her other struggles (relating to menopause, her daughter, her work), to the extent that the film ends before any of these can be settled. What is significant, from a feminist perspective, is that Ling has taken on her apartment, had a fight with it, and won. The film's other crises do not need resolving, because in this scene she has already demonstrated her capacity to overcome the challenges that life might throw her way. This might be understood as cathartic, for the character as much as the viewer, acknowledging the contested understandings of Aristotle's use of the term in *Poetics*.[32] Here, it seems apt to discuss Ling's climactic outpouring of emotion as cathartic *for her*, given that the Greek term literally referred to the evacuation of fluid through menstruation, the cessation of which is a subject that *Exit* dramatises. This is catharsis reimagined as a woman's rite-of-passage through menopause; the door is both a material opening and a threshold on an affective journey.

Seeking to question the dichotomy that identifies home with the female subject and voyage with the male, Giuliana Bruno challenges the idea that travel alone implies mobility: 'At home, one may indeed travel. Home itself is made up of layers of passages that are voyages of habitation.'[33] She elaborates her notion of the 'dwelling-voyage', a transformative emotional journey that can occur within the house which, like film, is a site of affective mobility:

> The house, with its material boundaries, is not a stationary tectonics. It is not a still architectural container but a site of mobile inhabitations. The house embraces the mobility of lived space. Like film, it is the site of an *emotion* and generates stories of dwelling.[34]

The films considered here depict mobile inhabitations; routes taken around the material geography of the home that recur, and thereby acquire the quality of routine. In *More than Blue*, we are shown the various locations within K and Cream's home that they frequent each day. There is the mattress in the bedroom, where they sleep; the counter in the kitchen, where they eat; the porch, where they enter and exit the interior. Within the home, Yi-Fu Tuan argues that pieces of furniture, for example,

> are points along a complex path of movement that is followed day after day. These points are places, centers for organizing worlds. As a result of habitual use the path itself acquires a density of meaning and a stability that are characteristic traits of place. The path and the pauses along it together constitute a larger place – the home.[35]

More than Blue embraces the mobility of lived space, continually revisiting the different places that exist along K and Cream's daily domestic route, thereby establishing their shared routine, the way they organise their world. In affective terms, the viewer grasps the comfort afforded by routine; the sense of stability it provides, something that both characters crave. Narratively, the depiction of habitual cycles reminds us what is at stake, as in the elegiacally beautiful sequence in which K moves around the house doing chores following his terminal cancer diagnosis. He enacts his routine – tidying up, doing the laundry, washing the dishes, sweeping the floor, making the bed – but now with the knowledge that he does not have long to live. The rooms are bathed in light that enters through the windows in chiaroscuro and as backlighting, resulting in misty images. These were intended by Director of Photography Kwan Pun-Leung (a regular cinematographer for Wong Kar-Wai) to lend the sequences a dreamlike quality.[36] Domestic habits that would typically be undertaken in a mindless manner suddenly register as something precious. In becoming aware of his own future absence from the space, K gains a heightened sense of his daily domestic movement.

Tuan proposes that 'local stations' within the home (places like the bedroom, kitchen, and porch) are important not just as places connected by an intricate path, but because they represent 'pauses in movement, markers in routine and circular time'.[37] The sofa is perhaps the most important location in *More than Blue*, and notably more prominent than in the South Korean original. It is a piece of furniture that necessitates a pause in movement, upon which the characters physically rest, and where the characters are located at some of the most transformative moments in their relationship. The sofa is also revisited during an extended flashback sequence as the site of a significant narrative moment that can only be appreciated in retrospect. Early in the film, K arrives home to find Cream sitting on the sofa covered with a blanket; she is upset, apparently following an argument with a client, and he comforts her. The later flashback to this scene, however, occurs after the revelation of the film's central twist, that Cream has known about K's illness all along. We learn that this was, in fact, the day she first found out about it, explaining her forlorn behaviour. The sofa is a shared place of happiness, but also central to the film's tragedy, underscored at the film's climax, when K dies there while sitting next to Cream. A previsualisation by the film's art director Yao Kuo-Chen clearly establishes the sofa as the main focal point of the living room (Figure 6.2a), and furthermore, along with another pre-production rendering of K's bedroom, evidences the planning of the lighting style (Figure 6.2b).

If the geography of the interior can be mapped in and of itself, then the films also dramatise the outside world as imagined from the material and psychological interior. From the confines of her small apartment, Ling in *Exit* fantasises about becoming a tango dancer, released into a world of sensual experience.

Figure 6.2a–b Art design previsualisations of the house interior in *More than Blue* (Lin Hsiao-Chien, 2018). Courtesy of Yao Kuo-Chen.

One abstract sequence portraying an imagined reality shows a woman dancing with her partner, accompanied by an accordion tango soundtrack. While referencing Argentina specifically, more important is the general impression of Ling's desire to escape. Her daily experience is very limited, spatially. Most of her time is spent in the apartment or in the hospital, or briefly in uninspiring locations such as her initial workplace and the bus. Noticeably little of Kaohsiung is depicted in the film, and certainly none of the city's lively central districts – and when Ling does venture out, this results in disappointment. She dresses up to go dancing, feeling rejuvenated, attractive, and empowered, but instead comes across her daughter, Mei-Mei (Wen Chen-Ling), and her boyfriend. Mei-Mei had told her mother that she was working in Taipei, and realising the extent of her daughter's deceit, Ling returns home, dejected. Something similar occurs in *Black Sheep*, in which Chi-Ping is desperate to leave the apartment, but once outside, soon realises that he has nowhere to go. His escape plan – speeding off on a motorbike to commence a life of petty crime – is no better than the status quo.

The outside world may be remembered rather than imagined, as occurs with Lili in *Sen Sen*, who is forced to give up her physically mobile occupation as a taxi driver and to stay at home, her voyages limited to memory. Sometimes, the outside world may be part-remembered, past-fantasised, as by Chieh in *Dear Ex*, whose apartment facilitates a journey into the past, articulated through surreal flashbacks. In one scene, Cheng-Hsi is talking with Chieh in his apartment. A shot from the boy's perspective shows Chieh begin to play his guitar, excluding Cheng-Hsi from the frame. A dreamlike scene then ensues, as Sung appears in what could either be a flashback or Chieh's fantasy. A further possibility is suggested by a shot visualising the outlines of the men in the foreground, heavily out of focus as they kiss, with Cheng-Hsi at the centre of the frame, watching. This is spatially and temporally impossible, given that Sung has already died and Cheng-Hsi never witnessed the pair embracing. A cut to the boy waking up in the morning suggests that it might have been his dream rather than Chieh's, a juvenile speculation on his father's double life.

Either way, the effect is one of transportation; within a confined space, the characters are moved into the past. This theme figures strongly in the film's climax, in which Chieh performs in a play about travel; a vacation trip to Bali. Details of the plot and characters are not provided, nor are they required to understand the thematic point: that Chieh undertakes an affective itinerary as he performs. The actors repeatedly sing musical lyrics about someone longing for the embrace of the 'magical' Bali. The Indonesian destination is here insignificant in itself, but registers as an exoticised dreamscape that evokes feelings of yearning and love. The play and the song accentuate the film's understanding of the theatrical as that which is transporting.

Domestic Stages: Theatricality at Home

In *Dear Ex*, Chieh's theatre production is meaningful to him because it facilitates affective travel, and more generally in these films, the characters' predilection for performance is framed in terms of a response to feelings of entrapment. This is less about a desire to lose oneself in fantasy, and more about a yearning for change. The characters want to move forward emotionally, and performance facilitates this; in one sense, it is therapeutic, reflecting the preoccupation with health issues. In *Exit*, the hospital ward has curtains that divide the beds, which Ling is constantly opening and closing, recalling the structural forms of the theatrical stage. The scenes set in the hospital focus on the care given by Ling to Mr Chang (Tung Ming-Hsiang), an injured patient emerging from a coma. When Ling decides to soothe Chang's pain by wiping him with a damp cloth, she closes the curtain for privacy. But later, when the patches are removed from his eyes, she hides behind the curtain to avoid his gaze. Ling is afraid of the man seeing her for the first time, which in the context of the film's thematic concern with menopause, can be understood as a fear of being rejected. The tactile intensity of the encounters between Ling and Chang rely on her knowing that she is unseen by him; once his capacity for sight returns, she hides behind the curtain.

In their final encounter, Ling wears a surgical face mask – unnecessarily, given that she has not previously worn one, and nothing has changed that would now require her to do so. She chooses to wear it because she is again seeking to conceal her appearance from Chang. As he slowly opens his eyes for the first time, Ling turns away, removes the mask, then places it over his eyes, an action that definitively prevents him from seeing what she looks like. The hospital, presented as a space of theatricality and disguise, contrasts with the apartment, in which Ling is unseen by others. But this is not to imply that she can consequently 'be herself', for within the apartment, she begins to perform – for herself. Developing a fascination with tango, Ling seeks to transport herself imaginatively, from within the confines of her apartment. She uses her sewing machine to make a dress, and applies bright red lipstick and rouge, before examining herself in the mirror. She fantasises about the woman she wants to be, and begins to act out the part.

Role play is depicted as a response to loneliness. At home, Ling dreams about being an object of desire, but once outside it, she cannot face the gaze of the stranger to whom she is attracted. The other protagonists similarly perform in order to connect with people, to be seen by others, yet are paradoxically committed to concealment. In *Sen Sen*, Lili attains minor fame as a webcast personality, but hides the severity of her illness from her fans. In *Dear Ex*, Chieh is utterly bereft following the death of his lover, but publicly masks his despair. The film draws direct parallels between the home and the theatre, an emphasis that partly derives from Hsu Yu-Ting's own interests and background. Known as a TV screenwriter and producer, she started her career working in theatre, and was mentored by the noted playwright and director, Lee Kuo-Hsiu.[38] The play *Happy Holiday* that Chieh rehearses is, in fact, a real-life work originally written and directed by Hsu herself. Hsieh was cast because the director was a fan of her stage performances, and it was also Hsu's decision to make Chieh a theatre actor; in Lu's original script, he was solely a director.[39]

Chieh's flat is virtually an extension of the theatre. In one scene, he takes Cheng-Hsi's homework and reads aloud from it, as if interpreting a script, making grand gestures, and using the text as a prompt for a dramatic monologue.

If the film portrays the movement of the theatrical into the domestic sphere, then this is a two-way process, emblematised by San-Lien's grand entrance into one of Chieh's rehearsals. She strides up the aisle, the centre of attention as she yells accusations: 'You gay asshole who stole my husband, listen carefully!' Realism is not the objective here; instead the film consciously constructs a space for melodramatic performance. Another scene in a temple has San-Lien talking to a god at the altar, almost directly to camera in an unbroken shot, enabling what resembles a stage soliloquy. Post-production flourishes accentuate our sense of the theatrical; after the horrific scene in which San-Lien discovers Chieh with his leg broken at ninety degrees by thugs working for loan sharks, there is an abrupt cut. Chieh now peers through long curtains, as if on stage, to underscore the dramatic showiness of the moment that has just transpired. We soon realise, however, that this is a flashback to the hospital in which Sung lies resting, his bed curtained off, recalling the ward-theatre metaphor from *Exit*.

The editing of *Dear Ex* warrants further consideration, given that the film was heavily reconstituted in post-production and was very nearly a disaster. The test audience version, edited according to the script, was 'awful', according to Hsu, and instantly rejected by five distributors – so she resolved to re-edit the film before the planned release date.[40] The re-edit was well-regarded in the industry, with the editor Lei Chen-Ching winning a Golden Horse for her efforts. The changes were substantial: the structure of the film was overhauled; the narrative perspective was shifted to the boy, whose voiceover was added; hand-drawn animations were sometimes superimposed over the footage; and many scenes were cut. These changes often have the effect of underscoring the thematic preoccupation with performance, and a focal point for this was the character of San-Lien, whom test audiences had found annoying:

> I felt this was actually a very serious problem – everyone felt the character was authentic, but truly hated her too. This was not my intention at all. What I'd been hoping was that the audience would see her pain. This screening signalled to me that there was some problem with the editing, which resulted in this kind of perception.[41]

The issue was not Hsieh's performance, but its contextualisation. Hsu felt it was problematic to have three points of view imposed on the viewer simultaneously, with nobody to lead them into the story, therefore 'wanted to find a main narrator for the story, and I instinctively thought of Cheng-Hsi'.[42] The addition of the boy's voiceover prompts the audience to view San-Lien from a tragicomic angle, as the son points out his mother's seemingly endless capacity for self-pity and melodrama.

An early scene, in which the voiceover helps reconfigure the home as a more performative space, demonstrates how this plays out in practice. San-Lien sits at the dinner table with Cheng-Hsi, complaining about his grades and threatening to speak to his teacher. Throughout this, the boy's thoughts are interspersed in voiceover. 'It's Hollywood's loss that she didn't become an actress', he remarks sarcastically, and after he storms out of the room in anger, he counts down to the moment when she will, as if on cue, begin shedding tears. 'She should have gone to Hollywood', he confirms acidly. Hsieh's performance is recontextualised, as the viewer is guided to view San-Lien's behaviour as amusing rather than irritating; this is achieved by putting emphasis on the character's performative qualities. The post-production decisions are not imposed inorganically on the material, but complement it: once her son is out of sight, San-Lien abruptly stops crying, suggesting that her tears were indeed a deliberate ploy to generate his sympathy. Once this tone is established, there is less need for the voiceover, which tails off almost entirely in the film's second half.

Dear Ex demonstrates a commitment to performance as an ongoing process. San-Lien queries how Chieh will be able to perform on opening night with a broken leg, but what matters is that he keeps going. The quality of Chieh's acting is really of no consequence, as he clumsily knocks things over with his wheelchair and causes accidents onstage. What matters is seeing the performance through, which will help him come to terms with his grief, through a moment of catharsis. Although the onscreen audience responds unenthusiastically, ironically it is San-Lien who grasps the significance of Chieh's actions, realising that the performance marks one hundred days since her husband died, which in Buddhist tradition connotes the end of the mourning period. San-Lien understands that this ill-advised performance is Chieh's way of saying goodbye.

Performance is here depicted as a response to death, as a grieving process in search of catharsis. It may be Cheng-Hsi who is in therapy, but ultimately, he is in least need of it: rather it is Chieh and San-Lien who are the focal points of what is ultimately a therapeutic narrative. This connection between performance and death is dramatised in all the other films considered here. In *More than Blue*, for example, K and Cream work for a record label, thus deal professionally with musicians every day, but the narrative focuses on a performance of another kind: K's decision not to inform Cream about his terminal cancer diagnosis. Instead, he pretends that he is fine, and that he is happy for her to start dating somebody else. Looking to protect Cream, K even schemes to set her up with another man, in order that she will not dwell on his passing when it comes. His pretence seems incomprehensive and even unreasonable to other characters, who tell him that Cream is stronger than he thinks. But in a later twist, it emerges that she knew about his illness all along, thus has herself been acting out a role. And when K dies, Cream kills herself. In the film's fatalistic universe, the melodramatic tragedy is that K's apparently misguided instincts were right: he knew her best.

HAPTIC GEOGRAPHIES: ATMOSPHERE AND MATERIAL TRACES

In *Sen Sen*, Lili acts out a persona in her uplifting webcast recordings, as she comes to terms with her mortality. More broadly, all these films dramatise ways in which digital technology has the capacity to reshape domestic experience. Mobile phones are omnipresent, altering the characters' perspectives on their interior environments by drawing their attention outwards, and always with narrative ends in mind: they are plot devices. Other kinds of technology, however, are cinematically depicted in a manner that is less concerned with plot, than with providing context for it through the construction of domestic atmosphere. Ben Highmore argues that 'mundane technologies' such as central heating should be scrutinised, alongside social change, when accounting for how people exist in postwar interiors.[43] This can be discussed in the context of fictional interiors; mundane technologies such as air-conditioning units, portable heaters, and electric fans help us understand how these characters narratively occupy their homes. Temperature, for example, is an important component of atmosphere, if understood in the meteorological sense of the term, and is evoked in all these films. Hsu remarks that she wanted the vivid, orange hues of *Dear Ex* to capture the experience of Taipei in summer: 'Under this July sun, everything is steaming, all the colours become vivid, and everyone feels sticky. This is just like the relationship between our inhabitants in Taipei – their passion can sometimes get clammy.'[44] The representation of atmospheric conditions is regularly facilitated by the depiction of heating and cooling technologies. In the chilly house in *Sen Sen*, a portable heater keeps Lili warm; in the stuffy apartment in *Exit*, Ling swelters in baking hot temperatures and relieves herself with an electric fan. In both cases, the evocation of temperature contributes to the depiction of domestic atmosphere, but is also intended to resonate thematically, as with Ling's overheating due to her experience of the menopause.

Heat is experienced through the sensitivity of the skin and body, and the visual depiction of this often lends the storytelling in these films a strongly haptic quality. In one scene in *Exit*, Ling removes her face mask, then sensually rubs its sticky moisture over her arms and chest. This tactile activity brings relief, given that she has hitherto been overheated and uncomfortable; moreover she becomes sexually aroused by the sensation of being lubricated. A similar impression is evoked in several scenes set in the hospital. Ling uses a damp cloth to wipe Chang's face and neck, trying to alleviate his pain, but later, in an overtly sexualised scene, she unbuttons his gown and rubs the cloth over his bare chest. A similar emphasis on sensual experience drives *Sen Sen*, and is closely connected with the film's portrayal of mourning. Sheng handles his brother's clothes with considerable tactility, carefully brushing and stroking them, even wearing them, to experience himself the sensations his brother would have felt against his body. Elsewhere, the sense of smell is strikingly evoked when Yi-An finds her mother's belt-bag and presses it tight against her face, deeply inhaling its scent.

More broadly, the narrative of *Sen Sen* is structured in terms of the haptic experience of interior geography. The film is bookended by two sequences showing Lili's house being emptied of its contents following her death. At the film's opening, Yi-An finishes packing up household objects into cardboard boxes while an estate agent values the property; at the end of the film, she invites Sheng into the empty home. These two sequences that chronologically occur after Lili's death are designed to contrast dynamically with the scenes set during her lifetime. For instance, in the opening section, Yi-An packs a portable heater into a cardboard box. This appears to be an ordinary piece of household technology, of no particular interest. Yet it appears repeatedly throughout the film. In a wide shot that lasts one minute twenty seconds, Lili sits eating at a table, facing away from the camera. The table is illuminated from above, but the foreground is gloomy. The calm stasis of the visualisation is undercut only by the consistent movement and whirring sound of the heater, which glows red and rotates on the floor in the bottom-left of the shot. Elsewhere, we observe Lili moving the heater between different rooms, in order to keep warm. An ordinary household object cumulatively acquires affective value and becomes associated with the character, her daily routine and the sensations she feels.

When Sheng first enters Lili's abode, he slowly looks around the lounge, at the plentiful ornaments and pictures, all of which stamp her personality onto the space, especially given that much of the bric-a-brac is highly idiosyncratic. The environment is shaped by Lili, a person in whom Sheng finds comfort and refuge. For this reason, when the boy visits the house at the end of the film, and discovers it devoid of contents, stripped of furniture and objects, the effect is devastating. As Tuan remarks, 'we think of the house as home and place, but enchanted images of the past are evoked not so much by the entire building, which can only be seen, as by its components and furnishings, which can be touched and smelled as well'.[45] Director Bon An discusses this in terms of how affective traces reside in material structures, citing the influence of Tsai and Michael Haneke:

> I think leaving a trace is inevitable if you have stayed in one place. That's why I feel sometimes the space itself can tell stories. This is how I feel Haneke seems to reflect on something ... It's all because the environment has told part of the story, and he doesn't need to make that much effort to elaborate that stuff. I think that a minimalist structure, in part, has conveyed some of it. For instance Tsai Ming-Liang also did this on *The River*.[46]

In the final scene, Sheng mourns Lili by trying to recall how her home used to look, slowly examining the space – visually *handling* it, in the sense of haptic theory.[47] The camera adopts his point of view as he scans the blank walls where pictures and the map of Taichung previously hung, his eyes following the route of the pipes and wires. But the infrastructure is all that remains.

Similar dynamics are at play in *More than Blue*, but while Sheng reflects on death, K anticipates it. The character is first introduced as a teenager in his family home, surrounded by cardboard boxes; his father has died and the contents of the house have been packed up. The house in which he and Cream live was inherited from his parents, and is cluttered with old objects, notably piles of records, CDs, and DVDs. The film's art director intended this to show the way the couple's regrets were accumulated; relics of their shared memories piled up, leading to love.[48] Years later, as he faces the prospect of his own mortality, K's attention again turns to the material items he will leave behind. Photographer Cindy (Chen Ting-Ni) asks if he will donate his belongings to her, as part of a gallery exhibit, but he refuses, explaining that everything he owns will go to Cream. 'You see the paradox here?' the exasperated Cindy retorts. 'If you want her to forget you, then you should leave her nothing.' K's intention to bequeath his material possessions to Cream connotes that deep down, despite what he says, he cannot bear the thought of his soulmate forgetting him after his death. Later, Cindy confronts him more forcefully, 'Do you want things to be like this? Leaving no trace, and just gone from the world?'

The final scene of *Sen Sen* gains affective power precisely because the last traces of Lili are in the process of being removed from her home. The film ultimately suggests that material environments are inadequate to the task of memorialising, because they will inevitably transform and come to bear the mark of others instead. An suggests that images offer a more reliable means of remembering, something that Lili seems to intuit before she dies; her webcast is a conscious attempt to preserve her memory for those she leaves behind. Nonetheless, the emptying of the home is made more difficult for Yi-An by the estate agent, who chatters away in the background, taking photos and referring to the space in abstract economic terms. The condition of the house is quite good, he tells her, and it will be easy to sell after a light brush-up; his clients like old houses, especially young people who might want to renovate one and perhaps open a coffee shop. Lili's house is destined for renovation – perhaps even a designer makeover – and with it will disappear her last material traces.

Cleaning: Mobile Inhabitations and Narrative Progress

The title *Sen Sen* derives from *sheng sheng bu xi*, which can loosely be translated as 'circle of life', but which more precisely connotes an endless cycle of change – birth, death, and regeneration – in a manner evoking the natural repetition of the seasons. In this respect, An's films demonstrate an interest in process, in how domestic experience constitutes itself, disintegrates, and reconstitutes itself over time. A preoccupation with the cleaning, tidying, and clearing of the home enables the director to dramatise these processes materially. An's interest in this topic is partly personal. His mother worked as a maid, helping with domestic chores, and he would often watch her cleaning the house; to clean and tidy, he says, 'means to transform'.[49] These remarks recall Guo-Juin Hong's analysis of residential spaces in Tsai's *Vive L'Amour* (1994) in that what is represented 'is neither what things were nor what they will be; it is change materialized by the cinematic capture of the in-between moment of transition'.[50]

In the films considered here, themes of domestic decay and renewal are made manifest in the movement of domestic material. This might entail, for example, the gathering and disposal of dust, the removal of empty beer bottles, or the rearrangement of furniture. Each of these acts involves the movement of tangible material within the domestic environment, a recurring trope in these films. In a bleak scene in *Exit*, Ling discovers that unused sanitary pads – now useless to her – serve rather well as dusters. In *More than Blue*, K does the household chores while Cream is at work. In *Dear Ex*, San-Lien is appalled by the state of Chieh's apartment, and revisits it laden with a vacuum cleaner, duster, and sprays. Cleaning is a small act of domestic reorganisation, but in several instances, the films dramatise the larger-scale reconfiguration of domestic objects and infrastructure. In both of his films, An utilises spaces that are gradually altered over the course of the running time; the apartment in *Black Sheep*, for example, comes near to total disintegration, with doors and windows removed, and the contents ultimately vandalised by debt collectors.

To map domestic environments cinematically is to account for the movement of material within and outside the home. If, as Bruno suggests, a house is not a static architectural container but a site of mobile inhabitations, then it follows that a house represented on film must be designed in a manner that dramatises that capacity to embrace the mobility of lived space.[51] Looking at this through the prism of atmosphere design illuminates a productive tension between stasis and movement. From the perspective of a designer advising her students, Weinthal observes,

> The interior relies upon the static nature of architecture as a base upon which temporary elements are located. These can be furniture, the movement of a door swing, or the decision by an occupant to open or close a window for comfort. The point of connection between the static and fleeting can be grounded in measured drawing, thereby acting as the hinge point between the measured and the poetic.[52]

Poetic is here understood as something subjective or emotive, defined in contrast to what is objective or measured. Different disciplinary understandings of terminology notwithstanding, as an overall approach this can be useful to film poetics, in the sense that it allows us to consider how the affective qualities of atmosphere might be constructed through production design taking account of movement. Weinthal examines architectural writings in which the understanding of atmosphere aligns 'with the general attributes of atmospheric conditions as defined by meteorology – light, materials, and gravity. These too are fleeting and change with time, especially in the interior, where elements are more difficult to predict because of the changing nature by which we occupy interiors.'[53]

The filmmakers considered here place particular emphasis on the points of connection between that which is static, and that which moves, with domestic material acting as a hinge point between the measurable and immeasurable: the poetic. Hinges feature as more than a critical metaphor in *Black Sheep*, in which Lu Ming unscrews the hinges of a door in order to remove it, while Chi-Ping, seeking escape, prises open a window and jumps through it. A melancholy sequence in which K undertakes household chores in *More than Blue* dramatises the relationship between that which endures, and that which does not. As he sweeps the floor, collecting the dirt in a dustpan, and gathers the clothes that are strewn untidily over the bed, K reflects on the terminal cancer diagnosis that he has recently been given. He seems to intuit that the material environment he inhabits in the present will endure in the future, long after his own fleeting existence has passed. Household cleaning appliances remind him of the ticking clock; he sits on the floor, staring at the numerical dial on the washing machine, inexorably counting down to the end of the wash cycle. In their production design, these shots acquire an otherworldly quality owing to the prominence of windows as natural light sources within each frame. Hazy white light shines into the different rooms, emphasising that this is an idyllic moment that will not last. One of the reasons art director Yao used a green colour palette in the home was the association of the colour with illness (see Figure 6.2b, a previsualisation of K's bedroom).[54]

Cleaning is ostensibly a response to mess, and in these transitional narratives, figuratively connotes resistance to unwanted change, or the pursuit of desired change. In *Dear Ex*, San-Lien is obsessed with cleanliness and order, something Cheng-Hsi complains about. When he moves in with Chieh, a comedic montage sequence depicts San-Lien bringing cleaning equipment and products to the flat, and tidying up the mess. She clears away empty drinks bottles and rubbish, airs the sheets and pillows, and neatly folds clothes, while complaining 'Why is everything so dirty?' Justifying this industrious activity, San-Lien cites her son's allergies to dust mites, but this seems to be a pretext. By cleaning up the flat, San-Lien is really attempting to understand why her husband left the family home and 'dirtied' himself with another man.

Her obsessive-compulsive efforts with the rubber gloves attest to a craving for order and tidiness that is noticeably lacking in her life, reminding us of Mary Douglas's work on pollution and constructions of cultural purity: 'if uncleanness is matter out of place, we must approach it through order. Uncleanness or dirt is that which must not be included if a pattern is to be maintained'.[55] San-Lien's tidying of Chich's living quarters is intrinsically connected to her views on what is pure and clean, which has implications for the character's perspective on same-sex relationships.

This reflects more generally how domestic mess is deployed narratively: as a means of enabling the characters to transition from a state of imbalance and confusion to one of equilibrium and comprehension. Both Chieh and San-Lien are motivated by grief, a need to come to terms with the death of their loved one. But their respective journeys are shaped by opposing perspectives on mess. While San-Lien has an aversion to it, Chieh embraces and produces mess. He even engenders it artistically, putting on a theatre play in which household clutter is again prominent. The eagle-eyed viewer will note that the stairwell area outside Chieh's flat is crammed full of appliances and domestic items, including a washing machine and a fan (Figure 6.3a). Many of these exact same objects also appear onstage in the theatre, as part of the set – arranged in a manner that recalls some of the designer recycling installations discussed in the previous chapter (Figure 6.3b). The gradual proliferation of domestic junk onstage underscores the porous boundary between theatre and home, confirming the theatrical as a means of sifting through of domestic mess, both material and emotional.

In *Black Sheep* and *Sen Sen*, the process of clearing things away is shown to be transformative, a necessary step in the psychological journeys of the characters. Lili's apartment in *Sen Sen*, filled with bric-a-brac and clutter, is clearly represented as a good mess, the idiosyncratic objects lending the space her personality and grace. The emptying of her home is portrayed as desperately sad, whereas in *Black Sheep*, the connotations of clearance are entirely different. The first half of the film deals with bad mess, specifically, Lu Ming's creation of it: unable to take any pride in the upkeep of his flat, he litters it with beer bottles, old food containers, and other rubbish. This accumulation of objects reflects his downward spiral, a loss of self-respect that will culminate in his suicide attempt. However, halfway through the film, the revelation that Chi-Ping has high blood pressure, and might not therefore be able to undertake his military service, brings about a change in Lu Ming. Recognising that he and his son may be forced to continue cohabiting, he resolves to change. Lu Ming takes a plastic bag and a cardboard box, and begins clearing up the empty beer bottles. Later, Chi-Ping reciprocates by scrubbing the bathroom tiles to remove the bloodstains that remain from his father's suicide attempt. Cleaning represents an attempt by both characters to begin healing their broken relationship.

Figure 6.3a–b Household appliances and clutter outside Chieh's apartment end up on the theatrical stage in *Dear Ex* (Hsu Yu-Ting, Hsu Chih-Yen, 2018).

Moving domestic material is a practice: a task that must be physically undertaken by the characters, but also by the actors and the filmmaker. This is illustrated by *Black Sheep*, which is fixated on portals, such as doors and windows, and their movement. At the start of the film, Chi-Ping slams his bedroom door shut to avoid contact with his father. For his part, Lu Ming is determined to prevent his son leaving the flat, so he locks the front door whenever he leaves. So the resourceful teenager removes the entire window in his bedroom, and exits that way instead, a task made easier by the frame being old and rotten. Lu Ming responds to this by upping the ante significantly: he unscrews the door to Chi-Ping's bedroom from its frame, removes it, then carries it down the street and dumps it. The result is to reconfigure space so that privacy no longer exists; a means of Lu Ming asserting control by subjecting his son to constant supervision. Doors and windows, and their removal, materialise emotion: the father's desire to confine his son, and the son's aspiration to freedom.

The removal of the door also signals the intervention of the filmmaker into the *mise en scène*, forcing the characters into proximity. An discusses the absent door with regard to his views on the relationships between Asian fathers and sons:

> I was wondering whether a more intimate interaction might occur once the door disappeared. On the contrary, I realised that an Asian father and son usually don't talk to each other. Hence, if you open the door between them, they become more uneasy, not closer.[56]

Several scenes capture this tense dynamic. One wide shot shows the pair eating, each sitting in his own room, but both visible within the frame due to the missing door. But while they occupy the same unbroken space, they sullenly fail to communicate. In a later scene, also shot in a wide shot, Lu Ming attempts to make amends by entering his son's bedroom, but Chi-Ping responds by silently moving to the lounge where his father was previously seated. Visually, they swop places. The symbolic resonance of the door recalls Tsai's comments that, for him, doors represent 'a channel of communication' but also enable people to shut themselves away and hide; he described the door as his most frequently used prop, not just in his film work but also in his theatre productions, such as *The Unopenable Door in the Dark*.[57]

In *Black Sheep*, Lu Ming and Chi-Ping's removal of doors and windows can certainly be viewed as performative interventions, actions intended to arouse the other's ire. Yet ultimately, the film differs from the others considered here in that the theatrical can be sought less at the level of character and more at the level of practice. For the film set comes literally to resemble a theatrical stage, upon which the actors remove and rearrange furniture and fixtures. This is partly evoked using wide shots. An recalls that he and the Director of Photography did not vary the camera positions very much, but aimed to tell the story using different means: 'I feel that in that space, I learned something very important: *mise en scène*. I could use blocking to achieve a variation of framing. It felt like theatre.'[58] Within the apartment, the cinematography tends to favour shots that are longer than average in duration, and often wide too; this allows the performances to play out within the environment, minimising the number of different camera setups required. This too results in a shift towards theatrical conventions; the director and cinematographer agreed that they would 'let the actors own the space, and the camera would work around them'.[59]

What seems significant here is not the adoption of any directing or acting technique, but rather that the overall approach was designed to shape performances inflected by the actors' responses to the environment.[60] The director's use of the film set exceeds any notion of *mise en scène* as a backdrop, as something unaltered by the people who appear onscreen. On the contrary, the space is constantly changed by the characters themselves, and always with thematic ends in mind. Ultimately, the debt-collecting thugs, having succeeded in tracking down Lu Ming, remove just about everything. The entire flat is trashed, furniture upturned and destroyed, and the walls graffitied, definitively capturing the utter degradation of the family, and the domestic values associated with it.

An Autobiographical Epilogue: Cleaning as Method

The hit film *I WeirDO* (Liao Ming-Yi, 2020) shares many of the characteristics of the films discussed above. Predominantly set in the interior of an apartment, it dramatises affective journeys within the materiality of the home, is preoccupied with tactility, and presents the domestic sphere in theatrical terms. Moreover, the protagonists Po-Ching (Lin Po-Hung) and Chen Ching (Hsieh Hsin-Ying) are absolutely obsessed with cleaning, given that both suffer from mysophobia, a fear of germs and contamination. This is why they are scared to leave their home. Formally experimental, *I WeirDO* was the first Taiwanese feature to be entirely filmed on an iPhone, using a narrow aspect ratio that heightens the sense of claustrophobia. It intended to portray the lives of two 'weirdos' who do not conform to typical stereotypes of domesticity.

The timing of the film's release, however – summer 2020 – certainly impacted on its reception. When Po-Ching and Chen Ching do occasionally exit their apartment to buy supplies, they wear protective plastic anoraks, rubber gloves, and surgical face masks. Neither this, nor their insistent fixation on antibacterial sanitation, was especially weird in 2020. What was intended as a drama about OCD had become a COVID-19 film. This was obvious to the cinema audience with whom I watched *I WeirDO* in London in December 2020, clad in a face mask and with hand sanitiser in my pocket. I remember wondering whether the film's newly acquired connotations would resonate more profoundly outside, rather than inside, Taiwan. The strength of the island's border controls had resulted in relatively fewer pandemic restrictions than elsewhere, not least in film production, which continued largely uninterrupted. For me, *I WeirDO* will always be one of the quintessential COVID films, even though it was never intended as such. Before the pandemic, I might have considered the characters in the film to be weird. But in 2020, I had spent most of the year stuck in an interior where, I remember, I used to clean things every day.

NOTES

1. An, Personal interview. This was equivalent to around £41,000 in 2016.
2. Taiwan Film Institute, *Taiwan Cinema Yearbook* 2019, 88.
3. Lin, 'If you knew it was sentimental'.
4. Thongchai, *Siam Mapped*, 130.
5. Guo-Juin Hong argues that 'the idea of the home in the Chinese cultural context is not antithetical to the collective but, rather, is in a congruent and mutually enabling relationship', with connections between nation (*guo*) and home/family (*jia*) 'deeply rooted in a long history of political cosmology, however problematic, even stifling, it may be'. Hong, '*Our Neighbors* (1963)', 27.
6. Lim, *Taiwan Cinema as Soft Power*, 3–6; 8–17.
7. *Taipei Times*, '2018 Referendums', 3.
8. Brown, 'This film is blessed by the Gods'.
9. Fell, 'The impact of social movements', 279.
10. Hsu, Personal interview.
11. Ibid.
12. See, for example, Yeh and Davis, *Taiwan Film Directors*, 26; Berry and Farquhar, *China on Screen*, 92–4; Lo, *The Authorship of Place*, 36.
13. Horng, 'Domestic dislocations', 30.
14. Tweedie, 'Morning in the new metropolis', 121.
15. See, for example, Hong, *Taiwan Cinema*, 164–6; Martin, *Situating Sexualities*, 166–9.
16. Yeh and Davis, *Taiwan Film Directors*, 241.
17. Chen and Hsieh, 'Defending the faith in melodrama'.
18. Yeh and Davis, *Taiwan Film Directors*, 35–42.
19. Berry and Farquhar, *China on Screen*, 77–82.
20. For these stylistic characteristics of melodrama, see Berry and Farquhar, *China on Screen*, 80.
21. Chen and Hsieh, 'Defending the faith in melodrama'.
22. Butler, 'Performative acts', 527–8.
23. Uhlin, 'Feeling depleted', 280.
24. Weinthal, 'Interior atmosphere', 158–9.
25. Ibid., 157, 161–2.
26. Ibid., 170.
27. Heskins, 'The *Exit* interviews'.
28. Ibid.
29. Martin, *Situating Sexualities*, 170.
30. Palmer, 'Chen Shiang-Chyi interview'.
31. Heskins, 'The *Exit* interviews'.
32. Aristotle, *Poetics*, 23.
33. Bruno, *Atlas of Emotion*, 103.
34. Ibid.
35. Tuan, *Space and Place*, 182.
36. Chen and Hsieh, 'Defending the faith in melodrama'.
37. Tuan, *Space and Place*, 182.
38. Hsu, Personal interview.
39. Ibid.
40. Brown, 'This film is blessed by the Gods'.
41. Ibid.
42. Ibid.
43. Highmore, 'Home truths', 182.

44. Brown, 'This film is blessed by the Gods'.
45. Tuan, *Space and Place*, 144.
46. An, Personal interview.
47. See Bolt, 'Heidegger, handlability and praxical knowledge'.
48. Chen and Hsieh, 'Defending the faith in melodrama'.
49. Brown, 'Life cycles', 137.
50. Hong, *Taiwan Cinema*, 168.
51. Bruno, *Atlas of Emotion*, 103.
52. Weinthal, 'Interior atmosphere', 168.
53. Ibid., 167.
54. Chen and Hsieh, 'Defending the faith in melodrama'.
55. Douglas, *Purity and Danger*, 41.
56. Brown, 'Life cycles', 134.
57. Martin, *Situating Sexualities*, 171.
58. Brown, 'Life cycles', 135.
59. Ibid., 135.
60. An, Personal interview.

7. QUIET PLACES

Introduction: Sound and Peripheral Masculinity

The stylistically diverse films considered in this chapter are about male characters who feel themselves to be distant from a geographical centre, finding themselves instead on the periphery. In *A Time in Quchi* (Chang Tso-Chi, 2013), schoolkid Pao (Yang Liang-Yu) is uplifted from his home in Taipei and sent to Quchi, in a river valley on the southern outskirts of the city, which he resents. The teenage protagonist of *Secrets in the Hot Spring* (Lin Kuan-Hui, 2018) must similarly leave Taipei and endure a stay with his grandparents in a run-down hotel in the mountains. A security guard in *The Great Buddha +* (Huang Hsin-Yao, 2017) languishes in a small township on the west coast, enjoying vicarious travel to urban centres by avidly watching his employer's dashcam footage with a friend. The geographical centre from which the characters feel excluded is either Taipei or another large city. Frustrated, they find themselves stuck in the provinces.

This narrative pattern reflects broader cinematic trends since 2008. Karen Ya-Chu Yang, drawing on the remarks of Lee Yuan, observed in 2015 the 'decentering disposition of Taiwan's latest cinematic revival', noting that films had tended to 'forgo Taiwan's national and metropolitan center, Taipei, in favor of other localities'.[1] Earlier in this book, I discussed the oft-deployed trope of an urban visitor returning to the provinces. The character arcs tend to be similar, tracing an outsider's integration in the community, as they gradually come to appreciate the way of life in a backwater that they initially thought they hated. To the extent that their narratives recognise the value of the local, many filmmakers demonstrate a commitment to regionalism – as might be expected, given the priorities of many funding sources. This is not necessarily the same as promotion, of course, and the years after 2015 have witnessed some noticeably bleaker portrayals of provincial life, in genre cinema such as horror, and in dramas including *The Great Buddha +*. The film offers an affectionate rendering of small-town life, but in the context of a cynical narrative depicting social inequity and corruption.

Yet despite the films' ostensible subject matter, framing a discussion in terms of an urban centre versus rural margins might ultimately be a distraction. There is first the question of where industrial modernity is perceived to sit, given the way in which Taiwan's industrial networks developed from the mid-1960s. As Daniel Buck has demonstrated, various economic factors combined to generate a rapid 'ruralization of industry' at this time, with a significant number of new enterprises taking the form of localised and specialised networks of rural family firms; these did not simply 'pull industry into the countryside', but 'drove the creation and growth of entirely new industrial sectors'.[2] Bearing this in mind, Xiao Cai seems justified in her instinct to argue that some of Hou Hsiao-Hsien's films depict what she terms 'border countryside', a liminal space where traditional rural lifestyles and values begin to blend with urban modernity.[3] But in relation to some geographical areas – the vast swathes of Taiwan's western seaboard spring to mind – I would perhaps go further and query the very premise of the rural being traditional, the urban being modern, and there being a border area, however porous, between them. A film like *The Great Buddha +* is set in exactly the kind of rural environment that was previously dominated by small and medium enterprises in the years of the economic miracle, and has since gone into decline. The characters are shaped by the legacy of rural modernity.

More fundamental, artistically, is that while these stylistically disparate films are apparently constructed in terms of a rural–urban dichotomy, this understanding of space is shown to be shaped by character psychology. The example of another film, *Father to Son* (Hsiao Ya-Chuan, 2018), is instructive. The protagonist Pao-Te (Huang Chung-Kun) lives in a large city, Chiayi, but feels distant from where he believes the action is really happening, in Taipei. Despite living in a developed urban area, he still feels himself to be on the periphery. In this sense, the films considered in this chapter are ultimately structured around imagined centres and the margins these imply. These might take external geographical form, but fundamentally depict internal psychological dynamics: the centre is associated with desire, change, and renewal, while the periphery conversely connotes resignation, stasis, and stagnation. To the extent that the filmmakers depict this understanding of place as misguided, they display a commitment less to rural life or regionalism than to asking why the characters consider themselves to be peripheral.

This is inextricably tied up with questions of masculinity. *A Time in Quchi* and *Secrets in the Hot Spring* are coming-of-age stories, about a boy and a teenager respectively; *The Great Buddha +* is about frustrated middle-aged men; and *Father to Son* portrays an older man facing a terminal illness. Masculine self-image is shown to shape the characters' perspective on physical geography, and curiously, allusions to the Western crop up in all these films, suggesting the enduring power of that genre to shape popular conceptions of manhood. As Kevin (Dai Li-Jen) drives around in search of women in *The Great Buddha +*, the narrator explains that the accompanying music was 'made specially as a theme song' for him by the film's composer and has an 'American west cowboy flavour'. In *Secrets in the Hot Spring*, Hsiao-Chin (Chang Ting-Hu) engages in a cleansing ritual to prove his virility prior to an exorcism, accompanied by a trumpet theme that might have come straight out of a Spaghetti Western. In *Father to Son*, handyman Pao-Te brandishes a large pipe wrench like a pistol, jokingly pulling it from his holster in a quick draw. In *A Time in Quchi*, Pao stares out at the forested mountain that lies beyond a picket fence, shot from behind and framed by a shadowed doorway (Figure 7.1). This recalls iconography of the domestic threshold and the wilderness associated with the Western, perhaps epitomised by the shot of John Wayne exiting his homestead in *The Searchers* (John Ford, 1956).

In one way or another, these are all stories about masculine repression, expressed geographically, for the periphery is where long-submerged secrets, fears, and vulnerabilities rise to the surface. This aquatic analogy is not my own but derived from the films themselves, all of which are set in environments where water is omnipresent. Despite the diversity in genre and style, water signifies death in all these films. A boy dies in the river in *A Time in*

Figure 7.1 Pao looks out at the landscape in *A Time in Quchi* (Chang Tso-Chi, 2013).

Quchi, and the titular village is engulfed by floodwater. Tu-Tsai (Chen Chu-Sheng) meets his end in a paddy field drainage ditch in *The Great Buddha +*. A flashback in *Secrets in the Hot Spring* informs the viewer that Hsiao-Chin's mother died in a hot spring bath. Two characters have ominous nightmares about watery inundation that foreshadow their deaths in *Father to Son*. Water is often depicted in the manner of pathetic fallacy; as *The Great Buddha +* builds up to Tu-Tsai's climactic death, the hitherto dry weather is replaced by a torrential downpour. The symbolic connotations of water are not solely destructive; water also offers the possibility of renewal. The haunted hot spring is ultimately therapeutic for Hsiao-Chin in *Secrets in the Hot Spring*, while in *Father to Son* water is associated with fertility as well as death. In these dramas of masculinity, water helps the boys come of age, and the men come to terms (with age, life, mortality).

This is elemental, classic, mythological stuff – and one might ask about the implications for women, who occupy secondary or minor roles in all these films. Male bonding dominates, as a theme but also a process, a narrative means of instigating change in the protagonist. The gendering of narrative form is hardly unique to Taiwan, yet a notable trend of the island's post-2008 film output has been stories extolling the virtues of homosocial relationships. Sheng-Mei Ma writes about a string of youth films that appeared in the years after 2008, all centred on 'Nezha-like protagonists', literally or figuratively fatherless, who bond in brotherhood against overwhelming social forces.[4] He argues that these tropes reflect a national identity crisis, though other factors might offer more concrete explanations for the cinematic recurrence of male bonding.[5] Hong-Chi Shiau, for example, has undertaken ethnographic work suggesting that millennials' understanding of Taiwanese masculinity is, in part, shaped by the homosocial experience of compulsory military service.[6] The films considered here offer far more critical, ironic, ambivalent depictions of male relationships than the examples discussed by Ma. But that does not mean that they offer compelling portrayals of women, or that the reiteration of masculine themes and preoccupations is necessarily unproblematic.

Given this context, it should be acknowledged that the inclusion of *A Time in Quchi* in this chapter requires me to put aside offscreen controversy, namely, that director Chang Tso-Chi served a prison term for a sexual assault that occurred shortly after the film's completion.[7] I have opted to analyse *A Time in Quchi* because of the important critical space the film occupies, as a geographically decentred articulation of male coming-of-age that refers directly back to a key work from the Taiwan New Cinema. This reflects my more general concern with the historical replaying of masculine narratives in recent Taiwanese cinema; the filmmakers considered here all dramatise contemporary masculinity in relation to the past, as something subject to reiteration, repetition, and reviewing. This is undertaken aesthetically, for example through pastiche in *Secrets in the Hot Spring*, as well as narratively: the protagonists of *The Great Buddha +* literally replay the past in the form of dashcam footage, while *Father to Son* depicts male behavioural cycles repeating themselves across generations. In questioning the apparently sacrosanct bonds between men, and the sexism this implies, Hsiao's film quietly makes a case for breaking the cycle. As the character Yu-Chin remarks, 'Is it really so important for a son to see his father?'

Hearing is not necessarily the same as seeing, however, and a final thing these films have in common is that the viewer is required to notice the soundtrack in order to understand the drama. The environments considered in this chapter lack urban noise, reflecting their geographical position and relatively sparse populations. But these places are also 'quiet' in the subjective sense of being tranquil and sleepy – or boring and stagnant, depending on the characters' perspective; quietude initially marks out these environments as peripheral to an imagined centre. This chapter will explore how affective journeys in these quiet places are articulated through the interplay of sound with the visuals; how the relationship between environment and masculinity undergoing change is explored through soundtrack components including ambient sound, music, voiceover, and sound effects. To observe that these films share quiet settings is not to imply that their soundtracks lack noise. *A Time in Quchi* comes closest to giving that impression, if we associate the absence of human noise with quietude; *The Great Buddha +* and *Secrets in the Hot Spring* are positively cacophonous; and *Father to Son* makes perhaps the most use of sonic contrast.

Ambient Sound in *A Time in Quchi* (2013)

A Time in Quchi is titled *Summer Vacation Homework* in Chinese, which refers to the essay-diary that the young urbanite Pao is required to complete while sojourning at his grandfather's home in Quchi. The title and the film's themes evoke Hou's 1984 classic *Summer at Grandpa's* (*Tung-Tung's Holiday* in Chinese), which offered a similarly unsentimental take on male coming-of-age. Chang's film is not a remake so much as a contemporary reimagining of the earlier film. In Hou's film there is a greater distance between the city and the rural village, geographically but also emotionally: the village *feels* far away from the city. This is of course nuanced by the presence of the railway, which acknowledges the reach of modernity; Cai suggests the train is a means of Hou 'linking the rural and the city', while June Yip argues that the roar of the train shatters the tranquillity of the early morning and is a reminder of technology's inevitable encroachment.[8] Nonetheless, the proximity of Quchi to the urban centre is of a different order. It is located just a few kilometres south of Xindian, the southern edge of Taipei where the metro line terminates.

Pao's character arc has him evolve from an arrogant outsider, frustrated with the slow pace of small-town existence, to someone integrated in the community. However, the geographical proximity to Taipei means that, unlike in *Summer at Grandpa's*, this does not feel like an excursion into a past way of life (the English title is somewhat misleading in this regard). The economic flows that link Quchi to the city are everywhere apparent. The affluence of Pao's father (Yan Yung-Heng) means that he has been able to move the grandfather (Kuan Yun-Lung) into a well-appointed new home, although the old man secretly pines for his dilapidated former residence. The reach of gentrification into Quchi reflects the earning power of former residents, while the reference to the guesthouse acknowledges the economic importance of tourism to the region; Quchi is situated along the route to the famed beauty spot of Wulai and its hot spring resorts. Recalling how he used to spend time in the area as a teenager, Chang explains that Quchi is 'a place that is overlooked by people' who pass through on their way to Wulai.[9]

An important element of the film's soundtrack is Pao's voiceover, compromising spoken excerpts from his essay-diary. Its inclusion is significant, as Chang has said that he does not generally like using voiceover but, aware that one of its functions is 'to explain what cannot be shot', he has used it with restraint in certain circumstances.[10] Here, it establishes the character's initial dissonance with his new environment, as he uses clichés to describe Quchi, and lies about his experiences there. He first characterises the village as 'a place with charming views and spectacular scenery' with 'so many beautiful things to see', yet this contrasts starkly with what the viewer has hitherto observed: Pao's utter indifference to his surroundings. Shortly afterwards, Pao explains that his classmates gave him a warm welcome and complimented him on his B-Box skills, when in truth they found him rude and aloof. The voiceover contradicts the visuals, as the essay-diary is written for purposes of self-justification to an external reader, the teacher. Each entry is peppered with clichéd expressions that he has been taught in school – all roads lead to Rome, mighty oaks from little acorns grow, time is like money – with each excerpt repetitively concluding that this was an 'unforgettable day'.

In this coming-of-age narrative, the voiceover confirms that Pao has yet to grow up. He can regurgitate what he has heard at school, but lacks a mature understanding of his environment and empathy for other people. After the first half hour, the essay-diary disappears entirely, but it returns an hour later, at a climactic moment shortly after Pao's new friend Ming-Chuan (Hsieh Ming-Chuan) dies. This time, however, its contents remain unspoken. Rather than using voiceover, which the viewer expects, Chang films Pao's hand as he writes: 'Today on the river where two waters meet, I had my best friend sink right into the bottom of my heart. Grandpa comforted me and says I have to get used to loneliness. He says that nobody is with us forever.' Pao's face is kept offscreen, but we hear sniffling, and a tear drops onto the lined workbook. The essay-diary has previously been heard but is now only seen, accompanied by silence. This moment confirms Pao's transition into adulthood: his experience of loss, and his newfound respect for his grandfather, are accompanied by a new ability to express his feelings through landscape metaphors in a mature way. He has come of age.

Ambient sound is similarly used to express the tensions between the character and his environment. Insects feature prominently on the soundtrack in the film's first third, and after arriving in Quchi, Pao suffers from mosquito bites. The grandfather explains that children who travel from the city always get bitten, but if they stay long enough won't be affected; Pao's susceptibility to insect bites marks him out as a stranger to the environment. This was also a consideration during the film's production; one of Chang's criteria when casting the child actors was that they should not be afraid of mosquitoes: 'There are mosquitoes everywhere there, it's really unbearable. Basically, children need time to adapt to the environment, and it really takes a lot of patience to integrate them.'[11] The film's frequent references to insects – a mantis captured by the children is a recurring metaphor – suggests that their presence on the soundtrack is designed to be noticed, something that is arguably true of the film's use of ambient sound more generally.

A Time in Quchi is not a work of slow cinema, but at times it draws on the conventions of this form, noticeably in the way quietude is constructed on the soundtrack, contributing to the viewer's perception of rhythm and pace.[12] Song Hwee Lim discusses how Tsai Ming-Liang constructs an aesthetic of slowness in his films through the use of sonic strategies including sparse dialogue, no voiceover, and the accentuation of sound effects including ambient noises.[13] *A Time in Quchi* does not continually imply silence in the comprehensive way that Lim argues Tsai's films do, but Chang does dramatise contrasts and transitions between the sonic presence and absence of human beings. The presence of the voiceover in the film's early sections, for example, is underscored by its conspicuous absence later. While several scenes are dialogue-heavy, others feature no dialogue at all; ambient sound is often accentuated, contributing to the impression that Quchi is 'quiet' due to the relative lack of human noise. Dynamics of distance and proximity to nature are central to the way that the film's visuals and sound are edited.

The three-minute sequence depicting Pao's first morning in Quchi is entirely wordless. It commences with different shots of the environment, with abrupt changes in ambient sound occurring on the cuts. It is early morning. A wide shot depicts clouds moving over the mountaintops, accompanied by the sound of insects and birds, and a dog faintly barking. This cuts to a much wider shot of the mountains filmed from ground level, along with buildings, a river and vegetation in the foreground. The birds can now barely be heard, which, along with the bubbling noise of the river, emphasises the change in altitude. The sound of insects has reduced in volume, and the noise of the dog is clearer, indicating greater proximity to the village. This cuts to an exterior shot of the grandfather's home. The insects are now much quieter, while a dog can be seen eating from a bowl, identifying the source of the sound heard previously. This cuts to a shot depicting the interior of the property, portraying Pao as he wakes up. Outside, a dog can be heard barking again, indicating the passing of time, and the whirring of an electric fan, seen on the right, is now highly prominent on the soundtrack. The next shot is filmed from the inside of the home, looking out at the neatly manicured lawn, on which the dogs can now be seen playing. The soundtrack, however, continues to be dominated by the hum of the electric fan.

Visually, the sequence commences with a series of establishing shots, and once the home is seen, the sequencing recalls what David Bordwell, Kristin Thompson, and Jeff Smith term an 'analytical' approach to editing, which breaks an establishing shot into closer views in order to analyse the space (as opposed to constructive editing, which builds up a sense of the space without an establishing shot).[14] However, the motivation for this approach here relates to the ambient soundscape as much as the visuals. The soundtrack charts thematic progression, as distance from the domestic realm gives way to proximity within it, and natural sounds are progressively replaced by the noise of an electronic household product. This dramatises Pao's initial reluctance to adapt to his surroundings, which the film connects to broader discourses around human attempts to attain ascendancy over nature. In the shot looking from the inside of the home outwards, a picket fence clearly demarcates the neatly tended lawn from the untended vegetation on the mountains in the background (Figure 7.1). As the sequence continues, Pao walks over to the fence and looks out at the mountains and lake, for the first time showing nascent signs of interest in his environment. The sound of insects heightens, suggesting he is closer to nature. But Pao is not yet ready to commit; he returns to his electronic tablet, and sits playing with it on the lawn, a willing captive within a space in which the natural is materially and sonically controlled. As if to underscore the point, the sequence ends with an empty shot of the interior, the fan still blowing with its continuous whirring sound – rather pointlessly and wastefully, given that nobody is now present in the space.

The ambient sound of water (from watercourses, rainfall, storms, flooding) is dominant in the film's final third. The sound design of water is used to foreshadow and build character arcs to elicit an affective response, and to symbolise themes such as death. At the film's climax a typhoon sweeps through the community, causing flooding, while Ming-Chuan's fatal accident occurs in the stream. Ironically it is Pao, rather than any of the adults present, who warns his friend to be careful when attempting to spear shrimps, observing that the currents are strong. Ming-Chuan ignores him, however. 'This what men do', he asserts, comically adopting a muscle man pose. The subtext here is the fragility of young masculinity, but also adult negligence: the pool worker played by Chen Jen-Shuo is apparently the closest Ming-Chuan has to a father figure. The scene depicting the accident begins with a wide shot of the river, with the heavy, threatening sound of rushing water. The boy is seen jumping across stones and almost reaches the other side, which generates relief given the previous dialogue about strong currents. Yet a cut to a slightly different angle of the river, now devoid of the boy or other people, is unsettling. This cuts to a shot of the empty yard above the gorge; the sound of water is now distant, implying safety. But after a moment of quiet, men are heard yelling about an accident. Chen's character is subsequently seen carrying Ming-Chuan from the river, covered in blood. The rapids indeed killed him, but not in the manner the viewer expected; he slipped and hit his head, and will die in hospital.

As a typhoon approaches, rainfall becomes more prominent on the soundtrack, while the weather event itself results in the sound of heavy rain and wind, then gushing water as the river overflows and properties are damaged. The film includes real-life footage of the rising river levels and localised flooding, probably that which followed Typhoon Saola in 2012, along with the clean-up operation. Temporally, this dramatic climax occurs around the same time as Ming-Chuan's offscreen death, and is followed by scenes in which family secrets are revealed: we learn that the grandfather has an illegitimate daughter whose family are noticeably poorer, calling into question the moral authority hitherto displayed by the character. Water causes repressed histories to rise to the surface, while the impact of the typhoon matches Pao's character arc in confirming the hopelessness of attempts to insulate oneself from nature. Sadly, the film was prescient in its depiction of the threat posed by water to the region; in 2015, Typhoon Soudelor caused utter devastation in nearby Wulai, with flooding and mudslides destroying buildings and resorts.

Heard Pastiche in *Secrets in the Hot Spring* (2018)

'Honestly, I'm past my arthouse days', remarks director Lin Kuan-Hui, recalling influences she absorbed at college, including the films of Andrei Tarkovsky and Krzysztof Kieślowski.[15] By contrast, her main reference points for the teen supernatural-comedy *Secrets in the Hot Spring* are popular genre cinema: Hollywood blockbusters such as *The Exorcist* (William Friedkin, 1973) and *E.T.* (Steven Spielberg, 1982), but primarily Hong Kong supernatural films from the 1980s and 1990s, which she first viewed as TV repeats broadcast on the Long Shong Film Channel.[16] These include the series of vampire films starring Lam Ching-Ying, and *A Chinese Ghost Story* (Tsui Hark, 1987). Lin sought to combine tropes from these older films with a contemporary sensibility, to appeal both to older viewers who would feel nostalgia for the classic works referenced, and younger viewers drawn to the antics of their TV idols.[17] She adopts production practices associated with commercial genre cinema and TV, rather than arthouse approaches, evident in her emphasis on meticulous planning over on-set spontaneity. Lin personally drew over a thousand shots for the film's storyboard to communicate the basis for the visualisations to the crew, and prefers the actors to memorise their lines than to improvise.[18]

Secrets in the Hot Spring centres on Hsiao-Chin, a teenager living in Taipei who returns to an unnamed mountainous province to stay with his grandparents (Law Kar-Ying and Mimi Chu), who run a dilapidated hot springs hotel. He is accompanied by two male classmates, Hsu Li-Han, known as Little Princess (Hung Yan-Hsiang), and Lu-Chun (Lin Ho-Hsuan), who discover that Hsiao-Chin's parents died many years ago, making him heir to the isolated property. The resort hotel is apparently haunted, however, and the ensuing terrorisation of the trio by the resident spectres gently pokes fun at adolescent conceptions of masculinity, and pastiches genre conventions, in line with Richard Dyer's understanding of pastiche as 'a kind of imitation that you are meant to know is an imitation'.[19] Lin explains,

> Some elements of horror films seem to have become rules, for example, that ghosts like to eat candles, or that if you hold your breath, zombies will not find you. The plot elements of previous films have become a kind of convention and rule, and I will definitely put these things in the film.[20]

However, in the film Lin does not simply enact generic conventions, but signals to the viewer that they are meant to be enjoyed as an imitation. Discussing pastiche in genre, Dyer distinguishes between 'knowing what you are doing (straightforward genre production), reflecting on this in a work and pastiche as a specific form of that reflexivity'.[21] *Secrets in the Hot Spring* operates mainly in the latter category, offering less a comprehensive imitation of 1980s Hong Kong supernatural cinema than an imitation of 'what it perceives to be characteristic of its referent, perceptions that are temporally and culturally specific'.[22] Ghosts eating candles, for instance, are a trope in East Asian horror, but not a feature of the genre globally. My analysis here will focus on the film's pastiche of soundtrack conventions.

The frenetically paced opening section of the film, set in Taipei, is accompanied by an insistent, cartoonish score intended to reinforce and cue comic moments. This assists in lending an upbeat feel to what could otherwise be quite disturbing subject matter. Hsiao-Chin is neglected by the uncle and aunt supposedly charged with his care, and has been fired from his job. He has been expelled from several schools, and in his new one, is publicly undermined by the teacher. Bullying, often with homophobic undertones, is rife. Hsiao-Chin has responded to these pressures by adopting a tough guy image; his hair is dyed blonde, codifying rebellion. Underlying the film's raucous humour are some serious points about bullying and bereavement, while rural poverty is similarly depicted in a comic manner. As the action moves to the hot springs, the film mocks the substandard facilities that characterise this cash-strapped backwater. Everything attracts an extra charge, to be paid through coin-operated machines (including, most incongruously, internet access). The water in the pool has not been changed for six years, but Hsiao-Chin's grandmother assures him that the froth and scum on the surface are, in fact, medicinal herbs.

The film demands not to be taken too seriously, and its mapping of space is entirely fantastical. The run-down hotel is in the generic 'middle of nowhere', and from the outset is situated in relation to cinematic, rather than real-life, geography; surrounded by an obviously fake backdrop, the hotel visually resembles the haunted house of the horror tradition (Figure 7.2). The musical score by Terdsak Janpan assists the film's pastiche of genre conventions, with one device used repeatedly: tense, menacing music primes the viewer to anticipate a scare or shock, but instead, the score abruptly stops as an unexpected moment of comedy transpires. The immediate silencing of the unsettling score reinforces the change in mood, focusing attention on whatever humorous incident is occurring; a tactic of discrepancy that is typical of pastiche.[23] Yet the music is itself the subject of comedy, in drawing the viewer's attention to the conventions of horror scoring – the overt and often clichéd mechanisms through which soundtracks are used to cue emotion.

Figure 7.2 The hotel and backdrop in *Secrets in the Hot Spring* (Lin Kuan-Hui, 2018).

The music also helps pinpoint the film's influences. Examining photos of the hotel while on the train, Lu-Chun remarks that it looks like Lanruo Temple – the haunted setting mentioned in the story by Pu Songling that later inspired *A Chinese Ghost Story* and various other film adaptations.[24] The scene on the train then cuts directly to a shot of the hotel on a dark, stormy night, while on the soundtrack, the theme song from the earlier film, performed by its star, Leslie Cheung, starts to play. A fantasised shot then depicts the teenagers first arriving at the hotel, wearing the same Qing-era costumes as the characters from Tsui's film. We later learn that Hsiao-Chin's grandfather originally emigrated from Hong Kong, and when he lectures the boys about how the family has been in the hotel business for generations, he shows them landscape paintings of China and photos of colonial Hong Kong. This captures the film's own lineage: a remediation of Hong Kong popular cinema that itself remediated Chinese literature and mythology. The film's influences are reinforced by the casting of the grandparents; Law and Chu are veteran actors from the territory, with Law having appeared in films including the gender-bending Cheung vehicle *He's a Woman, She's a Man* (Peter Chan Ho-Sun, 1994), and both parts of *A Chinese Odyssey* (Jeffrey Lau Chun-Wai, 1995) as Longevity Monk.

The lyrics of the Cheung song use the metaphor of travel, describing the journey of life being like a beautiful dream, the singer's experiences on the road, and questioning the directions a dream might take. The direct citation from *A Chinese Ghost Story* demonstrates Lin's intention to recreate the pleasures of the earlier classic for a contemporary audience. In one scene, Hsiao-Chin, Little Princess, and Lu-Chun creep along the hallway carrying candles, in search of ghosts, accompanied by ominous music that builds anticipation that something horrible is about to happen. Little Princess, unnerved by the (diegetic) silence, asks one of the others to say something; Hsiao-Chin sarcastically replies that Little Princess can sing a song if he is scared. The teenagers continue shuffling forward as the tense score builds. Suddenly, Little Princess begins singing the opening theme from *A Chinese Ghost Story*, and the score abruptly stops, completely breaking the tension. Hsiao-Chin rolls his eyes in irritation. There is then a cut to a shot of the ceiling, and the sound of a few slaps. The horror music then recommences as the trio continue creeping through the house, the chastened Little Princess sulkily nursing his cheek. The abrupt cutting of the score and its equally sudden recommencement exposes the artifice of genre conventions to comic effect, while signalling the film's debt to Tsui's earlier classic.

The homage to Cheung and the use of his vocals on the soundtrack also focuses attention on the legacy of the star's image, given that *Secrets in the Hot Spring* foregrounds questions of male sexuality. Little Princess – briefly imagined wearing Joey Wong's garb and whose name recalls the Little Beauty of Pu's original text – is effeminate and assumed by the others to be gay, although at the end of the film, it emerges that he is straight, consistent with the film's light-hearted challenge to conventional understandings of masculinity. The macho Hsiao-Chin initially considers his classmates' terror to be a sign of weakness – and resents sharing a bed with them – but gradually loses his qualms about publicly displaying his emotions. Over time, he becomes willing to admit that he is frightened, a stance that has implications beyond the immediate horrors he encounters. When confronting a sinister apparition at the film's climax, he admits 'I'm scared', confessing that he has felt afraid, alone, and powerless following the death of his parents.

Much of the film's humour results from the way it pushes a traditional subtext of the horror genre – repressed sexuality – to the forefront of the drama. In adopting a tough guy posture and denying his own fears, Hsiao-Chin is defending himself against perceived threats to straight masculinity. Sound is central to the way this is handled, again through a pastiche of genre conventions. In one scene, the teenagers prepare to attempt an exorcism. This involves a series of rituals, including the cleansing of the body. Slow-motion shots depict the semi-clothed Hsiao-Chin scooping water from a bucket and pouring it over his body. The shot tilts down, following the water as it runs over his naked chest, in a ludicrously fetishistic spectacle. The soundtrack at this moment features trumpets playing a Morricone-esque showdown theme, recalling 1960s Westerns and their associated machismo. This is a tactic of aural pastiche through deformation, the exaggeration and accentuation of a musical trait.[25] From the sidelines, Little Princess watches, bewildered, as Hsiao-Chin and Lu-Chun wring out their towels. This is a queer spectacle from which the pair are ironically keen to exclude any hint of queerness:

Little Princess:	This thing that you both have, that I don't – do you mean low IQ?
Lu-Chun:	It's masculinity.
Hsiao-Chin:	It's an air of confidence. It's just like fighting and claiming territory. Whoever shows confidence wins the game.
Lu-Chun (to Little Princess):	Go away! You're reducing our masculinity and confidence.

Hsiao-Chin associates confident masculinity with the claiming of territory – which is exactly what he is seeking to achieve by exorcising the ghosts. As heir to the hot springs resort, he is looking to reclaim his inheritance by chasing out the spectral inhabitants. Crucial to the claiming of any territory – in this case, familial space – is mapping, and in this respect, it is unsurprising that shortly afterwards, Hsiao-Chin produces a plan he has sketched of the hotel.

Roughly drawn, it nonetheless captures the overall geography of the interior and indicates where each ghost has been spotted (Figure 7.3).

The connection between environment and family is clearer in the film's Chinese title, *The Inn of Chieh Hsiao-Chin's Family*, in which *jia* means family and house. Ultimately, the classmates discover that the sinister apparitions are nothing but props – the work of the grandparents, who have constructed a system of winches and pulleys in the attic, enabling the ghosts and other horrific beings to appear. The hotel is conceived as a haunted house experience. Hsiao-Chin's deceased parents originally came up with the idea, which the grandparents have taken forward as a business venture, reasoning that their decidedly shoddy hotel will attract notoriety, and therefore more paying guests, if it appears to be haunted. Lin explains that the production design of the hotel, in blending traditional Chinese architecture with Japanese-style interiors (corridors lined with wood panelling and translucent windows; shoji doors and windows), is intended to reflect the backstory of the parents, who met in Japan.[26] What Hsiao-Chin remembers as 'playing house' with his parents – arranging figurines in a wooden dollhouse – was in fact the family's way of prototyping the design of a novelty hotel. Clues to this, and to Hsiao-Chin's forgotten involvement, are placed throughout the film. In a woodwork class at school, he fashions an exquisitely designed house, suggesting that he has inherited an interest in architectural planning. At the film's climax, a flashback scene shows him in bed reading a book entitled *Hotel Management: Theory and Practice*, indicating a long-repressed interest in space management.

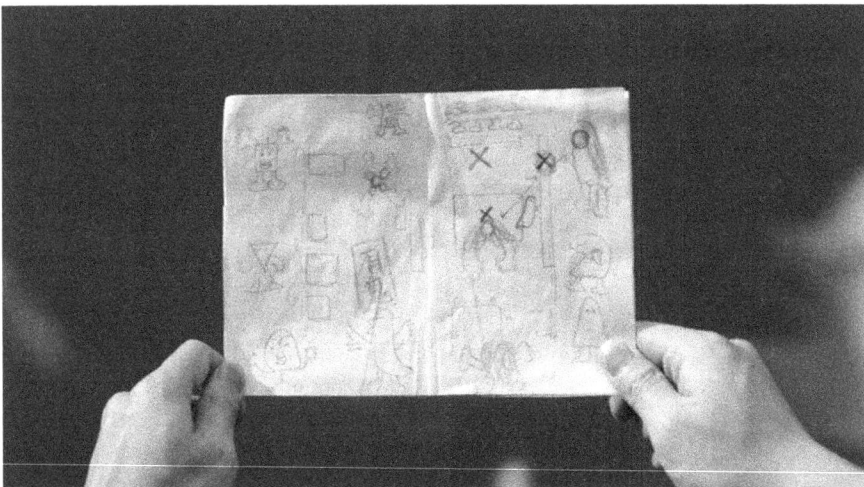

Figure 7.3 Hsiao-Chin's ghost-map in *Secrets in the Hot Spring* (Lin Kuan-Hui, 2018).

The solving of the mystery thus relies less on external revelations than on Hsiao-Chin coming to remember what he has found it easier to forget. Sound helps dramatise the character's reflections on his past family life, occasionally demonstrating the limitations of the film's allegiance to pastiche. In one scene, he discovers an old camcorder and scrolls through the footage, coming across a video of his deceased parents. Aware of his classmates in the background, he responds by quickly turning down the volume so that the others will not notice what he is watching. By adjusting the volume, he seeks to conceal the melancholy that lies beneath his tough-guy façade. Here, and elsewhere during the film's more sentimental moments, a piano composition is heard on the soundtrack. At some points, this too is abruptly cut for comic effect, but in the film's later scenes, as Hsiao-Chin comes to terms with the loss of his parents, it is allowed to play without interruption. Here, pastiche as a knowing imitation, mimicry that bespeaks a shrewd fondness for genre conventions, gives way to a more straightforward sonic enactment of conventions: in this deathly environment, the tropes of family melodrama are alive and well.

Auralism and Insulation in *The Great Buddha +* (2017)

The Great Buddha + is a dark comedy about security guard Tsai-Pu (Chuang Yi-Tseng), who guards the property of his boss, Kevin, in a rural area on the western seaboard. Tsai-Pu spends his evenings with his friend Tu-Tsai, a semi-destitute junk collector. Together they sit in Tsai-Pu's office watching dashcam video footage, recorded during Kevin's long drives around Taiwan; it ultimately transpires that the footage contains evidence that Kevin committed a murder. Despite striking cinematography and a prominent focus on visual technology, sound plays a crucial role throughout the film, from the opening shot of a brass band playing 'Amazing Grace' to the very last shot, when the sound of banging is heard from within a Buddha statue, suggesting that Kevin is about to be punished by divine retribution. Certain characters are defined entirely by sound, such as the mysterious Sugar Apple, a homeless friend of Tu-Tsai who never speaks but sleeps in an abandoned naval sentry post, because he needs to listen to the noise of waves in order to fall asleep.

A full analysis of the film's critique of different visual regimes and social spaces can be found elsewhere; notably, Carlos Rojas has analysed how *The Great Buddha +* reflects on the relationship between representation and reality and how it is impacted by technological mediation.[27] My focus here is on just one component of this rich audiovisual tapestry – the sound heard in the dashcam footage. A consideration of this enables us to understand how the film can be understood as a form of 'cartographic narration', which Giuliana Bruno has argued collapses Michel De Certeau's distinction between the map and the tour – between *seeing* (the knowledge of an order of places) and *going* (spatialising actions).[28] The film's narrative is apparently framed in darkly comic terms of the *voyageur* (the economically mobile Kevin, traversing Taiwan in his car) and the *voyeurs* (Tsai-Pu and Tu-Tsai, who watch the dashcam footage, unable to escape their impoverished provincial existence). A desire for escapism partly motivates Tu-Tsai and Tsai-Pu's video addiction. The film is entirely shot in black and white, except for the dashcam footage, which appears in colour; whenever the monitor is in shot, its contents are colourful, while the surroundings remain desaturated. As the film unfolds, it becomes increasingly difficult to conceive of Tsai-Pu and Tu-Tsai's pleasure in 'seeing' as separate from 'going', even though the pair never leave their rural environs. The dashcam footage sets them on an affective journey, enabling vicarious travel. Kevin passes through places they are unlikely to have a chance to visit themselves. They see downtown city districts, with their tall buildings, glitz and bright lights, and environments that are inaccessible to them economically, such as expensive drive-in hotels. The sheer profusion of colour and activity contrasts with the drab mundanity of the pair's lives. They are both single and live precariously, with Tsai-Pu barely able to make ends meet and Tu-Tsai on the verge of complete destitution, living in a makeshift shack.

When the narrator, in voiceover, ironically explains that the dashcam footage is intended to demonstrate that there is truth in images (recording traffic accidents and so on), he also draws attention to the enclosed sonic qualities of the recording. The dashcam microphone only records what is heard inside the car, he explains, not the sounds outside it. Sonically, the car is an insulated space, underscoring Kevin's detachment from the world around him. The environments he passes through are never heard, while visually, what unfolds is a seemingly endless, purposeless series of voyages around Taiwan. Kevin picks up women on the way, but apparently does so at random. As Tu-Tsai remarks, he 'keeps driving and driving', as if travel is an end in itself. Kevin's deep alienation is underscored by the sonic enclosure of his car, which can be contrasted with the numerous tracking shots of Tu-Tsai and others driving on scooters around the local area. These are all filmed from a similar angle: behind the vehicles driven by the characters, but facing the road ahead, accompanied by the noise of the engine and the external sounds of the environment. The characters are visually and sonically integrated into the landscape, and shown to be organically connected to it, unlike Kevin, who is stylistically abstracted from it.

Another aspect of Tsai-Pu and Tu-Tsai's vicarious living is pornographic interest, the nature of which further complicates questions of voyeurism. Kevin is apparently addicted to sex, and when travelling spends much of his time finding women – usually young or underage – who then have sex with him in his car, sometimes while he is driving. The security guard and his friend later skip through the footage in search of arousing content. At first sight, these scenes appear to dramatise voyeurism; Rojas, for example, refers to Tsai-Pu and Tu-Tsai's 'voyeuristic fascination as they surreptitiously watch the dashcam videos and listen to the sexual encounters that transpire out of the dashcam's line of sight'.[29] Yet it is debatable whether a discussion of voyeurism is the best way to frame critical analysis of these scenes. For the nature of Tsai-Pu and Tu-Tsai's erotic interest is unusual, in that during the sexual encounters, neither the women nor Kevin is ever seen; the dashcam continually looks out towards the road, while the sexual activity occurs behind the camera and is thus only heard. The security guard and his friend watch the footage intently, but it is through sound, rather than the landscape imagery, that they get aroused. 'Just from listening, you get hard', says Tu-Tsai, remarking elsewhere, 'that's a good sound', as he listens to the noise of oral sex and kissing. He likens one of Kevin's conquests to a musical performer as he listens to her moan, deploying a phallic metaphor: 'This girl's a good singer, once she gets the microphone she won't let go.' The sound of pleasure and bodily contact is sufficient to get him aroused. Despite their ostensible subject matter, these scenes in *The Great Buddha +* are ultimately less about voyeurism, which involves the gaining of sexual pleasure through covert looking, than auralism – a popular term that has recently entered academic discourse and refers to the gaining of sexual gratification through listening.[30]

Ultimately, whether we consider the film to dramatise voyeurism depends on our definition of the term; is it possible for someone to be voyeuristic without gaining sexual pleasure? If so, then Tsai-Pu and Tu-Tsai's compulsive viewing of diverse Taiwanese landscapes is voyeuristic, in that it prompts intense longing and vicarious experience. But in its depiction of sexuality, I would argue that the film is instead preoccupied with sound and auralism. The sound of the dashcam footage, for instance, provides a telling sexual motivation for the murder that later has life-changing implications for Tsai-Pu and the ill-fated Tu-Tsai. Kevin's killing of his onetime girlfriend Ms Yeh (Ting Kuo-Lin) occurs within the dashcam footage, as the injured woman struggles with him in front of the car bonnet. But it is their argument beforehand, unseen but recorded by the dashcam microphone, that provides context for the murder. Yeh is angry that Kevin forced her to have an abortion, and demands compensation, threatening to phone his wife and expose his affairs. But she says one specific thing that causes Kevin to become crazed with rage and to begin attacking her. She threatens to reveal that he has also been having sex with a man, baiting him by crudely asking if his asshole was tighter than hers. This revelation undermines the narrator's earlier claim that the dashcam recordings are somehow objective or truthful; based on the evidence of this footage, Kevin is entirely heterosexual. But the viewer learns that this is not the whole story.

Kevin's sexual encounters with a man occurred outside the car, confirming that there is knowledge that lies visually and sonically beyond the scope of the viewer. This reflects the broader aesthetic approach in *The Great Buddha +*, in that what lies spatially beyond what we see and hear onscreen places limits on our understanding of the characters. Tu-Tsai's home, for example, is not shown until the end of the film, after he has died in a traffic accident, presumably murdered by Kevin in a hit-and-run. When Tsai-Pu visits this shack filled with junk, he discovers it contains some bizarre things, such as a sleeping area filled to the brim with cuddly toys that Tu-Tsai had collected. Tsai-Pu realises, the narrator tells us, that there are things he never knew about his friend, knowledge the viewer is similarly not privy to. Another thing that remains obscure is the exact chain of events that leads to Tu-Tsai's death. Kevin seems strangely oblivious to technology; his call records easily alert a local cop to his likely involvement in Yeh's death, and it seems by no means certain that he himself realised that the murder would have been recorded by the dashcam. Did Tu-Tsai attempt to blackmail him? If so, this occurred offscreen, and might account for Tu-Tsai's behaviour when he appears alive for the last time. The narrator cryptically remarks that he 'stares at the scenery with faint longing' – which finds a parallel in his auralism, his vicarious consumption of the sounds heard within Kevin's car. Did Tu-Tsai's longing become acquisitive? We are none the wiser, but what remains certain is that sonically, as much as visually, the dashcam unleashes desire.

Listening to Water: *Father to Son* (2018)

Father to Son is about Fan Pao-Te, a handyman and amateur inventor who lives in Chiayi.[31] Coming to terms with a likely diagnosis for pancreatic cancer, he attempts to track down his long-lost father, assisted by his own son, Da-Chi (Fu Meng-Po). The film's complex plot sprawls far beyond this central character arc, spanning three generations and incorporating a wide range of secondary characters. Missed connections are prevalent: characters who should meet but do not, and characters who meet without understanding the significance of their encounter. *Father to Son* structurally resembles what Gary Bettinson refers to as the Hong Kong puzzle film, albeit in a manner stylistically executed with arthouse, rather than multiplex, audiences in mind. Puzzle films are 'apt to jumble story chronology, conflate objective and subjective reality, furnish unreliable flashbacks and untrustworthy narrators, spring deus ex machinas, and foreground other narrationally restricted devices'.[32] Fixated on repetition and doubling, *Father to Son* implies historical parallels, but also differences: most significantly, while his own father walked out on him as a young boy, Pao-Te chose to stay with his wife and child, despite wanting to leave. His decision to fulfil his family responsibilities meant that he had to forsake a potential career as an inventor. However, he has been rewarded with a father–son relationship that is basically healthy, a rarity in recent Taiwanese cinema. Da-Chi is grateful to his father for staying with him in this 'no-hope town', and cares for him as the illness worsens.

A full consideration of the film's extraordinarily detailed mapping of domestic, local, national, and international itineraries is outside the scope of this analysis. Instead, as a means of concluding the chapter, I will address how one place is heard: the patio behind Pao-Te's shop, a small courtyard surrounded by tall walls. The location becomes significant given the ubiquity of water in the film, depicted variously as traumatic, haunting, and therapeutic. A local laundry manager recalls a nightmare in which she stood next to a fish pond that began to flood, which finds a parallel in Pao-Te's nightmare in which a young boy stands isolated in a semi-inundated landscape. Pao-Te visits a mountain pool and waterfall where he bathes, nostalgically recalling that this is where he had his first cigarette and his first sexual encounter. Later, he and Da-Chi visit a hot springs hotel in Japan. Pao-Te has, by this point, become disillusioned by the discovery that his father worked as a 'broker', bringing Taiwanese women to clubs in Kabukichō in Tokyo to work as hostesses. Pao-Te concludes that his father, even if he is still alive, is not worth meeting or knowing. Perhaps his acquaintance, hotel proprietor Kuo Yu-Chin (Wang Hsiu-Feng), was correct when she queried the apparently sacrosanct bonds between men: 'Is it really so important for a son to see his father?'

The mystery at the heart of the narrative is gradually revealed during the scenes set in the patio courtyard, which require the viewer to focus on the act of listening to water. The first time we see the space, half an hour into the film, Pao-Te is hosing it down. There is a close-up of wet concrete, and the subtle sound of dripping water on the soundtrack, followed by a cut to an extreme close-up of Pao-Te's ear (Figure 7.4). He is listening, intently, to the sound. There are then close-ups of Pao-Te's eyes looking upwards, and his fingers holding the hose, and next a cut to a wide shot in which the camera rises – manoeuvred by a cable from above – offering an aerial perspective on the character (Figure 7.5).[33] The following shot returns to ground level, with a close-up of water droplets; the camera then circles around Pao-Te's head as the soundtrack crescendos into a cacophony of different dripping and fizzing sounds, which continue over a cut to black. In preparation for the shooting of this scene, cement coverings were added to the walls to suggest credibly that some of the noise is caused by the water being absorbed by concrete; the soundtrack was comprised of location sounds as well as other recordings such as the bubbling sound of carbonated drinks.[34]

The meaning of Pao-Te's intense audio experience is not immediately apparent. The second time the courtyard is seen, another half-hour later, the context has slightly changed. The viewer has been introduced to the enigmatic character of Newman (Samuel Ku), a young Taiwanese émigré to Hong Kong who is back visiting Yu-Chin, whom he refers to as Auntie. Yet it appears likely that

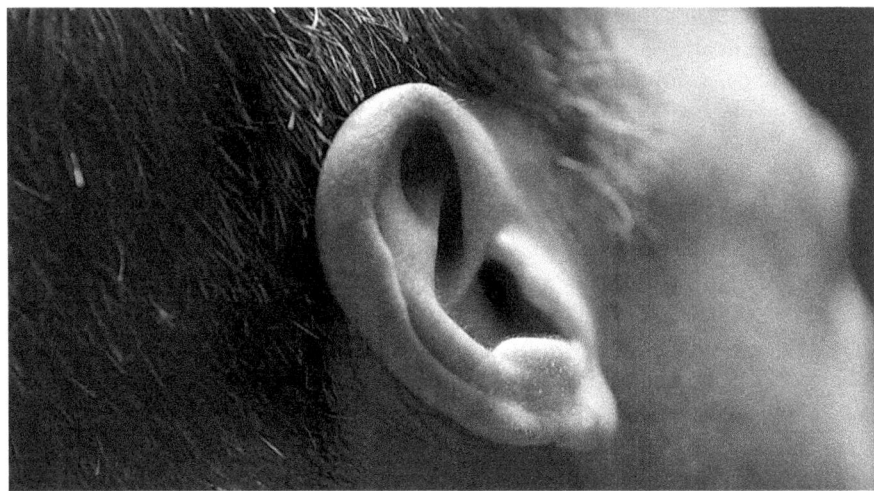

Figure 7.4 Close-up of Pao-Te's ear as he listens in *Father to Son* (Hsiao Ya-Chuan, 2018).

Figure 7.5 Pao-Te listens, filmed from above, in *Father to Son* (Hsiao Ya-Chuan, 2018).

she is really his mother. She has in her possession a baby tag indicating that she gave birth in November 1988, while Newman's words to her – 'You're not my auntie, my auntie would never say that' – are meant in jest, but perhaps indicate some awareness of his parentage. Moreover, Yu-Chin has given Newman the nickname Fan, leading us to suspect that Pao-Te, who shares the family name, is the father. What transpires when the patio appears for the second time might therefore be figurative. Rain pours down as Pao-Te stands holding an umbrella, sheltering his wife as she plants flowers in pots. This is odd behaviour given the weather, so it could be worth interpreting this imagery figuratively, in terms of shelter. Is Pao-Te protecting his wife from knowledge that will hurt her?

The final time the patio appears, after Pao-Te has died, water is again present. Da-Chi is hosing down the space, and shortly afterwards Newman arrives. By this point, it is clear that he must be Pao-Te's second son, and Yu-Chin the mother. He is momentarily left alone in the courtyard. In direct symmetry to the first scene in which Pao-Te listened to the sound of water, an aerial shot now tracks downwards, towards Newman, while he looks up in a reversal of the earlier camera movement. Again, there is a close-up of an ear, as Newman listens to the sound of dripping and bubbling water. His expression is one of recognition, possibly a memory being recalled. Hsiao has said that the patio scenes are intended to give a clue to the blood relationship between father and son, and were inspired by personal experience:

> My Beitou home also has a similar patio. I cleaned it at home one summer afternoon. At that time, the humidity was high and the weather was hot. The walls began to absorb water, and the patio emitted water droplets through evaporation, the sound of which echoed, getting louder and louder – it was magical and made me focus on listening ... I tried to describe it to my relatives and family using words, but I couldn't make them understand.[35]

Emphasising knowledge that is intuited through hearing as a bodily experience, rather than the hearing of stated dialogue, Hsiao deployed unusual production methods, reversing the typical approach of shooting first and scoring later. The soundtrack by Hou Chih-Chien and Lei Kuang-Hsia was composed prior to the shoot, and played on set for the actors to listen to as they performed in the courtyard.[36] Hsiao felt that if the two actors undertook the same activity, and listened to the same music, the result – entering a state of thinking about something – would be similar, thereby implying the characters' connection.[37]

In narrative terms, the climactic scene with Newman is at once revelatory – connecting him to Pao-Te through the shared experience of listening – and ambiguous. We do not know whether either man has been made aware of their blood connection. Much of this depends on what Yu-Chin has decided to tell them, and with hindsight her earlier remark – 'Is it really so important for a son to see his father?' – takes on a double meaning, suggesting that neither of them probably knows about it. Crucially, the knowledge that Pao-Te has fathered a second son paints the character in a less sympathetic light than previously.

The film's gender politics take a full pivot: while Pao-Te didn't abandon his wife and son, he does seem to have abandoned another woman who was pregnant with his child. Much of the history is unknown or implied, but it seems that Pao-Te's parents were hostile to Yu-Chin, which possibly explains why they didn't end up together.

Through the act of listening to water, two men intuit something, and experience a connection, the nature of which is beyond their own comprehension. Attempting to piece together the puzzle, the viewer experiences a similar bewilderment. For how is the sound of water connected to fatherhood? The film offers no clear answers. Certainly, there are Freudian possibilities in the dousing of space with hosed liquid. More convincing perhaps is the possibility that Newman is half-recalling a long-forgotten memory. As a baby or a young child, did he hear this space? Alternatively, it may well be that he was conceived near water. Pao-Te remembers losing his virginity in a mountainside pool, while Yu-Chin recalls that when she first arrived in Chiayi in 1987, the local men behaved like 'bored guys at the pool, surprised by sudden ripples in the water, all turning to see what made the splash'. Here, water is the stuff of memories, dreams and nightmares, and connects the characters to their environments in ways they cannot fully understand. Mapping starts with the body – in *Father to Son*, with the ears.

Notes

1. Yang, 'Passionately documenting', 44.
2. Buck, 'Growth, disintegration, and decentralization', 246–7.
3. Cai, 'Borders and trajectories', 39.
4. Ma, *The Last Isle*, 56.
5. Ibid., 56.
6. Shiau, 'Little new meat', 54–6.
7. For a summary, see *Taipei Times* (staff writer), 'Film director's sex assault conviction', 4.
8. Cai, 'Borders and trajectories', 38; Yip, *Envisioning Taiwan*, 199.
9. Wang, 'One must get used to loneliness'.
10. Berry, *Speaking in Images*, 411–12.
11. Wang, 'One must get used to loneliness'.
12. For silence as an element of slow cinema, see Lim, *Tsai Ming-liang*, 116–19.
13. Lim, *Tsai Ming-liang*, 117–18.
14. Bordwell et al., *Film Art*, 226, 234.
15. Tan, 'Shared feelings'.
16. Ibid.
17. Chien, 'Interview with Lin Kuan-Hui'.
18. Ibid.; Tan, 'Shared feelings'.
19. Dyer, *Pastiche*, 1.
20. Chien, 'Interview with Lin Kuan-Hui'.
21. Dyer, *Pastiche*, 92.
22. Ibid., 128.

23. Ibid., 58.
24. Pu, *Strange Tales*. The name is not given in the English translation, probably because the original text is ambiguous regarding whether Lanruo refers to the temple itself, or to a place where a temple exists.
25. Dyer, *Pastiche*, 56–7.
26. Tan, 'Shared feelings'.
27. Rojas, '*The Great Buddha +*'.
28. Bruno, *Atlas of Emotion*, 245.
29. Rojas, '*The Great Buddha +*', 430.
30. Taylor, 'Taking it in the ear', 604.
31. The film's Chinese title is the character's name.
32. Bettinson, 'Hong Kong puzzle films', 121.
33. Huang, 'Affectionate family letter'.
34. Ibid.
35. Lan, 'Interview: *Father to Son*'.
36. Huang, 'Affectionate family letter'.
37. Ibid.

CONCLUSION: MAPPING THE FUTURE

This book has argued for the importance of mapping in shaping recent Taiwanese cinema (2008–20), focusing on the impulse of filmmakers to map: to chart the island as a distinct geographical environment. My intention has not been to conceive of screen cartography as a theory, but instead to develop an approach to film poetics in which mapping, as a conceptual framework, might enhance our understanding of cinematic histories, themes, stylistics, and large-scale form. In analysing a broad, diverse range of case studies, I have sought to redress some of the imbalances of previous scholarship, which has tended to prioritise films by *auteurs* and noted directors. Throughout the book, I have worked on the assumption that screen mapping is fundamentally a practice, an ongoing process of making and becoming – something that requires us to contemplate what we understand by cinematic novelty.

I began the book by asking whether there was anything new about post-2008 Taiwanese cinema. Its commercial orientation is often given as an answer to this question, yet the box office record has been decidedly patchy. In assessing novelty, therefore, it is arguably less illuminating to focus on commerce in the economic sense, than on the aesthetic results of commercial intent. Post-2008 filmmakers have sought to adopt themes, styles, and forms that they believe will appeal to a wider market than was generally the case with earlier modes of Taiwanese art cinema. This is a broad-brush statement and there will always be nuances and exceptions: filmmakers who retain allegiance to the aesthetics of art cinema, or the occasional art film that manages to reach a wide viewership. But this has been the general direction of travel. In proliferating aesthetic forms that were different from those of previous cinematic traditions, post-2008 filmmaking in Taiwan spearheaded something new.

This book offers no evidence, however, of a new 'national style' in post-2008 Taiwanese cinema. The stylistic diversity of the case studies, the heterogenous influences and practices on display, resolutely attest to there being no such thing (nor any single global commercial style, for that matter). Yet in adopting the methods of film poetics, in identifying and analysing patterns across a wide range of cinematic output, one begins to see the reiterative effect of certain themes and forms being repeated over time. It is possible, I think, to consider these dynamics in relation to concepts of national cinema – whereby the national lies less in constituent parts than in the repetition of composite patterns. Each chapter has examined an aesthetic trend comprised of elements that, in and of themselves, are not necessarily unique to recent Taiwanese cinema. But in combination, and repeated over time, they form patterns that do seem quite specific to filmmaking in the Taiwanese context. The novelty of post-2008 cinema does not lie in any thematic, formal, or stylistic trope, but in the way multiple tropes coalesce.

Mapping is a structuring impulse in many kinds of filmmaking, but in specific contexts and at certain moments it can become extremely prominent, as I have argued was the case in post-2008 Taiwanese cinema. This may now be changing. Onscreen maps, for instance, now seem to be in retreat. As a new kind of cinema emerged in the years around 2006–8, cartographic artefacts were all over the place, appearing in a wide range of films. This confirms the old truth that maps are instruments of power; here, perhaps soft power, as a new kind of cinematic expression, still in the process of being consolidated, sought legitimacy and confidence. By 2020, onscreen cartography was appearing less frequently, while the onset of the COVID-19 pandemic in that year likely signals a more general turning point in Taiwanese filmmaking, the full impact of which has yet to be fully understood or researched.

The tail-end of the period under consideration witnessed the emergence of two significant trends that seem to be changing the nature of Taiwanese cinema. The first of these was accelerated by the pandemic; the notable rise in Taiwanese films acquiring distribution online. When I first started writing this book, *Dear Ex* was unusual, in that it was among a tiny handful of Taiwanese films released on Netflix in the UK. As I finish writing the book, there are now many films from Taiwan available on this and other online platforms for UK audiences to watch. Some films bypass festival screenings altogether, while others, even by noted directors, might premiere at just one national festival before being released online. This again focuses attention on questions of commercial intent, especially in relation to international viewers, and will have an impact on aesthetics. The second trend has been the massive proliferation of genre filmmaking in Taiwan, with a significant increase in horror, thriller, and science-fiction work. This is notable in terms of volume – the sheer quantity of genre output where previously this was patchy – and promises to become interesting in terms of aesthetic innovation and industry practices, as infrastructure and expertise around genre filmmaking continue to develop.

In connecting these future areas of research to my own work in this book, it seems apt to conclude with sci-fi. Sci-fi's emergence as a film genre (as opposed to a literary genre) in Taiwan is intriguing because there is very little precedent for it in Taiwanese cinema. When analysing filmmakers' speculative mapping of the island's future, a useful starting point might be design, both a practice and an intent that seeks fundamentally to inhabit what is yet to come. *As We Like It* (Chen Hung-I and Wei Ying-Chuan, 2021) relocates Shakespeare's play *As You Like It* to a futuristic Taipei, using an all-female cast to reverse Elizabethan stage practices, and to further queer the play's cross-dressing premise. Seeking to map the future city in line with a designer vision, the film represents the logical culmination of concepts that Chen developed earlier in *Design 7 Love*. In *As We Like It*, the Forest of Ardern exists in the courtyard of an old, repurposed block, while huge aerial internet transmitters float in the sky, suspended above the city. This creates districts with constant wireless access, but campaigns for regulation have meant that some areas lack any internet connection at all. Orlando (Hsieh Pei-En) works for a boutique agency offering a nostalgic service, the delivery of paper letters. Entering an internet-free zone, he is unable to locate the delivery address using the digital map on his phone. So incongruously, Orlando pulls out an old paper map of Taipei, and uses it to find his way: an artefact of the past, hidden in a vision of the future.

BIBLIOGRAPHY

Written Works

Airey, John, 'Graham Greene's *Journey Without Maps* and the Fascination of the Abomination', e-*Rea* 7.1 (2009). <http://journals.openedition.org/erea/849>

Aristotle, *Poetics*. Translated by Anthony Kenny (Oxford: Oxford University Press, 2013 [c. 335 BC]).

Bao, Hongwei, *Queer Comrades: Gay Identity and Tongzhi Activism in Postsocialist China* (Copenhagen: NIAS Press, 2018).

Benn, James A., *Burning for the Buddha: Self-Immolation in Chinese Buddhism* (Honolulu: University of Hawai'i Press, 2007).

Berry, Chris, 'Imagine there's no China: Wei Te-Sheng and Taiwan's "Japan Complex"', in Chiu, Rawnsley, and Rawnsley (eds), *Taiwan Cinema* (2017), 111–21.

Berry, Chris, 'Taiwan's indigenous peoples and cinema: From colonial mascot to Fourth Cinema?', in Chang and Lin (eds), *Positioning Taiwan in a Global Context* (2019), 228–41.

Berry, Chris, '*Cape No. 7* (2008): A Taiwan Structure of Feeling', in Yeh, Davis, and Lin (eds), *32 New Takes on Taiwan Cinema* (2022), 316–31.

Berry, Chris and Mary Farquhar, *China on Screen: Cinema and Nation* (New York: Columbia University Press, 2006).

Berry, Michael, *Speaking in Images: Interviews with Contemporary Chinese Filmmakers* (New York: Columbia University Press, 2005).

Bettinson, Gary, *The Sensuous Cinema of Wong Kar-Wai: Film Poetics and the Aesthetic of Disturbance* (Hong Kong: Hong Kong University Press, 2015).

Bettinson, Gary, 'Hong Kong Puzzle Films: The Persistence of Tradition', in Bettinson and Udden (eds), *The Poetics of Chinese Cinema* (2016), 119–46.

Bettinson, Gary and Richard Rushton, *What Is Film Theory?* (Maidenhead, Berkshire: Open University Press, 2010).

Bettinson, Gary and James Udden (eds), *The Poetics of Chinese Cinema* (New York: Palgrave Macmillan, 2016).

Bhabha, Homi K., *The Location of Culture* (London: Routledge, 2004 [1994]).

Bolt, Barbara, 'Heidegger, Handlability and Praxical Knowledge'. Australian Council of University Art & Design Schools Conference, Canberra, 23–5 September 2004. <http://acuads.com.au/conference/article/heidegger-handlability-and-praxical-knowledge/>

Bordwell, David, *Planet Hong Kong: Popular Cinema and the Art of Entertainment* (Cambridge, Massachusetts: Harvard University Press, 2000).

Bordwell, David, 'Transcultural spaces: toward a poetics of Chinese film', in Lu and Yeh (eds), *Chinese-Language Film* (2005), 141–62.

Bordwell, David, *Poetics of Cinema* (London: Routledge, 2007).

Bordwell, David, Kristin Thompson, and Jeff Smith, *Film Art: An Introduction*, twelfth edition (New York: McGraw-Hill Education, 2020). First edition 1979.

Braester, Yomi, *Painting the City Red: Chinese Cinema and the Urban Contract* (Durham: Duke University Press, 2010).

Brown, Christopher, 'Performance enhancement: identity, surface aesthetics, and the direction of actors in *Yang Yang* 陽陽 (Cheng Yu-Chieh, 2009)', *Asian Cinema*, 28.1 (2017), 23–37.

Brown, Christopher, '"Even if you have nothing, you should keep filming": an interview with Cheng Yu-Chieh on *Wawa No Cidal* (2015)', *Senses of Cinema*, 83 (2017). <https://www.sensesofcinema.com/2017/movements-filmmaker-interviews/cheng-yu-chieh-interview/>

Brown, Christopher, '"This film is blessed by the Gods": Talking with Mag Hsu, Director of *Dear Ex* (Netflix, 2018)', *Bright Lights Film Journal*, 25 October 2019. <https://brightlightsfilm.com/this-film-is-blessed-by-the-gods-talking-with-mag-hsu-director-of-dear-ex-netflix-2018/#.Yfa9qPXP124>

Brown, Christopher, '"By introducing my culture to someone else, I learnt to understand it again somehow": an interview with filmmaker Laha Mebow', *East Asian Journal of Popular Culture*, 6.2 (2020), 293–303.

Brown, Christopher, 'Life cycles: an interview with director Bon An', *Film International*, 18.4 (2020), 132–9.

Bruno, Giuliana, *Atlas of Emotion: Journeys in Art, Architecture, and Film* (London: Verso, 2002).

Buck, Daniel, 'Growth, disintegration, and decentralization: the construction of Taiwan's industrial networks', *Environment and Planning A: Economy and Space* 32 (2000), 245–62.

Butler, Judith, 'Performative acts and gender constitution: an essay in phenomenology and feminist theory', *Theatre Journal* 40:4 (1988), 519–31.

Cai, Xiao, 'Borders and trajectories: Remapping cities in Hou Hsiao-Hsien's films', *Journal of Urban Cultural Studies* 5.1 (2018), 35–52.

Cao, Xue-Qin, *The Story of the Stone*. Volumes 1–5. Translated by David Hawkes (London: Penguin, 1973–86 [c.1760]).

Caquard, Sébastien, 'Foreshadowing contemporary digital cartography: a historical review of cinematic maps in films', *Cartographic Journal* 46:1 (2009), 46–55.

Caquard, Sébastien and D. R. Fraser Taylor, 'What is cinematic cartography?', *Cartographic Journal* 46:1 (2009), 5–8.

Caquard, Sébastien, and William Cartwright, 'Narrative cartography: from mapping stories to the narrative of maps and mapping', *Cartographic Journal* 51.2 (2014), 101–6.

Castro, Teresa, 'Cinema's mapping impulse: questioning visual culture', *Cartographic Journal* 46:1 (2009), 9–15.

Castro, Teresa, 'Mapping the city through film: from "Topophilia" to urban mapscapes', in Richard Koeck and Les Roberts (eds), *The City and the Moving Image: Urban Projections* (London: Palgrave Macmillan, 2010), 144–55.

Chang, Anita Wen-Shin, 'In the realm of the indigenous: local, national, and global articulations in *Fishing Luck*', *positions* 17:3 (2009), 643–53.

Chang, Bi-Yu, *Place, Identity and National Imagination in Postwar Taiwan* (Abingdon: Routledge, 2015).

Chang, Bi-Yu and Pei-Yin Lin (eds), *Positioning Taiwan in a Global Context: Being and Becoming* (Abingdon: Routledge, 2019).

Chang, Chia-Ju, 'Documenting life in the era of climate change: Huang Hsin-Yao's *Nimbus* and *Taivalu*', *Asian Cinema* 30.2 (2019), 235–54.

Chang, Hsi-Wen (Lenglengman Rovaniyaw), 'Indigenous attitudes toward nuclear waste in Taiwan', in Ashley Esarey, Mary Alice Haddad, Joanna I. Lewis, and Stevan Harrell (eds), *Greening East Asia* (2020), 197–212.

Chang, Ivy I-chu, *Taiwan Cinema, Memory, and Modernity* (Singapore: Palgrave Macmillan, 2019).

Chen, Hung-Wei and Hsieh Chia-Chin, 'Defending the faith in melodrama: interview with director Lin Hsiao-Chien and screenwriter Lu An-Hsien of *More Than Blue*', *Funscreen* 636 (2018). <https://funscreen.tfai.org.tw/article/9794>

Chen, Jui-Hua, 'Building a new society on the base of locality: transformation of social forces in Taiwan during the 1990s', *Inter-Asia Cultural Studies* 15.2 (2014), 291–305.

Chen, Yuan, 'Taiwan, abandoned', *Neocha: Culture and Creativity in Asia*, 24 February 2021. <https://neocha.com/magazine/taiwan-abandoned/>

Chi, Chun-Chieh, and Chin Hsang-Te, 'Knowledge, power, and tribal mapping: a critical analysis of the "return of the Truku people"', *GeoJournal* 77 (2012), 733–40.

Chien, Ying-Jou, 'Interview with Lin Kuan-Hui, director of *Secrets in the Hot Spring*: Movies must be able to entertain the audience', *Up Media*, 12 July 2018. <https://www.upmedia.mg/news_info.php?Type=5&SerialNo=44370>

Chiu, Kuei-Fen, Ming-Yeh T. Rawnsley and Gary D. Rawnsley (eds), *Taiwan Cinema: International Reception and Social Change* (London: Routledge, 2017).

Chulphongsathorn, Graiwoot, 'The cinematic forest and Southeast Asian cinema', *JCMS: Journal of Cinema and Media Studies* 60.3 (2021), 182–7.

Conley, Tom, *Cartographic Cinema* (Minneapolis: University of Minnesota Press, 2007).

Cottenie, Tyler, 'A geographical oddity in Chiayi', *Taipei Times*, 11 September 2020, p. 13.

Cummings, E. E., 'somewhere i have never travelled, gladly beyond', in *Selected Poems* (New York: Liveright, 1994), 65.

Davis, Darrell William, and Wu Nien-Chen, 'A new Taiwan person? A conversation with Wu Nien-Chen', *positions: east asia cultures critique* 11:3 (Winter 2003), 717–34.

Davis, Darrell William, 'Second coming: the legacy of Taiwan New Cinema', in Zhang, Yingjin (eds), *A Companion to Chinese Cinema* (Chichester: Blackwell, 2012), 133–50.

Douglas, Mary, *Purity and Danger: An Analysis of Concepts of Pollution and Taboo* (London: Routledge, 2003 [1966]).

Dung, Kai-Cheung, *Atlas: The Archaeology of an Imaginary City*. Translated by Dung Kai-Cheung, Anders Hansson, and Bonnie S. McDougall (New York: Columbia University Press, 2012).

Dunne, Anthony, and Fiona Raby, *Speculative Everything: Design, Fiction, and Social Dreaming* (Cambridge, MA: MIT Press, 2013).

Dyer, Richard, *Pastiche* (Abingdon: Routledge, 2007).
Esarey, Ashley, Mary Alice Haddad, Joanna I. Lewis, and Stevan Harrell (eds), *Greening East Asia: The Rise of the Eco-Developmental State* (Seattle: University of Washington Press, 2020).
Eskildsen, Robert, *Transforming Empire in Japan and East Asia: The Taiwan Expedition and the Birth of Japanese Imperialism* (Singapore: Palgrave Macmillan, 2019).
Executive Yuan. *Republic of China Yearbook 2014*.
Fan, Victor, '*Godspeed* (2016): Memories, Transindividuation, and Becoming Taiwanese', in Yeh, Davis, and Lin (eds), *32 New Takes on Taiwan Cinema* (2022), 385–97.
Fell, Dafydd, 'The impact of social movements', in Kharis Templeman, Yun-Han Chu, and Larry Diamond (eds), *Dynamics of Democracy in Taiwan: The Ma Ying-Jeou Years* (Boulder, Colorado: Lynne Rienner Publishers, 2020), 271–90.
Fox, James J., 'Place and landscape in comparative Austronesian perspective', in James J. Fox (ed.), *The Poetic Power of Place: Comparative Perspectives on Austronesian Ideas of Locality* (Canberra: Australian National University E-Press, 2006 [1997]), 1–22.
Frow, John, 'Invidious distinction: waste, difference, and classy stuff', in Gay Hawkins and Stephen Muecke (eds), *Culture and Waste: The Creation and Destruction of Value* (Oxford: Rowman and Littlefield, 2003), 25–38.
García Márquez, Gabriel, *One Hundred Years of Solitude*, trans. Gregory Rabassa (London: Penguin, 2007 [1967]).
Ghermani, Wafa, '*Super Citizen Ko* (1994): a cartography of memory and oblivion', in Yeh, Davis, and Lin (eds), *32 New Takes on Taiwan Cinema* (2022), 219–30.
Greene, Graham, *The End of the Affair* (London: Vintage, 2001 [1951]).
Haddad, Mary Alice, 'East Asian environmental advocacy', in Ashley Esarey, Mary Alice Haddad, Joanna I. Lewis, and Stevan Harrell (eds), *Greening East Asia* (2020), 32–43.
Hara, Kenya, *Designing Design*. Translated by Maggie Kinser Hohle and Yukiko Naito (Baden, Switzerland: Lars Müller Publishers, 2011 [2007]).
Harley, J. B., 'The map and the development of the history of cartography', in J. B. Harley and David Woodward (eds), *The History of Cartography, Volume 1: Cartography in Prehistoric, Ancient and Medieval Europe and the Mediterranean* (Chicago: University of Chicago Press, 1987), 1–42.
Harley, J. B., 'Maps, knowledge, power', in Denis Cosgrove and Stephen Daniels (eds), *The Iconography of Landscape: Essays on the symbolic representation, design and use of past environments* (Cambridge: Cambridge University Press, 1988), 277–312.
Harley, J. B. and David Woodward (eds), *The History of Cartography, Volume 2, Book 2: Cartography in the Traditional East and Southeast Asian Societies* (Chicago: University of Chicago Press, 1994).
Harrell, Stevan, 'The eco-developmental state and the environmental Kuznets curve', in Ashley Esarey, Mary Alice Haddad, Joanna I. Lewis, and Stevan Harrell (eds), *Greening East Asia* (2020), 241–65.
Harrison, Ariane Lourie, 'Ruin Academy: Casagrande Lab', in Ariane Lourie Harrison (ed.), *Architectural Theories of the Environment: Posthuman Territory* (London: Routledge, 2012), 304–12.
Henderson, John B., 'Chinese cosmographical thought: the high intellectual tradition', in Harley and Woodward (eds), *The History of Cartography, Volume 2* (1994), 203–27.
Heskins, Andrew, 'The *Exit* interviews: Chienn Hsiang and Chen Shiang-Chyi', *Eastern Kicks*, 21 April 2015. <https://www.easternkicks.com/features/the-exit-interviews-chienn-hsiang-and-chen-shiang-chyi>

Highmore, Ben, 'Home truths: identity and materiality in the postwar interior', in Massey (ed.), *A Companion to Contemporary Design since 1945* (2019), 173–88.

Hong, Guo-Juin, *Taiwan Cinema: A Contested Nation on Screen* (Basingstoke, Hampshire: Palgrave, 2011)

Hong, Guo-Juin, '*Our Neighbors* (1963): Historiography of Home and Emerging Realism in Post-1949 Taiwan', in Yeh, Davis, and Lin (eds), *32 New Takes on Taiwan Cinema* (2022), 22–35.

Horng, Meng-Hsin C., 'Domestic dislocations: healthy realism, stardom, and the cinematic projection of home in postwar Taiwan', *Journal of Chinese Cinemas* 4:1 (2010), 27–43.

Hou, Jeffrey, 'Governing urban gardens for resilient cities: Examining the 'Garden City Initiative' in Taipei', *Urban Studies* 57.7 (2020), 1398–416.

Hsieh, Hsuan, 'Wading into the deep water of obstacles, and turning into an avatar: an interview with Hsin Chien-Tsung, director of *Aground*', *Funscreen* 606 (2017). <www.funscreen.com.tw/feature.asp?FE_NO=1675>

Hsieh, Hsuan, and Hung Chien-Lun, 'Design Game of City and Love: interview with Chen Hung-I, director of *Design 7 Love*', *Funscreen* 487 (2014). <https://funscreen.tfai.org.tw/article/9644>

Hu, Tai Shan, and Kuang Chieh Chen, 'Creative talent drive transformation of professionals' constitution in the modern city: a case study of fashion talent flow in Taipei', *European Planning Studies* 22.5 (2014), 1081–105.

Hu, Brian, *Worldly Desires: Cosmopolitanism and Cinema in Hong Kong and Taiwan* (Edinburgh: Edinburgh University Press, 2018).

Huang, Chun-Hao, 'Affectionate family letter from father to son: Interview with Hsiao Ya-Chuan, director of *Father to Son*', *DC Film School*, 21 August 2018. <https://dcfilmschool.com/article/DC%20TALKS專欄｜父予子的深情家書—《范保德》導演蕭雅全專訪>

Huang, Peter I-Min, 'Taiwanese mountain and river literature from a postcolonial perspective', in Chia-Ju Chang and Scott Slovic (eds), *Ecocriticism in Taiwan: Identity, Environment, and the Arts* (London: Lexington Books, 2016), 29–40.

Huang, Ya-Ju, 'Interview with Fu Tien-Yu, director of *Somewhere I Have Never Travelled*', *Taiwan Cinema*. 5 October 2009. <https://taiwancinema.bamid.gov.tw/Infofeatures/InfofeaturesContent/?ContentUrl=59422>

I Ching, or Book of Changes (Yi Jing). Translated by Richard Wilhelm (London: Penguin, 2003 [1951]).

Ingram, David, 'The aesthetics and ethics of eco-film criticism', in Stephen Rust, Salma Monani, and Sean Cubitt, *Ecocinema Theory and Practice* (London: Routledge, 2012), 43–62.

Jameson, Fredric, 'Remapping Taipei', in Nick Browne et al. (eds), *New Chinese Cinemas: Forms, Identities, Politics* (Cambridge: Cambridge University Press, 1994), 117–50.

Jou, Sue-Ching, Eric Clark, and Hsiao-Wei Chen, 'Gentrification and revanchist urbanism in Taipei?', *Urban Studies* 53.3 (2016), 560–76.

Juan, Yi-Kai, Yu-Ching Cheng, and Yeng-Horng Perng, 'Preparations for developing a world design capital: the case of Taipei city transformation process in Taiwan', *Sustainability* 11.21 (2019), Article No. 6064, 1–19.

Kaldis, Nick, 'Submerged ecology and depth psychology in *Wushan yunyu*: aesthetic insight into national development', in Lu and Mi (eds), *Chinese Ecocinema* (2009), 57–72.

Karvelyte, Kristina, 'Shifting meanings in changing contexts: the role of the creative city in Shanghai, Hong Kong and Taipei', *International Journal of Cultural Policy*, 26.2 (2020), 166–83.

Kikuchi, Yuko (ed.), *Refracted Modernity: Visual Culture and Identity in Colonial Taiwan* (Honolulu: University of Hawai'i Press, 2007).
Kitchen, Rob, Justin Gleeson, and Martin Dodge, 'Unfolding mapping practices: a new epistemology for cartography', *Transactions of the Institute of British Geographers*, 38.3 (2013), 480–96.
Kohn, Eduardo, *How Forests Think: Toward an Anthropology beyond the Human* (Berkeley: University of California Press, 2013).
Lan, Tsu-Wei, 'Interview: *Father to Son* and masculinity of the Taiwan economic miracle: Hsiao Ya-Chuan challenges the audience', *Liberty Times Net*, 12 August 2018. <https://talk.ltn.com.tw/article/paper/1223709>
Lay, Jinn-Guey, Yu-Wen Chen and Ko-Hua Yap, 'Mapping Taiwan from an alternative angle', *Journal of Maps* 7.1 (2011), 244–8.
Lee, Sang Eun Eunice, 'Taiwan from below', in Pickowicz and Zhang (eds), *Locating Taiwan Cinema in the Twenty-First Century* (2020), 133–50.
Liao, Hsin-Tien, 'The beauty of the untamed: exploration and travel in colonial Taiwanese landscape painting', in Kikuchi (ed.), *Refracted Modernity* (2007), 39–65.
Liao, Jimmy (Ji-Mi), *The Starry Starry Night* (New Taipei City: Locus Publishing, 2009).
Lifshey, Adam, 'Translating Taiwan southward', in Chang and Lin (eds), *Positioning Taiwan in a Global Context* (2019), 30–44.
Lim, Song Hwee, *Celluloid Comrades: Representations of Male Homosexuality in Contemporary Chinese Cinemas* (Honolulu: University of Hawai'i Press, 2006).
Lim, Song Hwee, 'Taiwan New Cinema: small nation with soft power', in Carlos Rojas and Eileen Cheng-Yin Chow (eds), *The Oxford Handbook of Chinese Cinemas* (Oxford: Oxford University Press, 2013), 152–69.
Lim, Song Hwee, 'The voice of the Sinophone', in Yue and Khoo (eds), *Sinophone Cinemas* (2014), 62–76.
Lim, Song Hwee, *Tsai Ming-liang and a Cinema of Slowness* (Honolulu: University of Hawai'i Press, 2014).
Lim, Song Hwee, *Taiwan Cinema as Soft Power: Authorship, Transnationality, Historiography* (Oxford: Oxford University Press, 2022).
Lin, Cheng-Yi, 'Local and trans-local dynamics of innovation practices in the Taipei design industry: an evolutionary perspective', *European Planning Studies* 26.7 (2018), 1413–30.
Lin, Chih-An, '"If a society does not face its fears, there will be taboos": the Golden Bell Award team, determined to create a horror film that represents Taiwan', *News Lens*, 6 October 2015. <https://www.thenewslens.com/article/25059>
Lin, Mei-Mei, *Taiwanese Ghost Stories* (Taipei: Moon Bear Publishing, 2017).
Lin, Mei-Mei, and Li Chia-Gai, *The Anthropological Imagination of the Demon God* (Taipei: Wunan, 2014).
Lin, Ting-Ying, 'Charting the transnational within the national: the case of contemporary Taiwan popular cinema', in Chang and Lin (eds), *Positioning Taiwan in a Global Context* (2019), 196–210.
Lin, Yih-Ren, 'Politicizing nature: the Maqaw National Park controversy in Taiwan', *Capitalism Nature Socialism* 22.2 (2011), 88–103.
Lin, Hsiao-Chien, 'If you knew it was sentimental, then why did you still burst into tears? The director of the 5 billion dollar box office hit *More than Blue*: Filming like this allows the audience to participate in the tragedy of the century', *Common Wealth Magazine*. 27 October 2021. <https://www.cw.com.tw/article/5118686>
Liu, Ssu-Fang Jessie, 'From visual fantasies to bodily trajectories: the insular epistemology of around-the-island journeys in Taiwan cinema', *East Asian Journal of Popular Culture*, 3.2 (2017), 199–213.

Lo, Dennis, *The Authorship of Place: A Cultural Geography of the New Chinese Cinemas* (Hong Kong: Hong Kong University Press, 2020).
Lu, Sheldon H., 'Genealogies of four critical paradigms in Chinese-Language film studies', in Yue and Khoo (eds), *Sinophone Cinemas* (2014), 13–25.
Lu, Sheldon H., and Emilie Yueh-Yu Yeh (eds), *Chinese-Language Film: Historiography, Poetics, Politics* (Honolulu: University of Hawai'I Press, 2005).
Lu, Sheldon H., and Jiayin Mi (eds), *Chinese Ecocinema: In the Age of Environmental Challenge* (Hong Kong: Hong Kong University Press, 2009).
Lu, Tonglin, *Confronting Modernity in the Cinemas of Taiwan and Mainland China* (Cambridge: Cambridge University Press, 2002).
Ma, Sheng-Mei, *The Last Isle: Contemporary Film, Culture and Trauma in Global Taiwan* (London: Rowman & Littlefield, 2015).
Makeham, John, and A-Chin Hsiau, *Cultural, Ethnic, and Political Nationalism in Contemporary Taiwan* (New York: Palgrave Macmillan, 2005).
Mao, Ya-Fen, 'The meaning of travel: interview with Fu Tien-Yu, director of *Somewhere I Have Never Travelled*', *Funscreen* 223 (2009). <https://funscreen.tfai.org.tw/article/9376>
'Maple', 'Interview with Yeh Tien-Lun, director of *West Side Fairy Tale*', *Punchline*, 28 December 2016. <https://punchline.asia/archives/37702>
Marchetti, Gina, 'On Tsai Mingliang's *The River*', in Chris Berry and Feii Lu (eds), *Island on the Edge: Taiwan New Cinema and After* (Hong Kong: Hong Kong University Press, 2005), 113–26.
Martin, Fran, *Situating Sexualities: Queer Representation in Taiwanese Fiction, Film and Public Culture* (Hong Kong: Hong Kong University Press, 2003).
Massey, Anne (ed.), *A Companion to Contemporary Design since 1945* (Oxford: John Wiley, 2019).
Mi, Jiayin, 'Framing ambient *Unheimlich*: Ecoggedon, ecological unconsciousness, and water pathology in new Chinese cinema', in Lu and Mi (eds), *Chinese Ecocinema* (2009), 17–38.
Misawa, Mamie, 'The national anthem film in the early 1950s Taiwan', in Lin Pei-Yin and Su Yun Kim, *East Asian Transwar Popular Culture: Literature and Film from Taiwan and Korea* (Singapore: Palgrave Macmillan, 2019), 179–206.
Miyazawa, Kenji, *Night Train to the Stars, and other stories*. Translated by John Bester (London: Vintage Classics, 2022 [1924–33]).
Mon, Ya-Feng, *Film Production and Consumption in Contemporary Taiwan: Cinema as a Sensory Circuit* (Amsterdam: Amsterdam University Press, 2016).
Monmonier, Mark, *How to Lie with Maps*, third edition (Chicago: University of Chicago Press, 2018).
Palmer, Stephen, 'Chen Shiang-Chyi interview: "Tsai Ming-liang is a weirdo!"', *Eastern Kicks*, 20 August 2015. <https://www.easternkicks.com/features/chen-shiang-chyi-interview-tsai-ming-liang-is-a-weirdo>
Pickowicz, Paul G., 'The protest film genre in twenty-first-century Taiwan cinema', in Pickowicz and Zhang (eds), *Locating Taiwan Cinema in the Twenty-First Century* (2020), 113–32.
Pickowicz, Paul G. and Yingjin Zhang (eds), *Locating Taiwan Cinema in the Twenty-First Century* (New York: Cambria Press, 2020).
Pu, Songling, *Strange Tales from a Chinese Studio*. Translated by John Minford (London: Penguin, 2006 [1740]).
Roberts, Les, 'Cinematic cartography: projecting place through film', in Les Roberts (ed.), *Mapping Cultures: Place, Practice, Performance* (Basingstoke, Hampshire: Palgrave, 2012), 68–84.
Rocamora, Agnès, *Fashioning the City: Paris, Fashion and the Media* (London: I. B. Tauris, 2009).

Rojas, Carlos, 'The Great Buddha + (2017): Tracing the Limits of the Visible' in Yeh, Davis, and Lin (eds), 32 New Takes on Taiwan Cinema (2022), 426–38.

Roth, Robin, 'The challenges of mapping complex indigenous spatiality: from abstract space to dwelling space', cultural geographies 16:2 (2009), 207–27.

Saury, Alain, Back to the Wild: A Practical Manual for Uncivilized Times. Translated by Rachael Levalley (Port Townsend, Washington: Process Media, 2015).

Shanley, Kathryn W., '"Mapping" indigenous presence: the Declaration on the Rights of Indigenous Peoples at rhetorical turns and tipping points', in Kathryn W. Shanley and Bjørg Evjen (eds), Mapping Indigenous Presence: North Scandinavian and North American Perspectives (Tucson: University of Arizona Press, 2015), 5–26.

Shi, Flair Donglai, 'Reconsidering Sinophone Studies: The Chinese Cold War, multiple sinocentrisms, and theoretical generalisation', in International Journal of Taiwan Studies 4.2 (2021), 311–44.

Shiau, Hong-Chi, '"Little New Meat" and "Korean Warm Men": performance of regional heterosexual masculinities among Taiwanese millennials', East Asian Journal of Popular Culture 6.1 (2020), 45–58.

Shih, Shu-Mei, Visuality and Identity: Sinophone Articulations across the Pacific (Berkeley: University of California Press, 2007).

Shih, Shu-Mei, and Ping-Hui Liao (eds), Comparatizing Taiwan (London: Routledge, 2015).

Shimazu, Naoko, 'Colonial encounters: Japanese travel writing on colonial Taiwan', in Kikuchi (ed.), Refracted Modernity (2007), 21–37.

Steinberg, Philip, 'Of other seas: metaphors and materialities in maritime regions', Atlantic Studies 10.2 (2013), 156–69.

Steinberg, Philip, and Kimberley Peters, 'Wet ontologies, fluid spaces: giving depth to volume through oceanic thinking' Environment and Planning D: Society and Space 33 (2015), 247–64.

Sterk, Darryl, 'Romancing the Formosan Aborigine: colonial interethnic romance and its democratic revision in postwar film and fiction', in Ann Heylen and Scott Sommers (eds), Becoming Taiwan: From Colonialism to Democracy (Wiesbaden: Harrassowitz Verlag, 2010), 49–62.

Sterk, Darryl, 'Ironic indigenous primitivism: Taiwan's first 'native feature' in an era of ethnic tourism', Journal of Chinese Cinemas 8:3 (2014), 209–25.

Stevenson, Robert Louis, Treasure Island (London: Penguin, 1999 [1883]).

Su, Huang-Lan, 'Multi-layered reconciliations in the imagined Diqiucun in Cape No. 7', East Asian Journal of Popular Culture 3:1 (2017), 99–113.

Taiban, Sasala, Hui-nien Lin, Kurtis Jia-chyi Pei, Dau-jye Lu, and Hwa-sheng Gau, 'Indigenous conservation and post-disaster reconstruction in Taiwan', in Ashley Esarey, Mary Alice Haddad, Joanna I. Lewis, and Stevan Harrell (eds), Greening East Asia (2020), 122–36.

Taipei Times staff writer, 'Film director's sex assault conviction, sentence upheld', Taipei Times, 13 March 2015, p. 4.

Taipei Times staff writer, '2018 Referendums: Rights plebiscite results draw opposing views', Taipei Times, 26 November 2018, p. 3.

Tan, Tang-Mo, 'Shared feelings of the Long Shong Film Channel generation: Interview with Lin Kuan-Hui, director of Secrets in the Hot Spring', Funscreen 626 (2018). <https://funscreen.tfai.org.tw/article/9784>

Taylor, Damon, 'Design futures', in Massey (ed.), A Companion to Contemporary Design since 1945 (2019), 51–71.

Taylor, Jodie, 'Taking it in the ear: on musico-sexual synergies and the (queer) possibility that music is sex', Continuum: Journal of Media & Cultural Studies 26.4 (2012), 603–14.

Teo, Stephen, *Chinese Martial Arts Cinema: The Wuxia Tradition* (Edinburgh: Edinburgh University Press, 2009).
Teng, Emma Jinhua, *Taiwan's Imagined Geography: Chinese Colonial Travel Writing and Pictures, 1683–1895* (Cambridge, MA: Harvard University Press, 2004).
Thompson, Michael, *Rubbish Theory: The Creation and Destruction of Value*, second edition (London: Pluto Press, 2017).
Thongchai Winichakul, *Siam Mapped: A History of the Geo-Body of a Nation* (Honolulu: University of Hawai'i Press, 1994).
Tong, Chris, 'Toward a Hong Kong ecocinema: the *dis-appearance* of "Nature" in three films by Fruit Chan', in Lu and Mi (eds), *Chinese Ecocinema* (2009), 171–93.
Trotter, David, *Cooking with Mud: The Idea of Mess in Nineteenth-Century Art and Fiction* (Oxford: Oxford University Press, 2000).
Tsai, Bor-Wen and Yung-Ching Lo, 'The spatial knowledge of indigenous people in mountainous environments: a case study of three Taiwanese indigenous tribes', *Geographical Review* 103:3 (July 2013), 390–408.
Tsai, Lin-Chin, 'Mapping Formosa: settler colonial cartography in Taiwan cinema in the 1950s', in Shu-Mei Shih and Lin-Chin Tsai (eds), *Indigenous Knowledge in Taiwan and Beyond* (Singapore: Springer, 2021), 295–319.
Tuan, Yi-Fu, *Space and Place: The Perspective of Experience* (Minneapolis: University of Minnesota Press, 1977).
Tweedie, James, 'Morning in the new metropolis: Taipei and the globalization of the city film', in Darrell William Davis and Ru-Shou Robert Chen (eds), *Cinema Taiwan: Politics, popularity and state of the arts* (London: Routledge, 2007), 116–30.
Udden, James, 'Taiwanese comedies under the shadow of the Chinese market', *Journal of Chinese Cinemas* 12:2 (2018), 174–86.
Uhlin, Graig, 'Feeling depleted: ecocinema and the atmospherics of affect', in Kyle Bladow and Jennifer Ladino, *Affective Ecocriticism: Emotion, Embodiment, Environment* (Lincoln, Nebraska: University of Nebraska Press, 2018), 279–98.
Wang, Chialin Sharon, 'Memories of the future: remaking Taiwanese-ness in *Cape No. 7*', *Journal of Chinese Cinemas* 6:2 (2012), 135–52.
Wang, Yi-Chen, 'Demon and ghost stories, seeing people's joys and sorrows', *Academia Sinica: Research*, 13 July 2018. <https://research.sinica.edu.tw/lin-mei-rong-folklore-mosina-ghost-taiwan/>
Wang, Yun-Yan, 'One must get used to loneliness: an interview with Chang Tso-Chi, director of *Summer Vacation Homework*', *Funscreen* 436 (2013). <https://funscreen.tfai.org.tw/article/9590>
Weinthal, Lois, 'Interior atmosphere', in Massey (ed.), *A Companion to Contemporary Design since 1945* (2019), 157–72.
Weng, Ching-Min, Shu-Ming Hsu, and Chun-Chi Yang, 'Concentration ratio in Taiwan's film market: A case study', *Asian Journal of Communication* 9:2 (1999), 116–28.
Weng, Huang-Te, 'See a ruin amidst the bustle, vitality in ruin: Interview with Yeh Tien-Lun, director of *West Side Fairy Tale*', *Funscreen* 587 (2016). <https://funscreen.tfai.org.tw/article/9744>
Wicks, James, *Transnational Representations: The State of Taiwan Film in the 1960s and 1970s* (Hong Kong: Hong Kong University Press, 2014).
Williams, Tony, 'Wang Yu – the Taiwan years', *Asian Cinema* 23:1 (2012), 75–104.
Wood, Denis, *Rethinking the Power of Maps* (London: Guildford Press, 2010).
Wu, Chia-Rong, 'Re-examining extreme violence: historical reconstruction and ethnic consciousness in *Warriors of the Rainbow*: *Seediq Bale*', *ASIANetwork Exchange* 21:2 (Spring 2014), 24–32.

Wu, Meiling, 'Postsadness Taiwan new cinema: eat, drink, everyman, everywoman', in Lu and Yeh (eds), *Chinese-Language Film* (2005), 76–95.

Wu, Ming-Yi, *The Man with the Compound Eyes*. Translated by Darryl Sterk (London: Vintage Books, 2014).

Yan, Yuan-Chen, 'One island, one movie: interview with Tsui Yung-Hui, director of *Long Time No Sea*', *Funscreen* 624 (2018). <https://funscreen.tfai.org.tw/article/9782>

Yang, Ta-Ching, 'Log into the film to go travelling #1: *Godspeed*', *Catchplay*, 24 February 2017. <https://edsays.catchplay.com/tw/article-860-rsgtv2gj>

Yang, Karen Ya-Chu, 'Passionately documenting: Taiwan's latest cinematic revival', *Journal of Film and Video* 67.2 (Summer 2015), 44–54.

Yang, Nai-Chen, 'Interview with director Chen Hung-I: *Design 7 Love* was inspired by *Massage*', *Fenghuang Entertainment News*, 25 December 2014. <https://ent.ifeng.com/a/20141225/42119163_0.shtml>

Yee, Cordell D. K., 'Reinterpreting traditional Chinese geographical maps', in Harley and Woodward (eds), *The History of Cartography, Volume 2* (1994), 35–70.

Yee, Cordell D. K., 'Chinese cartography among the arts: objectivity, subjectivity, representation', in Harley and Woodward (eds), *The History of Cartography, Volume 2* (1994), 128–69.

Yee, Cordell D. K., 'Traditional Chinese cartography and the myth of westernization', in Harley and Woodward (eds), *The History of Cartography, Volume 2* (1994), 170–202.

Yeh, Emilie Yueh-Yu, 'Poetics and politics of Hou Hsiao-Hsien's films', in Lu and Yeh (eds), *Chinese-Language Film* (2005), 163–85.

Yeh, Emilie Yueh-Yu, 'Taiwan: popular cinema's disappearing act', in Anne Tereska Ciecko (ed.), *Contemporary Asian Cinema: Popular Culture in a Global Frame* (Oxford: Berg, 2006), 156–68.

Yeh, Emilie Yueh-Yu, and Darrell William Davis, *Taiwan Film Directors: A Treasure Island* (New York: Columbia University Press, 2005).

Yeh, Emilie Yueh-Yu, Darrell William Davis, and Wenchi Lin (eds), *32 New Takes on Taiwan Cinema* (Ann Arbor: University of Michigan Press, 2022).

Yip, June, *Envisioning Taiwan: Fiction, Cinema, and the Nation in the Cultural Imaginary* (Durham: Duke University Press, 2004).

Yorke, John, *Into the Woods: How Stories Work and Why We Tell Them* (London: Penguin, 2013).

Yu, Tai-Lang and Jason Pan, 'Aborigines now make up 28% of Hualien County', *Taipei Times*, 17 February 2014, p. 3.

Yue, Audrey, and Olivia Khoo (eds), *Sinophone Cinemas* (Basingstoke, Hampshire: Palgrave, 2014).

Zhang, Yingjin, *Cinema, Space, and Polylocality in a Globalizing China* (Honolulu: University of Hawai'i Press, 2010).

Zhang, Yingjin, 'Taiwan film market in the new millennium', in Pickowicz and Zhang (eds), *Locating Taiwan Cinema in the Twenty-First Century* (2020), 21–40.

Zhang, Zhen, 'Migrating hearts: the cultural geography of Sylvia Chang's Melodrama', in Lingzhen Wang (ed.), *Chinese Women's Cinema: Transnational Contexts* (New York: Columbia University Press, 2011), 88–110.

Zhou, Xuelin, *Youth Culture in Chinese Language Film* (Abingdon: Routledge, 2016).

Video Sources

Camcorder footage of *Little Girl in Red*. 1998. <https://www.youtube.com/watch?v=5E2Oau4ayYA&app=desktop>

Lin, Shu-Yu, 'Thomas Lin Shu-Yu Series: Director's Q&A', at Taiwan Post New Wave Cinema Project, SOAS University of London, Centre of Taiwan Studies. 6 November 2020. <https://www.youtube.com/watch?v=g7WMkOdk1VA>

Lin, Ting-Ying, 'New auteurs in Taiwan post-New Wave cinema: Hou Chi-Jan, Lin Shu-Yu, and Cheng Yu-Chieh', at Taiwan Post New Wave Cinema Project, *SOAS University of London, Centre of Taiwan Studies*. 5 November 2020. <https://www.youtube.com/watch?v=t5VhW9tn0Ms&t=2513s>

Taiwan Cinema Yearbooks

Chinese Taipei Film Archive (1991–2013)
Taiwan Film Institute (2014–19)
Taiwan Film and Audiovisual Institute (2020–1)

Personal Interviews

An, Bon. 28 June 2019.
Cheng, Yu-Chieh. 27 June 2016.
Hsu, Yu-Ting. 2 July 2019.
Kuo, Cheng-Chui. 11 August 2021.
Lu, Yen-Chiu. 13 July 2019.
Mebow, Laha. 2 July 2019.
Wang, Jen-You. 3 June 2019.

FILMOGRAPHY

Films Cited from Taiwan, Including Co-productions

20:30:40, 二十三十四十 (Sylvia Chang, 2004).
52Hz I Love You, 52赫茲我愛你 (Wei Te-Sheng, 2017).
Aground, 澤水困 (Hsin Chien-Tsung, 2017).
Alifu, the Prince/ss, 阿莉芙 (Wang Yu-Lin, 2017).
Amour-Legende, 松鼠自殺事件 (Wu Mi-Sen, 2006).
Anywhere Somewhere Nowhere, 到不了的地方 (Li Ting, 2014).
As We Like It, 揭大歡喜 (Chen Hung-I, Wei Ying-Chuan, 2021).
Au Revoir Taipei, 一頁台北 (Arvin Chen, 2010).
Beautiful Treasure Island, 美麗寶島 (Chen Wen-Chuan, 1952).
Beyond Beauty: Taiwan from Above, 看見台灣 (Chi Po-Lin, 2013).
Black Sheep, 兒子老子 (Bon An, 2016).
Blue Gate Crossing, 藍色大門 (Yee Chih-Yen, 2002).
Borrowed Life, A, 多桑 (Wu Nien-Jen, 1994).
Boys from Fengkuei, The, 風櫃來的人 (Hou Hsiao-Hsien, 1983).
Brighter Summer Day, A, 牯嶺街少年殺人事件 (Edward Yang, 1991).
Ça fait si longtemps, 漂流遇見你 (Laha Mebow, 2017).
Cape No. 7, 海角七號 (Wei Te-Sheng, 2008).
Da Yu: The Touch of Fate, 指間的重量 (Pan Chih-Yen, 2006).
Dear Ex, 誰先愛上他的 (Hsu Yu-Ting, Hsu Chih-Yen, 2018).
Dear Tenant, 親愛的房客 (Cheng Yu-Chieh, 2020).
Design 7 Love, 相愛的七種設計 (Chen Hung-I, 2014).
Design & Thinking, 設計與思考 (Tsai Mu-Ming, 2012).
Do Over, 一年之初 (Cheng Yu-Chieh, 2006).
Eternal Summer, 盛夏光年 (Leste Chen, 2006).
Exit, 迴光奏鳴曲 (Chienn Hsiang, 2014).
Exit No. 6, 六號出口 (Lin Yu-Hsien, 2006).

Father to Son, 范保德 (Hsiao Ya-Chuan, 2018).
Finding Sayun, 不一樣的月光 (Laha Mebow, 2011).
Forêt Debussy, 德布西森林 (Kuo Cheng-Chui, 2016).
Fourth Portrait, The, 第四張畫 (Chung Mong-Hong, 2010).
God Man Dog, 流浪神狗人 (Chen Singing, 2007).
Godspeed, 一路順風 (Chung Mong-Hong, 2016).
Great Buddha +, The, 大佛普拉斯 (Huang Hsin-Yao, 2017).
Heroic Pioneers, The, 唐山過台灣 (Lee Hsing, 1986).
Hidden Treasures in the Mountain, 山的那一邊 (Wang Tao-Nan, 2018).
Homecoming Pilgrimage of Dajia Mazu, The, 大甲媽祖回娘家 (Huang Chun-Ming, 1974).
Husband's Secret, The, 丈夫的秘密 (Lin Tuan-Chiu, 1960).
I Didn't Dare to Tell You, 不敢跟你講 (Mou Tun-Fei, 1969).
Island Etude, 練習曲 (Chen Hwai-En, 2007).
I WeirDO, 怪胎 (Liao Ming-Yi, 2020).
Lokah Laqi, 只要我長大 (Laha Mebow, 2016).
Long Time No Sea, 只有大海知道 (Tsui Yung-Hui, 2018).
Love, 愛 (Niu Cheng-Tse, 2012).
L-O-V-E, 愛到底 (various, 2009).
Mad King of Taipei, The, 西城童話 (Yeh Tien-Lun, 2017).
Man from Island West, 西部來的人 (Huang Ming-Chuan, 1991).
More than Blue, 比悲傷更悲傷的故事 (Lin Hsiao-Chien, 2018).
Most Distant Course, The, 最遙遠的距離 (Lin Ching-Chieh, 2007).
My Little Honey Moon, 野蓮香 (Cheng Yu-Chieh, 2012).
My Missing Valentine, 消失的情人節 (Chen Yu-Hsun, 2020).
Nimbus, 帶水雲 (Huang Hsin-Yao, 2009).
One Day, 有一天 (Hou Chi-Jan, 2010).
On Mount Hehuan, 合歡山上 (Pan Lei, 1958).
Orz Boyz, 囧男孩 (Yang Ya-Che, 2008).
Our Times, 我的少女時代 (Chen Yu-Shan, 2015).
Pakeriran, 巴克力藍的夏天 (Lekal Sumi, 2017).
Pongso No Tao, 人之島 (Wang Chin-Kuei, 2008).
Rebels of the Neon God, 青少年哪吒 (Tsai Ming-Liang, 1992).
Riding the Breeze (Southern Wind), 南風 (Kôji Hagiuda, 2014).
Scenery Through the Smog, The, 風從哪裡來 (Shih Ho-Feng, 2018).
Secrets in the Hot Spring, 切小金家的旅馆 (Lin Kuan-Hui, 2018).
Sen Sen, 生生 (Bon An, 2018).
Somewhere I Have Never Travelled, 帶我去遠方 (Fu Tien-Yu, 2009).
Soul, 失魂 (Chung Mong-Hong, 2013).
Starry Starry Night, 星空 (Lin Shu-Yu, 2011).
Story of the Stone, The, 紅樓夢 (Wu Hsing-Hsiang, 2018).
Super Citizen Ko, 超級大國民 (Wan Jen, 1994).
Tag-Along, The, 紅衣小女孩 (Cheng Wei-Hao, 2015).
Tag-Along 2, The, 紅衣小女孩2 (Cheng Wei-Hao, 2017).
Taipei Exchanges, 第36个故事 (Hsiao Ya-Chuan, 2010).
Take Me to The Moon, 帶我去月球 (Hsieh Chun-Yi, 2017).
Tarzan and the Treasure, 泰山寶藏 (Liang Che-Fu, 1965).
Terrorizers, 恐怖分子 (Edward Yang, 1986).
Thanatos, Drunk, 醉.生夢死 (Chang Tso-Chi, 2015).
Time in Quchi, A, 暑假作業 (Chang Tso-Chi, 2013).
Tropical Fish, 熱帶魚 (Chen Yu-Hsun, 1995).
Turn Around, 老師你會不會回來 (Chen Ta-Pu, 2017).
Unwritten Rules, 潛規則 (Cheng Yu-Chieh, 2012).

Vive L'Amour, 愛情萬歲 (Tsai Ming-Liang, 1994).
Warriors of the Rainbow: Seediq Bale, 賽德克·巴萊 (Wei Te-Sheng, 2011).
Wawa No Cidal, 太陽的孩子 (Cheng Yu-Chieh, Lekal Sumi 2015).
When a Wolf Falls in Love with a Sheep, 南方小羊牧場 (Hou Chi-Jan, 2012).
White Ant, 白蟻—慾望謎網 (Chu Hsien-Che, 2016).
Winds of September, 九降風 (Tom Lin Shu-Yu, 2008).
Wish of the Ocean Rice, 海稻米的願望 (Lekal Sumi, 2013).
Yang Yang, 陽陽 (Cheng Yu-Chieh, 2009).
You Are the Apple of My Eye, 那些年，我們一起追的女孩 (Giddens Ko Ching-Teng, 2011).
Young Dudes, 騷人 (Chen Yin-Jung, 2012).
Your Name Engraved Herein, 刻在你心裡的名字 (Liu Kuang-Hui, 2020).
Zone Pro Site, 總舖師 (Chen Yu-Hsun, 2013).

Other Films Cited

Amélie (Jean-Pierre Jeunet, 2001). France, Germany.
Chinese Ghost Story, A (Tsui Hark, 1987). Hong Kong.
Chinese Odyssey, A (Jeffrey Lau Chun-Wai, 1995). Hong Kong, China.
E.T. (Steven Spielberg, 1982). USA.
Exorcist, The (William Friedkin, 1973). USA.
Grudge, The (Takashi Shimizu, 2002). Japan.
He's a Woman, She's a Man (Peter Chan Ho-Sun, 1994). Hong Kong.
Love Actually (Richard Curtis, 2003). UK, USA, France.
Once Upon a Time in China (Tsui Hark, 1991). Hong Kong.
Only God Forgives (Nicholas Winding Refn, 2013). USA, Denmark, France.
Persona (Ingmar Bergman, 1966). Sweden.
Ring, The (Hideo Nakata, 1998). Japan.
Sayon's Bell (Hiroshi Shimizu, 1943). Japan.
Searchers, The (John Ford, 1956). USA.
Singin' in the Rain (Gene Kelly and Stanley Donen, 1952). USA.
Umbrellas of Cherbourg, The (Jacques Demy, 1964). France, West Germany.

Films Consulted

This select filmography lists fiction films from Taiwan, including co-productions, that were released from the year 2000 onwards. Due to considerations of space, this list omits documentaries and short films.

10 + 10 (various, 2011).
9th Precinct, The, 第九分局 (Wang Din-Ling, 2019).
A Choo, 打噴嚏 (Ko Meng-Jung & Peter Tsi, 2020).
Assassin, The, 刺客聶隱娘 (Hou Hsiao-Hsien, 2015).
At Café 6, 六弄咖啡館 (Wu Tzu-Yun, 2016).
Best of Times, The, 美麗時光 (Chang Tso-Chi, 2002).
Black & White Episode 1: The Dawn of Assault, 痞子英雄首部曲：全面開戰 (Tsai Yueh-Hsun, 2012).
Blowfish, 河豚 (Lee Chi-Yuarn, 2011).
Bold, The Corrupt and The Beautiful, The, 血觀音 (Yang Ya-Che, 2017).
Boluomi, 菠蘿蜜 (Lau Kek-Huat, Chen Hseuh-Chen, 2019).
Bridge Curse, The, 女鬼橋 (Shih Yue-Lung, 2020).
Café Lumière, 珈琲時光 (Hou Hsiao-Hsien, 2003).

FILMOGRAPHY

Candy Rain, 花吃了那女孩 (Chen Hung-I, 2008).
Cannot Live Without You, 不能沒有你 (Dai Li-Jen, 2009).
Cities of Last Things, 幸福城市 (Ho Wi-Ting, 2018).
Classmates Minus, 同學麥娜絲 (Huang Hsin-Yao, 2020).
Crouching Tiger, Hidden Dragon, 臥虎藏龍 (Ang Lee, 2000).
Days, 日子 (Tsai Ming-Liang, 2020).
Detention, 返校 (Hsu Han-Chiang, 2019).
Din Tao: Leader of the Parade, 陣頭 (Kai Fung, 2012).
Double Vision, 雙瞳 (Chen Kuo-Fu, 2002).
Drifting Flowers, 漂浪青春 (Zero Chou, 2008).
Falls, The, 瀑布 (Chung Mong-Hong, 2021).
Fish out of Water, A, 上岸的魚 (Lai Kuo-An, 2017).
Formula 17, 17歲的天空 (Chen Yin-Jung, 2004).
Gangs, the Oscars, and the Walking Dead, The, 江湖無難事 (Kao Pin-Chuan, 2019).
Gatao, 角頭 (Lee Yun-Chieh, 2015).
Gatao 2: Rise of the King, 角頭2:王者再起 (Yen Cheng-Kuo, 2018).
Gatao: The Last Stray, 角頭—浪流連 (Chiang Jui-Chih, 2021).
Girlfriend, Boyfriend/Gf*Bf, 女朋友。男朋友 (Yang Ya-Che, 2012).
Girl's Revenge, 哈囉少女 (Wang Wei-Hsiang, 2020).
Go Go G-Boys, 當我們同在一起 (Yu Jong-Jong, 2006).
Goodbye, Dragon Inn, 不散 (Tsai Ming-Liang, 2003).
Help Me Eros, 幫幫我，愛神 (Lee Kang-Sheng, 2007).
High Flash, 引爆點 (Chuang Ching-Shen, 2018).
How Are You, Dad?, 爸，你好嗎 (Chang Tso-Chi, 2009).
How To Train Our Dragon, 有五個姊姊的我就註定要單身了啊 (Su Wen-Shang, 2018).
I Don't Want to Sleep Alone, 黑眼圈 (Tsai Ming-Liang, 2006).
Ice Poison, 冰毒 (Midi Z, 2014).
I Missed You, 我沒有談的那場戀愛 (Hsu Yu-Ting, Hsu Chih-Yen, 2021).
Increasing Echo, 修行 (Chienn Hsiang, 2021).
Juliets, 茱麗葉 (various, 2010).
Jump Ashin!, 翻滾吧！阿信 (Lin Yu-Hsien, 2011).
Kano (Umin Boya, 2014).
Kara-Orchestra, 很久沒有敬我了妳 (Wu Mi-Sen, 2015).
Last Painting, The, 自畫像 (Chen Hung-I, 2017).
Laundryman, The, 青田街一號 (Chung Lee, 2015).
Leaving Virginia, 破處 (Lin Li-Shu, 2020).
Life of Pi, 少年Pi的奇幻漂流 (Ang Lee, 2012).
Little Big Women, 孤味 (Hsu Chien-Chieh, 2020).
Losers, The, 廢物 (Lou Yi-An, 2013).
Lust, Caution, 色，戒 (Ang Lee, 2007).
Magnificent Bobita, The, 最乖巧的殺人犯 (Ching Shen-Chuang, 2018).
Make Up, 命運化妝師 (Lien Yi-Chi, 2011).
Man in Love, 當男人戀愛時 (Yin Chen-Hao, 2021).
Maverick, 菜鳥 (Cheng Wen-Tang, 2015).
Miao Miao, 渺渺 (Cheng Hsiao-Tse, 2008).
Millennium Mambo, 千禧曼波 (Hou Hsiao-Hsien, 2001).
Mirror Image, 命帶追逐 (Hsiao Ya-Chuan, 2000).
Miss Andy, 迷失安狄 (Teddy Chin, 2020).
Missing Johnny, 強尼．凱克 (Huang Xi, 2017).
Missing, The, 不見 (Lee Kang-Sheng, 2003).
Mom Thinks I'm Crazy to Marry a Japanese Guy, 雖然媽媽說我不可以嫁去日本 (Akihisa Yachida, 2017).

Mon Mon Mon Monsters, 報告老師！怪怪怪怪物！ (Giddens Ko Ching-Teng, 2017).
Murmur of the Hearts, 念念 (Sylvia Chang, 2015).
Nina Wu, 灼人秘密 (Midi Z, 2019).
Night Market Hero, 雞排英雄 (Yeh Tien-Lun, 2011).
Nobody, 有鬼 (Lin Chuan-Hua, 2020).
On Happiness Road, 幸福路上 (Sung Hsin-Yin, 2017).
Our Island, Our Dreams, 星月無盡 (Tong Chan-Yu, 2009).
Paradise in Service, 軍中樂園 (Niu Cheng-Tse, 2014).
Parking, 停車 (Chung Mong-Hong, 2008).
Passage, The, 經過 (Cheng Wen-Tang, 2004).
Poor Folk, 窮人。榴槤。麻藥。偷渡客 (Midi Z, 2012).
Receptionist, The, 接線員 (Jenny Lu, 2016).
Return to Burma, 歸來的人 (Midi Z, 2011).
Ripples of Desire, 花漾 (Zero Chou, 2012).
Road to Mandalay, The, 再見瓦城 (Midi Z, 2016).
Salute! Sun Yat-Sen/Meeting Dr Sun, 行動代號:孫中山 (Yee Chih-Yen, 2014).
Saving Mother Robot, 瑪德2號 (Chu Chia-Lin, 2013).
Scoundrels, The, 狂徒 (Hung Tzu-Hsuan, 2018).
Secret, 不能說的·秘密 (Jay Chou, 2007).
(Sex) Appeal, 寒蟬效應 (Wang Wei-Ming, 2014).
Silk, 詭絲 (Su Chao-Pin, 2006).
Soul of a Demon, 蝴蝶 (Chang Tso-Chi, 2008).
Soul, The, 緝魂 (Cheng Wei-Hao, 2021).
Spider Lilies, 刺青 (Zero Chou, 2007).
Splendid Float, 艷光四射歌舞團 (Zero Chou, 2004).
Stray Dogs, 郊遊 (Tsai Ming-Liang, 2013).
Sweet Alibis, 甜蜜殺機 (Lien Yi-Chi, 2014).
Sumimasen, Love, 對不起，我愛你 (Lin Yu-Hsien, 2011).
Sun, A, 陽光普照 (Chung Mong-Hong, 2019).
Synapses, 那個我最親愛的陌生人 (Chang Tso-Chi, 2019).
Tag-Along, The: The Devil Fish, 人面魚: 紅衣小女孩外傳 (Chuang Hsuan-Wei, 2018).
Tale of the Lost Boys, 他和他的心旅程 (Joselito Altarejos, 2017).
Teacher, The, 我的靈魂是愛做的 (Chen Ming-Lang, 2019).
Tears, 眼淚 (Cheng Wen-Tang, 2009).
Tenants Downstairs, The, 樓下的房客 (Tsuei Jehn-Dung, 2016).
Three Times, 最好的時光 (Hou Hsiao-Hsien, 2005).
Trick or Treat, 詭扯 (Hsu Fu-Hsiang, 2021).
Twa-Tiu-Tiann, 大稻埕 (Yeh Tien-Lun, 2014).
Village of No Return, The, 健忘村 (Chen Yu-Hsun, 2017).
Visage, 臉 (Tsai Ming-Liang, 2009).
Wayward Cloud, The, 天邊一朵雲 (Tsai Ming-Liang, 2005).
We Are Champions, 下半場 (Chang Jung-Chi, 2019).
What on Earth Have I Done Wrong?!, 情非得已之生存之道 (Niu Cheng-Tse, 2007).
What Time Is It There?, 你那邊幾點 (Tsai Ming-Liang, 2001).
When Geek Meets Serial Killer, 野狼與瑪莉 (Chin Pei-Chen, 2015).
When Love Comes, 當愛來的時候 (Chang Tso-Chi, 2010).
Who Killed Cock Robin, 目擊者 (Cheng Wei-Hao, 2017).
Wild Sparrow, 野雀之詩 (Li Shih, 2019).
Wrath of Desire, 愛情殺人紀事 (Zero Chou, 2020).
Xiao Mei, 小美 (Hwang Ma-Ren, 2018).
Yi Yi, 一 一 (Edward Yang, 2000).
Zinnia Flower, 百日告別 (Lin Shu-Yu, 2015).

INDEX

Note: entries in *Italic* are film titles, and page numbers in *italic* refer to figures.

achromatopsia, 35
actors, indigenous, 95–101, 102
Aground, 33–4, 45–51, *46*, *47*
   Chi, 46, 47, 49, 50, 51
   Chin, 46, 47, 50, 51
   drone shots, 47, 51
   Teng, 46, 50
   water in, 48–50
AIDS metaphor, 14
Alifu, the Prince/ss, 142
Altman, Robert, 125
Amélie, 114
Amour-Legende, 1–3, *2*, *4*, 28, 31, 50
   Bomba del Corazón, La, 1–3
   Oshima, 1–3
An, Bon, 139, 141, 157, 158–9, 163
Angaw, Bauki, 85
animism, 68, 69
Anywhere Somewhere Nowhere, 29
Apo', Kofid Talo, 101
Aristotle, 16, 149
around-the-island (*huandao*) trend, 9
art installations
   'Next Play: Green Factory', 135
As We Like It, 192
   Orlando, 192
atmospheric conditions, 156
Au Revoir Taipei, 63
auralism, 183
auteurs, 4, 14–15

Ban, Tie-Hsiang, 46
Bao, Hongwei, 117
Baozangyan, Taipei, 137
Basang, Yawei, 79
Beautiful Treasure Island, 9

Beijing, 125
bentuhua (indigenisation), 15
bereavement, 177
Bergman, Ingmar, 46
Berry, Chris, 6, 15, 58, 79–80, 84, 97
Bertoia, Harry, 110
Bettinson, Gary, 16, 57–8, 61, 184
Beyond Beauty: Taiwan from Above, 91
Bi, Feiyu, 124
bilocation, 27, 38
biodiversity, 70, 77
Black Sheep, 139–40, 141, 144, 146, 152, 159, 161–4
   Chi-Ping, 141, 152, 160, 161, 162–3
   Lu Ming, 141, 144, 160, 161, 162–3
Blue Gate Crossing, 147
Bokeh, Kosang, 88, 97
Bordwell, David, 16, 19, 112, 174
Borges, Jorge Luis, 77
Borrowed Life, A, 99
Boya, Umin, 84
Boys from Fengkuei, The, 14
Braester, Yomi, 132
Brighter Summer Day, A, 125
Bruno, Giuliana, 30, 32, 34, 149, 159, 181–2
Buck, Daniel, 168
Buddhism, 41, 45, 155
bullying, 177
buluo zhuyi (tribalism), 83
Butler, Judith, 100, 146
Buya, Watan, 87

Ça fait si longtemps, 105
Cai, Xiao, 14, 168, 171
Cao, Xueqin, 115–16, 124

209

Cape No. 7, 4, 5, 9, 28–9
  Ah-Chia, 15, 29
  and *bentuhua* (indigenisation), 15
Caquard, Sébastien, 19, 32
cartography
  cinematic cartography, 11–13
  as film practice, 19
  KMT, 2, 7, 9–10
Casagrande, Marco, 128
Castro, Teresa, 11, 17, 30
censorship, 8, 10
Certeau, Michel de, 30, 181–2
Chan, Ho-Sun, Peter, 178
Chang, Anita Wen-Shin, 83, 105
Chang, Bi-Yu, 7, 24n
Chang, Chin-Chen, 86
Chang, Hsi-Wen, 102, 103, 106
Chang, Hsiao-Chuan, 59
Chang, Hsiao-Hung, 127
Chang, Ivy I-Chu, 42, 69
Chang, Shu-Hao, 32, 143
Chang, Sylvia, 124, 131, 147
Chang, Ting-Hu, 169
Chang, Tso-Chi, 136–7, 167, 170, 171, 172, 173
Chang, Yang-Yang, 31
Chao, Yu-Ting, 123
Chen, Arvin, 63
Chen, Chien-Nien, 105
Chen, Chu-Sheng, 170
Chen, Hung-I, 110, 116, 118, 119, 120, 124, 192
Chen, Hwai-En, 5, 67
Chen, Jen-Shuo, 175
Chen, Kai-Ting, 114
Chen, Leste, 5
Chen, Shiang-Chyi, 68, 141, 147, 148–9
Chen, Singing, 5
Chen, Ting-Ni, 158
Chen, Wen-Chuan, 9
Chen, Yan-Ming, 122
Chen, Yi-Han, 143–4
Chen, Yi-Wen, 43
Chen, Yin-Jung, 111
Chen, Yu-Hsun, 29–30, 32, 42, 111, 147
Cheng, Wei-Hao, 55, 56, 58
Cheng, Yu-Chieh, 5, 8, 26, 30, 83, 84–5, 88, 96–8, 99–100, 119, 142
Cheng, Yu-Ching, 117
Cheung, Leslie, 178
Chi, Pei-Hui, 29
Chi, Po-Lin, 91
Chi, Yan-Kai, 118
Chiang Kai-Shek regime, 50
Chiang, Kuo-Pin, 115–16
Chien, Shih-Keng, 72
Chienn, Hsiang, 139, 147, 148–9
Chin Han, 115–16
Chinese Ghost Story, A, 175, 178
Chinese Odyssey, A, 178
Chiu, Tse, 142, 143
Chou, Yung-Hsuan, 37
Christianity, 89
Chu, Hsien-Che, 113
Chu, Mimi, 176, 178
Chu, Shan, 142
Chuang, Juan-Ying, 122
Chuang, Yi-Tseng, 181
Chulphongsathorn, Graiwoot, 59
Chung, Mong-Hong, 33, 41, 42, 43, 56, 69
Chung, Yao, 46
cinematic space, definition of, 20
colour blindness, 34, 35
Conley, Tom, 12, 33, 117
  bilocation, 27, 38
cosmology, 45–51
Council of Indigenous Peoples, 94
counter-mapping, 91–5, 140
COVID-19 films, 164
COVID-19 pandemic, 191
Cultural and Creative Park, Huashan, 135–6
Cummings, E. E., 34, 39–40
Curtis, Richard, 124

Da Yu: The Touch of Fate, 5, 31
  Da-Yu, 31
Dai, Li-Jen, 40, 169
Dao, Helen Thanh, 26
Davis, Darrell William, 6, 15, 145
Dear Ex, 31, 137, 139–40, 142–3, 144, 146, 152, 153–5, *162*, 191
  atmospheric conditions, representation of, 156
  Cheng-Hsi, 142, 152, 154–5, 160
  Chieh, 142, 146, 152, 153–4, 155, 161
  Liu San-Lien, 31, 142, 146, 154–5, 159, 160–1
  Sung Cheng-Yuan, 142, 146, 152
Dear Tenant, 142
deforestation, 70
Demy, Jacques, 116

Design 7 Love, 110–11, *112*, 114–15, *115*, 116–17, 118, 119–24, *121*
  Andrew, 117
  cab driver, 119, 123
  Chi-Tzu, 114, 117, 118
  Chiang, 114–15, 117, 118
  construction projects, 132
  Doris, 110, 117, 119–20, 123, 124, 127, 132
  Emma, 114–15, 117, 119, 123
  Mark, 110, 117, 123, 124
  Pa-Tzu, 110–11, 117, 119, 123, 124, 127, 132, 133
  urban vegetation, 132
Design & Thinking, 123
digital technology, 58–9, 156–8
disabilities, 87
  colour blindness, 34, 35
Do Over, 5, 30
  Kao, 30
  Ting-An, 30
Dodge, Martin, 19
Dogme 95 manifesto, 49
domestic dramas, 139–64
  atmosphere, construction of, 146–52, 156
  cleaning, 158–64
  decay and renewal, 158–64
  digital technology, 156–8
  health problems, 144–6
Donen, Stanley, 124
Douglas, Mary, 161
Dream of the Red Chamber, The, 115–16, 124
drone shots
  Aground, 47, 51
  Godspeed, 43–4
  The Tag-Along 2, 55
Dung, Kai-Cheung, 3, 120
Dunne, Anthony, 110, 124
Dyer, Richard, 58, 176

eco-cinema, 60, 61
  Soul, 69–70
  Starry Starry Night, 64
environmentalism, 13
environments
  definition of, 13
  Taiwan, 13–16
Eskildsen, Robert, 7
E.T., 175
Eternal Summer, 5

Exit, 139–40, 141, 144, 147–9, *148*, 150–3, 156
  atmosphere, construction of, 147, 156
  Chang, 153, 156
  Ling, 141, 144, 147–9, 150–3, 156, 159
  Mei-Mei, 151–2
  Mei-Mei's boyfriend, 151–2
Exit No. 6, 5
Exorcist, The, 175

Family Viewing, 78
Fan, Van, 15, 29, 45
Fang, Chih-Yu, 100
Fang, Wen-Shan, 136
Farquhar, Mary, 6
Father to Son, 168, 169, 170, 184–8, *186*
  Da-Chi, 184–5, 187
  Kuo Yu-Chin, 185
  Newman, 185–8
  Pao-Te, 168, 169, 184–5, 186–8
  sounds, 185, 187, 188
  water, 185, 187, 188
  Yu-Chin, 171, 185–8
feng shui, 44, 49–50
52Hz I Love You, 111, 116, 117, 118, 120–2, 129–30, *129*
  An, 118, 122, 123, 129, 131
  Hsin, 122, 123, 129, 131
  Ta-Ho, 124
film poetics, 16–18, 57, 58, 61, 74, 112–13
  large-scale form, 16, 17–18, 20, 112
film mapping, 20
film practice, 18–20
  cartography as, 19
Finding Sayun, 83, 84, 86, 96, 100
  clothing, 107
  Hsiao-Ju, 100, 107
  non-professional actors, 98
  root-tracing journey, 86
  Yukan, 86, 98, 100
  Yukan's grandfather, 86, 98, 100
Fishing Luck, 83, 105
Ford, John, 169
forests, 20–1, 55–80
  Forêt Debussy, 72–9, 76
  indigenous protagonists, 79–80
  return of, 55–6
  Soul, 67–9
  Starry Starry Night, 61–7

forests (cont.)
　The Tag-Along, 67–8, 69–70, 71–2
　and Taiwanese identity, 56–61
Forêt Debussy, 56, 59, 60–1, 72–9
　forests, 72–9
　mother, 72–4
　woman (classical pianist), 60, 72–4, 78
Fourth Portrait, The, 42
Fox, James J., 86
Friedkin, William, 175
Fu, Meng-Po, 184
Fu, Tien-Yu, 33, 34, 35, 37–8, 39
Fukushima disaster, 52
Funes the Memorious (Borges), 77

García Márquez, Gabriel, 38
Gleeson, Justin, 19
globes, 40, 40, 41, 62, 62
God Man Dog, 5
Godspeed, 33–4, 40–5, 40, 51
　Ah-Wen, 43, 44
　Buddhist themes and subtext, 41, 45
　drone shots, 43–4
　Hsu, 40–1, 42–3, 45
　Na-Tou, 40, 42–3, 44, 45
　spatial patterning and design, 43–4, 45
　Ta-Pao, 40, 41, 43, 44, 45
　Tou, 40, 41, 43, 44, 45
　Wu, 44
Great Buddha +, The, 41, 167, 168, 169, 171, 181–4
　auralism, 183
　Kevin, 169, 181, 182–4
　sounds, 181, 182–3
　Sugar Apple, 181
　Tsai-Pu, 167, 181, 182–3, 184
　Tu-Tsai, 170, 181, 182–3, 184
　voyeurism, 182–3
　Yeh, 183
Greene, Graham, 38
Gwei, Lun-Mei, 60, 65

Hagiuda, Kôji, 29
Han, Chang, 141
Haneke, Michael, 157
Hara, Kenya, 110, 112
Hark, Tsui, 175
Harley, J. B., 12, 30
healthy realism, 14, 144, 145
Hérberlé, Antoine, 73
Heroic Pioneers, The, 83, 96

He's a Woman, She's a Man, 178
Highmore, Ben, 156
Homecoming Pilgrimage of Dajia Mazu, The, 12–13
homosexuality, 34, 35–7, 183
Hong, Guo-Juin, 14, 159, 165n
Horng, Meng-Hsin C., 144
horror films, 56, 59, 67–72, 79, 176, 177, 178–9
Hou, Chi-Jan, 19, 31, 113
Hou, Chih-Chien, 187
Hou, Hsiao-Hsien, 14, 18, 99, 168, 171
Hou, Jeffrey, 130
Hsia, Yu-Chiao, 134–5
Hsiao, Ya-Chuan, 63, 168, 171, 187
Hsieh, Hsin-Ying, 31–2, 164
Hsieh, Ming-Chuan, 172
Hsieh, Pei-En, 192
Hsieh, Ying-Hsuan, 31, 142, 143, 153, 154–5
Hsin, Chien-Tsung, 33, 46, 47, 48–9, 50, 51
Hsu, Chih-Yen, 31, 137
Hsu, Kai-Hsin, 46
Hsu, Wei-Ning, 59, 110, 117
Hsu, Yu-Ting, 31, 137, 139, 143, 153, 154, 156
Hu, Brian, 56, 63, 64
huandao (around-the-island) trend, 9
Huang, Bo-Wen, 42
Huang, Chien-Wei, 30
Huang, Ching-I, 26–7, 87
Huang, Chun-Ming, 12–13
Huang, Chung-Kun, 168
Huang, He, 29, 69
Huang, Hsin-Yao, 41, 167
Huang, Ming-Chuan, 97
Huang, Shang-Ho, 102, 107
Huang, Sheng-Chiu, 142
Huashan 24, 136
　Hsin-Yu, 136
　music video director, 136
Huayi Brothers, 125
Hui, Koon-Man, Michael, 40–1
Hung, Yan-Hsiang, 176
Husband's Secret, The, 10

I Didn't Dare To Tell You, 9, 10
　Ta-Yuan, 9
I WeirDO, 164
　Chen Ching, 164
　Po-Ching, 164

identity, 34, 57–8
  Chinese, 29, 38
  indigenous, 84, 87, 88, 89, 91, 101
  national, 6, 16, 38, 141, 170
  regional, 31
  taike, 15
  Taiwanese, 15, 28, 56–61, 72, 102
indigenisation (*bentuhua*), 15
indigenous Austronesian peoples, 82–107
  eastern regions, 84–6
  indigenous actors, 95–101
  identity, 84, 87, 88, 89, 91, 101
  land rights, 86–91
  non-professional actors, 95–101, 102
  television documentaries, 100
Indigenous People's Action Coalition, 86–7
Ingram, David, 67–8
interior space, 139–64
International Council of Societies of Industrial Design (later World Design Organization), 111
island-circuit films, 28–9
Island Etude, 5, 9, 28–9, 29, 67
  Ming, 28

Jameson, Fredric, 11
Japan
  and Taiwan, 7–8
Jeunet, Jean-Pierre, 114
jigsaw puzzles, 62, 65–6, 66
Journey to the West
  Sun Wukong, 46
Juan, Ching-Tien, 122
Juan, Yi-Kai, 117

Kacaw, Dongi, 87
Kantana (post-production company), 72
Kao, Ming, 10
Kao, Ying-Hsuan, 30
Karvelyte, Kristina, 117
Kavalan of Bird Stepping Stone Village, 85
Kelly, Gene, 124
Kieślowski, Krzysztof, 175
King, Hu, 128
Kitchen, Rob, 19
Ko, Ching-Teng, Giddens, 31
Ko, Wen-Je, 130
Kohn, Eduardo, 61, 74, 77, 79
Ku, Samuel, 185

Kuan, Yun-Lung, 172
Kubozuka, Yôsuke, 1
Kuo, Cheng-Chui, 56, 73, 75, 78
Kuo, Shu-Yao, 113–14
Kuo, Tsai-Chieh, 125
Kuo, Yi-Dai, 46
Kuomintang (KMT), 40
  education system, 9
  maps/cartography, 2, 7, 9–10
Kurakawa, Mei, 29
Kwan, Pun-Leung, 150

Lam, Ching-Ying, 175
Lan, Cheng-Lung, 136
land ownership issues
  surveying, 21, 86–91
Lau, Chun-Wai, Jeffrey, 178
Law, Kar-Ying, 176, 178
Lay, Jinn-Guey, 85
Lee, Hsing, 83, 144
Lee, Kuo-Hsiu, 153
Lee, Lee-Zen, 114
Lee, Pei-Yu, 32
Lee, Sang Eun Eunice, 91
Lei, Chen-Ching, 154
Lei, Kuang-Hsia, 187
Lekal, Kaco, 87
Lekal, Sumi Cilangasan, 82, 83, 84, 88, 96, 97–8, 101
LGBT issues, 142–3
Li, Chia-Gai, 72
Li, Jet, 8
Li, Ting, 29
Li, Yun-Yun, 34
Liang, Che-Fu, 10
Liao, Ching-Yao, 104
Liao, Jimmy, 61, 62
Liao, Ming-Yi, 164
Liaodong Peninsula, 7–8
Lifshey, Adam, 102
Lim, Song Hwee, 4, 5–6, 142, 173
Lin, Ching-Chieh, 5
Lin, Chung-Yu, 118
Lin, Ho-Hsuan, 176
Lin, Hsiao-Chien, 139, 145
Lin, Hui-Min, 61
Lin, Kuan-Hui, 167, 175–6, 180
Lin, Mei-Mei, 72
Lin, Na-Tou, 40
Lin, Po-Hung, 34, 39, 164
Lin, Shu-Yu, Tom, 5, 56, 61, 64–5, 66, 67, 73

Lin, Ting-Ying, 6, 33
Lin, Tuan-Chiu, 10
Lin, Yu-Hsien, 5
Ling, Chang, 104
Liu, Chin, 10
Liu, Hsin-Yu, 136
Liu, Jou-Ying, 61
Liu, Kuan-Ting, 32
Liu, Kuang-Hui, 142
Liu, Ssu-Fang Jessie, 23n, 28
Liu, Yi-Hao, 143–4
Liu, Yin-Shang, 69
Lo, Dennis, 14, 18, 96
Lo, Yung-Ching, 94
location shooting
  as place making, 18–19
Lokah Laqi, 26–7, 83, 86, 87, 90, 96, 100–1
  clothing, 107
  Hu, 26–7, 87, 88, 89–90, 91, 98–9, 107
  Hu's grandmother, 87, 89, 98–9
  Lawa, 26–7, 87, 88
  location, 98–9
  Watan, 87, 88, 98–9, 107
Long Time No Sea, 83, 102–7
  Chin-Yi, 104
  Chung-Hsun, 102, 103, 104–6, 107
  clothing, 107
  Manawei, 102, 103, 104, 105, 106–7
  Manawei's father, 102, 105, 106–7
  Manawei's grandmother, 102, 104, 105
  Tears in the Sea (song), 105
  water, 102–4, 105–7
love, 119, 124, 125, 126
L-O-V-E, 111, 136
  Huashan 24, 136
Love, 111, 113, 117, 120–2, 124, 125–7, *126*, 130–1, *131*
  Daan Forest Park, 127
  Hsiao-Kuan, 122, 127, 130–1
  Hsiao-Ni, 125, 135–6
  Jou-Yi, 122, 127, 130–1
  Kai, 123, 135–6
  Lu, 122
  Mark, 123, 125, 126
  Xiao-Ye, 125, 126
Love Actually, 124
Lu, Chin-Hsiang, 122
Lu, Huang, 114
Lu, Shih-Yuan, 143, 153

Lu, Yen-Chiu, 73, 75, 77
Lu, Yi-Ching, 72–3

Ma, Sheng-Mei, 23n, 28–9, 170
Mad King of Taipei, The, 111, 115–16, 120–2, 127–8, *134*
  Fei Mao-Chiang, 115–16, 128
  Hsiao-Hu, 113–14, 115–16, 118, 128, 133, 134
  Hsiao-Hu's mother, 134
  Ximen-King, 114, 127–8, 133–4
male characters, 167–88
Man from Island West, 97
Man with the Compound Eyes, The (Wu), 60, 90–1
mapping
  counter-mapping, 91–5, 140
  east coast, 84–6
maps
  map-reading, 3, 7, 32–3
  rugs, 35, 36–7, *36*, 39
  of Taiwan, 7–11
Martin, Fran, 113, 127, 148
Massage (Bi), 124
Matam, Hidaw, 82
Mebow, Laha, 26, 83, 84, 86, 87, 88, 96, 97, 98, 99, 100, 105
medical themes
  Black Sheep, 161
  Dear Ex, 154
  in domestic dramas, 144–6
  Exit, 147, 152–3, 156
  mental health, 144, 147, 161
  More than Blue, 143, 160
  recuperation, 144–5
  Sen Sen, 153
  Soul, 68
melodrama, 145–6
Miyazawa, Kenji, 64
Mo, Tzu-Yi, 110, *121*
Monmonier, Mark, 35, 93, 95
More than Blue, 139–40, 143–4, 149–50, *151*, 155
  Cindy, 158
  Cream (Sung Yuan-Yuan), 143–4, 149–50, 155
  K (Chang Che-Kai), 143–4, 149–50, 155, 158, 159, 160
  Yu-Hsien, 143
Most Distant Course, The, 5, 28
Mou, Tun-Fei, 9
MRT Love, 119

My Little Honey Moon, 26, 27
   Chiung-E, 26
My Missing Valentine, 32–3, *33*
   Ah-Tai, 32
   Hsiao-Chi, 32
myths/legends, 57, 58, 68, 69, 72, 71, 74, 79, 135
   spirits/demons, 55, 56, 61, 68, 69–70, 79

national anthem films, 9
national identity, 6
nationalism, 8, 9, 15, 28, 85–6
nativism (*xiangtu*), 15
Netflix, 140, 191
New Cinema, 5–6, 10, 14–15, 56, 60, 145
   aesthetics, 99
   and nativism (*xiangtu*), 15
   post-New Cinema, 5–6
Ngan, Rachel, 1
'Night Train to the Stars' (Miyazawa), 64
Nimbus, 41
Niu, Cheng-Tse, 111, 122

Okubo, Mariko, 46
Omi, Wilang, 86–7
On Mount Hehuan, 83
Once Upon a Time in China
   Wong Fei-Hung, 8
One Day, 31–2
   Hsin-Ying, 31–2
   Tsung, 32
One Hundred Years of Solitude (García Márquez), 38
Only God Forgives, 41
Opium War (1839–42), 7
Orphan of Asia (Wu), 102
Orz Boyz, 5

Pacidal, Ado Kaliting, 87, 97
Pai, Ching-Jui, 144
Paik, Nam June, 134
Pakeriran, 82, 83, 101
   Futing, 82, 101, 106
   Kacaw, 101
Palmieri, Eddie, 3
Pan, Chih-Yen, 5
Pan, Chih-Yuan, 31
Pan, Chin-Yu, 141
Pan, Lei, 83

Pangaro, Paul, 123
parenthood, 70–1
parks, 127
   Cultural and Creative Park, Huashan, 135–6
   Daan Forest Park, 127
   Rock Park, 40, *40*, 41, 42, 43
   Songshou Square Park, 113, 117, 125, 135
pastiche, 176
Paw, Hee-Ching, 139
Peng, Yu-Yan, 123
Penghu Islands, 7–8
Perng, Yeng-Horng, 117
Persona, 46
perspective militaire, 43
Pickowicz, Paul G., 88–9
Pingelap Atoll, 34, 35, 52
Po, Ivy Ling, 115–16
poetics
   film poetics, 16–18, 57, 58, 61, 74, 112–13
   historical poetics, 16
Poetics (Aristotle), 149
Pongso No Tao, 83
Price, Thomas, 110, 117
Pu, Songling, 178
puzzle films, 184

Qing dynasty, 7, 13, 85
Qiong Yao melodramas, 145

Raby, Fiona, 124
Rahic, Gulas, 87
Rams, Dieter, 110
realism, 14, 144, 145
Rebels of the Neon God, 14
recursive imperialism, 7
Refn, Nicholas Winding, 41
regionalism, 168–9
religion, 41, 45, 88–9, 155
Roberts, Les, 11
Rocamora, Agnès, 118
Rojas, Carlos, 181, 183
Roth, Robin, 93, 94–5
rural poverty, 177

same-sex marriage, 142–3
Sayon's Bell, 83
Scenery Through the Smog, The, 41
sci-fi, 192
Searchers, The, 169

215

Secrets in the Hot Spring, 167, 169, 170–1, 175–81, *177, 180*
   Hsiao-Chin, 167, 169, 170, 176–81
   Hsiao-Chin's grandfather, 178, 178, 180
   Hsiao-Chin's grandmother, 176, 177, 180
   Little Princess (Hsu Li-Han), 176, 178–9
   Lu-Chun, 176, 178, 179
   masculinity, 176–7, 178–9
   pastiche of soundtrack conventions, 176, 177–8, 179, 181
Seediq Bale, 83
   Hanaoka Ichiro, 88
Sejima, Kazuyo, 110
self-censorship, 8, 10
self-reflexivity, 71
Sen Sen, 139–40, 141, 144, 152, 153, 156–9, 161
   Lili, 139, 141, 144, 152, 153, 156, 157, 158
   Yi-An, 141, 157, 158
   Yu-Sheng, 141, 156–7, 158
Shanley, Kathryn W., 87
Shi, Flair Donglai, 17
Shiau, Hong-Chi, 170
Shih, Ho-Feng, 41
Shih, Shu-Mei, 16–17, 57, 75, 85
Shimizu, Hiroshi, 83
Shimonoseki, Treaty of, 7–8
Shu Qi, 122
Si, Pangoyod, 102
Silk, 5
Singin' in the Rain, 124
Sino-Japanese war (1894–5), 7–8
Smith, Jeff, 174
Somewhere I Have Never Travelled, 33–40, *36*, 51
   Ah-Hsien, 34, 35–8, 39–40
   Ah-Hsien's boyfriend, 37–8
   Ah-Kuei, 34–5, 36–7, 38, 39
   Mori, 37
'somewhere i have never travelled' (Cummings), 34, 39–40
Soul, 56, 60, 67–9
   Chuan, 59, 68, 69, 70–1
   Chuan's sister, 68, 69
   eco-cinema, 68–70
   forests, 67–9
   parenthood, 70–1
   self-reflexivity, 71
   Wang, 68, 69, 71
   sounds
Father to Son, 185, 187, 188
The Great Buddha +, 181, 182–3
Southern Wind, 29
   Aiko, 29
Spielberg, Steven, 175
Spilsbury, John, 62
Starck, Philippe, 110
Starry Starry Night, 56, 60–7, 62, 80
   Chieh, 61–3, 64, 65–7, 71
   eco-cinema, 64
   forests, 61–7
   jigsaws, 62, 65–6, 66
   location, 73
   Mei, 59–60, 61–3, 64, 65–7, 71
Steinberg, Philip, 103, 105
Sterk, Darryl, 83, 84
Story of the Stone, The, 111, 116, 117, 118
   flower arranging, 132
   Josh, 122, 123
   Lin, 122, 132
   Sean, 118, 122, 123
Su, Chao-Pin, 5
Suming, 124
Summer at Grandpa's, 171
Swordsman, The, 128

Tag-Along, The, 56, 58, 60, 61, 67–8, 69–70, 71–2
   forests, 67–8, 69–70, 71–2
   parenthood, 70
   Wei, 69, 70
   Wei's grandmother, 69, 70
   Yi-Chun, 59, 69, 70
Tag-Along 2, The, 55–6
   drone shots, 55
   forest environment, 55–6
   Li Shu-Fen, 55
Taiban, Sasala, 80, 83
Taichung City Government Information Bureau, 139
Taichung Film Development Foundation, 139
Taipei, 21
   Farming Urbanism Network, 130
   Garden City Initiative, 130
   Ruin Academy, 128
   2016 World Design Capital, 111
   Urban Regeneration Office, 135
Taipei as designer city, 110–37
   boutiques, 116–19

colour schemes, 111–16
plotting, 119–27
urban installations, 132–6
urban vegetation, 127–32
Taipei Exchanges, 63
Taiwan
environments, 13–16
maps of, 7–11
Taiwan Design Museum, 135
Taiwan expedition (1874–5), 7
Tanaka, Chie, 136
Tao people, 102–3, 106
Tarkovsky, Andrei, 175
Tarzan and the Treasure, 10
Tarzan, 10
Tenn Siok-Hun, 10
Taylor, D. R. Fraser, 19
Taylor, Damon, 116
Tears in the Sea (song), 105
Teng, Emma Jinhua, 74, 79, 85
Teo, Stephen, 71
Terdsak, Janpan, 177
Terrorizers, 11, 125
Thompson, Kristin, 16, 174
Thongchai, Winichakul, 13, 50, 86, 89, 140
Tiersen, Yann, 114
Time in Quchi, A, 167, 169–70, *169*, 171–5
Ming-Chuan, 172, 174–5
Pao, 167, 169, 171–5
Pao's father, 172
Pao's grandfather, 172, 173, 175
pool worker, 175
sounds in, 171–5
water, 175
Ting, Kuo-Lin, 183
Tōhoku earthquake, 52
Tong, Chris, 60, 64, 69
topogeny, 86
Tou, Tsung-Hua, 40
tourism, 9, 10–11, 29, 60–1, 88, 100–1, 103, 104
travelogues, 28, 29
tribalism (*buluo zhuyi*), 83
Tropical Fish, 29–30
Trotter, David, 133
Tsai, Bor-Wen, 94
Tsai, Lin-Chin, 9–10, 11
Tsai, Ming-Liang, 14, 49, 113, 127, 145, 147, 148, 157, 159, 163, 173
Tsai, Mu-Ming, 123–4

Tsao, Shih-Huei, 26–7, 86, 87
Tseng, Han-Hsien, 71–2
Tseng, Wen-Chen, 83
Tsui, Hark, 8
Tsui, Yung-Hui (Heather Tsui), 83, 84, 102, 104
Tuan, Yi-Fu, 61, 70, 78, 79, 149, 150, 157
Tung, Ming-Hsiang, 28, 153
Tweedie, James, 118–19, 145
20:30:40, 124–5, 131, 147
Typhoon Morakot, 41, 52, 66, 80
Typhoon Soudelor, 175

Udden, James, 4–5, 29–30
Uhlin, Graig, 146
Umbrellas of Cherbourg, The, 116
unhealthy realism, 145
Unwritten Rules, 8, *8*
urban gardening, 129–30
Urban Regeneration Office, Taipei, 135
urban vegetation, 127–32

Vithaya, Pansringarm, 41
Vive L'Amour, 159
Daan Forest Park, 127
May Lin, 127
voyeurism, 182–3

Waisanding sandbar, 47, 48, 50, 52
Wanders, Marcel, 110
Wang, Chin-Kuei, 83
Wang, Hsiu-Feng, 185
Wang, Jen-You, 75
Wang, Ta-Lu, 114
Wang, Yu, 68, 71
Wang, Yu-Lin, 142
water
Aground, 48–50
and death, 169–70, 174–5
Father to Son, 185, 187, 188
Long Time No Sea, 102–4, 105–7
A Time in Quchi, 175
Wawa No Cidal, 83, 84, 87, 88, 92, 94, 96, 97, 100
camera equipment, 99
counter-mapping, 91–5
Nakaw, 87, 88–9, 92–3, 104
Panay, 87, 88, 91, 93–5
Panay's father, 87
Sera, 87
Sheng, 88, 93

Wayne, John, *169*
Wei, Te-Sheng, 4, 5, 58, 83, 111, 130, 131
Wei, Ying-Chuan, 192
Weinthal, Lois, 146–7, 159–60
Wen, Chen-Ling, 151–2
When a Wolf Falls in Love with a Sheep, 113
White Ant, 113
Williams, Tony, 71
Winds of September, 5
Wish of the Ocean Rice, 96
Wong, Kar-Wai, 150
Wood, Denis, 7
World Design Organization (previously International Council of Societies of Industrial Design), 111
Wu, Chih-Hsuan, 141
Wu, Chung-Tien, 44
Wu, Chuo-Liu, 102
Wu, Hsing-Hsiang, 111
Wu, Mi-Sen, 1
Wu, Ming-Yi, 60, 90–1
Wu, Nien-Jen, 34, 99, 134–5, 147
wuxia films, 56, 57, 71

Xia, Xianlun, 85
xiangtu (nativism), 15
Xici zhuan (3rd-century commentary on *Yi Jing*), 48
Xu, Jiao, 59–60

Yan, Yung-Heng, 172
Yang, Cheng-Lin, 55
Yang, Edward, 11, 113, 125

Yang, Karen Ya-Chu, 28, 67, 167
Yang, Kuei-Mei, 127, 134
Yang, Liang-Yu, 167
Yang, Ya-Che, 5
Yang, Yo-Ning, 30
Yang Yang, 100
Yao, Kuo-Chen, 150, 160
Ye, Lou, 124
Yee, Chih-Yen, 147
Yee, Cordell D. K., 12, 19, 48
Yeh, Emilie Yueh-Yu, 145
Yeh, Hsiao, 126
Yeh, Tien-Lun, 111, 119, 128–9
Yeh, Yueh-Yu, 18
Yen, Yi-Wen, 141
Yi Jing (text), 33
 hexagrams, 45–6, 47–9
 3rd-century commentary, 48
Yip, June, 171
Yorke, John, 59
You Are the Apple of My Eye, 31
Young Dudes, 111
Your Name Engraved Herein, 142
Yu, Cheng-Ching, 61
Yu, Chien-Sheng, 9
Yu, Hsin, 34

Zhang, Yingjin, 6, 113
Zhang, Zhen, 124–5, 138n
Zhao, Wei, 125
Zone Pro Site, 30–1, 111, 134–5, 147
 Ai Feng, 30
 Hai, 30
 Hsiao-Wan, 134–5
 Master Silly Mortal, 134–5

EU representative:
Easy Access System Europe
Mustamäe tee 50, 10621 Tallinn, Estonia
Gpsr.requests@easproject.com